ISSUES
BEFORE THE 42ND
GENERAL
ASSEMBLY OF THE
UNITED NATIONS

THE UNITED NATIONS ASSOCIATION IS MAKING THE U.N. WORK. THROUGH POLICY RESEARCH, PUBLIC OUTREACH, AND INTERNATIONAL DIALOGUE, UNA–USA IS BUILDING A NATIONAL AND INTERNATIONAL CONSTITUENCY FOR GLOBAL CO-OPERATION. A NONPROFIT, NONPARTISAN MEMBERSHIP ORGANIZATION, UNA–USA PARTICIPATES ACTIVELY IN THE PUBLIC DEBATE ABOUT AMERICA'S ROLE IN THE WORLD, SERVING AS A MAJOR SOURCE OF INFORMATION FOR CONGRESS, THE EXECUTIVE BRANCH, STUDENTS, AND THE MEDIA. STEP BY STEP, UNA–USA IS BRINGING THE U.S., THE U.N., AND THE GLOBAL COMMUNITY CLOSER TOGETHER.

ISSUES
BEFORE THE 42ND
GENERAL
ASSEMBLY OF THE
UNITED NATIONS.

*An annual publication of the
United Nations Association
of the United States of America*

John Tessitore and Susan Woolfson, Editors

Lexington Books
D.C. Heath and Company/Lexington, Massachusetts/Toronto

jet

Published simultaneously in Canada
Printed in the United States of America
ISSN: 0193-8096
Library of Congress Catalog Card Number: 82-640811

The paper used in this publication meets the minimum requirements of American National Standard for Information Sciences—Permanence of Paper for Printed Library Materials, ANSI Z39.48-1984.∞ ™

88 89 90 8 7 6 5 4 3   8/24/90

Contents

Contributors

Libby Bassett (Energy and Environment sections) is a writer and editor on international environment and development issues for, among others, the United Nations Environment Programme and Women in Defense of the Environment (World/WIDE).

Hannah Bentley (Legal Issues chapter), an associate with the firm of Morrison & Foerster in Washington, D.C., is a recent graduate of Columbia Law School.

Michael J. Berlin (Making and Keeping the Peace, Central America, Afghanistan, Indochina, Cyprus, and Other Colonial and Sovereignty Issues sections) writes on the United Nations for *The Washington Post* and *The InterDependent*, and is the diplomatic correspondent of *The New York Post*.

Emily Copeland (Refugees section, with Susan Forbes) is Research Assistant at the Refugee Policy Group in Washington, D.C., an independent, nonprofit organization engaged in policy analysis and research on refugee issues.

David Dell (Transnational Corporations, Science, and Technology section) is President of the Information Interface Institute, a research and consulting organization specializing in information technology.

Susan Forbes (Refugees section, with Emily Copeland) is Senior Associate at the Refugee Policy Group.

John W. Harbeson (Africa section), Director of International Studies and Professor of Political Science at City College, City University of New York, is the author of *Nation-Building in Kenya: The Role of Land Reform* and a forthcoming book on the Ethiopian revolution, among many books and articles on Africa.

Aaron Karp (Arms Control and Disarmament chapter) is Director of Arms Trade Research at the Stockholm International Peace Research Institute (SIPRI).

Lee Kimball (Law of the Sea and Antarctica sections) is the Executive Director of the Council on Ocean Law and serves as a consultant on Antarctic issues to the International Institute for Environment and Development.

Maggie Nicholson (Human Rights section, with Margo Picken) has observed the General Assembly for several years, just recently taking her leave from Amnesty International's office at U.N. headquarters.

Margo Picken (Human Rights section, with Maggie Nicholson), like her coauthor, left New York just recently after spending several years observing the General Assembly from Amnesty International's office at U.N. headquarters.

Sterett Pope (The Middle East and the Persian Gulf section) writes a monthly column on the Middle East for *World Press Review*.

Ruth D. Raymond (The Information Issue and Other Social Issues sections and Administration and Budget chapter), a former Research Associate for UNA-USA's U.N. Management and Decision-Making Project, is the newly appointed Public Affairs Officer of the International Board for Plant Genetic Resources in Rome.

Neal Spivack (Food and Agriculture and Population sections), Research Associate for UNA-USA's Multilateral Project, is coauthor of the 1987 briefing book, *Food on the Table—Seeking Global Solutions to Chronic Hunger*.

John Tessitore (Co-Editor) is Director of Publications at UNA-USA.

Stuart K. Tucker (The World Economy in 1987, Trade, and Money and Finance sections) is a Fellow at the Overseas Development Council, carrying out research and writing in the areas of international trade policy and Latin American development.

Susan Woolfson (Co-Editor) is Managing Editor of Publications at UNA-USA.

Preface

Each year the Publications Department of the United Nations Association of the United States produces *Issues Before the General Assembly*—a unique compendium of U.N. activities involving the General Assembly, the Security Council, the U.N. Specialized Agencies, and other U.N. bodies. As those who consult this series know full well, the organization's activities are complex, ongoing, varied, and worldwide. Naturally, such a summary is not intended to be exhaustive, nor could it hope to be. But as a timely reference work that permits examination of the many concerns of the world body, *Issues* performs a service for all members of the international affairs community— students and diplomats alike.

Preparation of this volume involves many stages and the energies of many people. Foremost, of course, are the scholars, journalists, and professionals whose efforts and skills are central to the project. To these generous and committed men and women we extend our deepest gratitude.

As is the case each year, *Issues*/42 authors were assisted by a team of stalwart editorial interns—young people who gave freely and unflaggingly of their time. Without the assistance of Russell M. Dallen, Jr., Carrie Pastor, and Helene Rosen, who spent several months unearthing documents, sorting through mounds of publications and reports, interviewing, fact-checking, and proofreading, this volume would not have been possible. Nor could we have done without the yeoman efforts of our colleague Deborah Scroggins, whose always sharp pencils contributed greatly to the editing.

Finally, we once again acknowledge our debt to the many men and women of the United Nations who so readily and warmly cooperated in the production of this volume, providing documents, assisting authors and interns, and offering constructive criticism of the early drafts of each chapter.

John Tessitore
Susan Woolfson

I
Dispute Settlement and Decolonization

1. Making and Keeping the Peace

The U.N. Role in Conflict Resolution

In February 1987 United Nations Secretary-General Javier Pérez de Cuéllar convened an unannounced meeting of the **five permanent members of the U.N. Security Council** and urged them to take joint action to force an end to the seven-year-long war between Iran and Iraq. The five—the United Kingdom, China, France, the Soviet Union, and the United States—have special responsibilities under the U.N. Charter as well as special privileges (such as veto power in the Council); and the **system of collective security** that was envisioned by the U.N.'s founders was based on the assumption that the five would be able to act in concert to maintain or restore the peace whenever it—and thus their collective interests—was threatened. In the case of the Persian Gulf war, all five shared a common interest in containing the fighting and bringing it to a balanced end. Yet the status of the United Nations and the universal assumptions as to its potential capacities had altered so completely in the four decades since it began operations that the five powers had not themselves considered using it as a mechanism for fulfilling their joint interests.

In fact, it had been more than fifteen years since the major powers had gathered together in the United Nations or any other forum to undertake jointly any substantive political exercise. (The last such occasion was in the early 1970s, when the U.N. ambassadors of the United Kingdom, France, the Soviet Union, and the United States tried to draft the text of an Arab-Israeli peace treaty. Beijing was not yet an active U.N. participant.) The long hiatus says as much about the **relationships among the big powers** as it does about the status of the United Nations and the perceptions of the institution's role. It also signals that Soviet-American and Sino-Soviet relationships have reached a stage where joint actions are finally conceivable, if only on limited issues.

In the absence of a system of collective security, the U.N.'s political organs—the Council, the Assembly, the World Court, and the Secretary-General—have been assigned **marginal roles in dispute settlement** in recent years: the defining of goals, perhaps the sketching of a framework of agreement, the prodding of parties, and (in the case of the Secretary-General) the role of mediator.

Most of the dozen or so issues now on the Secretary-General's plate are hopeless causes for the moment. It is rare that he is tossed a softball like the France–New Zealand arbitration that resolved the affair of the Greenpeace ship *Rainbow Warrior*, in July 1986, with advance assurance from both sides that the verdict would be accepted.

The Big Five meeting convened by Pérez de Cuéllar followed several years in which he tried without success to find a formula that would entice Iran to enter negotiations. In January he suggested the appointment of an international commission to determine the causes of the Gulf war—a condition set for the international community by Iran. "If the issue of who started the war acts as a knot to stifle mediation, is it not time to cut the knot?" the Secretary-General asked at an Islamic Conference meeting in Kuwait. He also proposed a Security Council meeting on the issue at the ministerial level. The idea that Pérez de Cuéllar set before the five powers was that a joint approach sponsored by them all, channeled through the Security Council, would be difficult for Iran to refuse—especially if the approach had a potential threat behind it, such as an effective **moratorium on arms deliveries**.

The five-power meetings that ensued for several months (about one a week, half of them at the ambassadorial level) involved more than posturing for the record, participants indicated [Interviews with *Issues Before the 42nd General Assembly*]. They said the ambassadors acted as true plenipotentiaries, often operating without precise instructions, and were awed by the extent of their common ground. The Council agreed unanimously on July 20 to a five-power resolution demanding a cease-fire under Chapter 7 of of the U.N. Charter. There was agreement in principle that a second resolution—to "put teeth" into the five-power demand—would be considered if either protagonist rejected the cease-fire. But the Chinese were reluctant to impose an arms embargo, and Soviet support for it was contingent on an understanding with Washington on the level of the big-power military presence in the Persian Gulf.

The Secretary-General prepared to travel to the area in August 1987 on the basis of a Security Council request that he mediate the conflict, help set up the commission on the causes of the war, and report on implementation of the cease-fire.

The five-power meetings on the Gulf war were not, in fact, the only ones. The group met on a far less difficult matter in October 1986 to formalize a political reality that was already universally assumed: that Pérez de Cuéllar would be appointed by acclamation to **a second five-year term as Secretary-General**. The appointment, made by the Assembly [A/Res/41/1] on the recommendation of the Security Council [S/Res/589 (1986)], was formalized on October 10.

The only doubt about the outcome was whether the sixty-six-year-old Peruvian diplomat would be able or willing to serve, having undergone a quadruple coronary bypass operation in July 1986.

Pérez de Cuéllar won generalized promises of support in his attempt to resolve the U.N. budget crisis. That year-long dispute had preempted much of the time the Secretary-General would have preferred to devote to dispute settlement, and it weakened the institution politically as well as administratively by leaving it vulnerable to critics on the right. The reforms agreed upon by the 41st Assembly enabled Pérez de Cuéllar to make political changes in the structure of the Secretariat, under the guise of administrative efficiency, during the first half of 1987.

The **office of secretary-general** appeared to have weathered another threat to its status: the **charges leveled against Kurt Waldheim**, Pérez de Cuéllar's predecessor, who became president of Austria in 1986. The evidence that surfaced piecemeal throughout much of 1986 made clear that Waldheim had not revealed his role as a German Army officer in the Balkans during World War II, suggesting that his active military service had ended when he was wounded on the Russian front in 1941. It was alleged that he played a role in reprisals against Yugoslav villagers, in the deportation of Greek Jews, in measures taken against Allied war prisoners, and in the dissemination of anti-Semitic literature. Some of the data was contained in files that the now-defunct seventeen-member **U.N. War Crimes Commission** deposited in **U.N. archives.** Israel asked that the files be opened to inspection by historians and the press. But after consulting the seventeen former commission members, Pérez de Cuéllar announced in March 1987 that all but Australia had failed to support the idea, and he decided against it. A majority of the seventeen, including the United States, have since reconsidered and endorsed some increase in access. U.N. officials indicated the possibility that some access might be accorded for scholarly research [*The New York Times*, 7/15/87].

Another issue that rocked the United Nations in the months preceding the 41st Assembly was a **U.S. demand that the Soviet Union reduce the staff of its U.N. Mission** from 275 to 170 in three stages over a two-year period, ending in March 1988. Washington defended this unprecedented move on the ground that Soviet diplomats had habitually engaged in espionage in the United States. Moscow denounced the move as illegal, and the Secretary-General concurred. The matter became part of a more serious dispute over the August 23, 1986, arrest in New York of Gennadi Zakharov, a Soviet employee of the Secretariat, on espionage charges. Several days later American reporter Nicholas Daniloff was detained in Moscow on similar charges. One U.S. response to his detention was a decision to specify twenty-five Soviet Mission staff members who were required to leave the United States. This led to a tit-for-tat series of expulsions by both sides known as "Spy Wars." But the second stage of the Soviet cutdown passed uneventfully in March 1987.

A third five-power meeting, again unannounced, was convened by Pérez de Cuéllar in April 1987 to consider prospects for an **international conference to tackle the Arab-Israeli dispute**. General Assembly resolutions adopted since 1983 had rigidly defined the ground rules for such a conference to include the creation of a Palestinian state as one of its goals. And a 1986 provision urged the establishment of a preparatory committee to set up just such a conference [A/Res/41/43D; vote: 123–3, with 19 abstentions]. The five powers' reactions to such a conference format—unacceptable to the West—were scarcely worth asking. But Pérez de Cuéllar went further and canvassed the five as well on the terms under which they would favor convening any Middle East conference, in hopes that a process leading to negotiations might emerge from such a discussion.

Most of the other issues on the Secretary-General's long but frustrating list of mediations had a similar status: complex, remote, and delicate.

In Latin America he was authorized to promote British-Argentine negotiations on the **Falklands/Malvinas** issue, but the parties were not ready to talk. He was to define the means of resolving an age-old **Guyana-Venezuela** territorial dispute, but the parties were quite happy to leave it unresolved. He was urged to keep the United Nations briefed on the Central America crisis but not to displace other mediators.

In Africa, there was a U.N. operation of major proportions waiting in the wings to help guide the territory of **Namibia** to independence but little chance of edging it toward reality. In the dispute over the territory of **Western Sahara**, Pérez de Cuéllar and his aides were joint mediators (with the president of the Organization of African Unity) between **Morocco and the Popular Front for the Liberation of Saguia el Hamra and Rio de Oro (POLISARIO)**. What the U.N. could offer was a face-saving cover for a political decision that had already been made by Morocco and by Algeria, the patron of Polisario. The effort had reached the stage where the U.N.'s proposals for a compromise (the temporary relinquishing of sovereignty to the U.N., until a referendum decides the final status of the territory) were being tried out on the parties. However, Polisario representatives told Pérez de Cuéllar in July that they believed conditions were not yet ripe for a referendum.

Pérez de Cuéllar also played a pivotal mediating role in **Cyprus**, where the two communities were far apart after coming close to agreement in January 1985. In Asia, he retained the confidence of both parties in the Persian Gulf war, but lacking a mechanism to bring Iran to the table, this fact was of little immediate value. Elsewhere, the Secretary-General was quietly trying to avert the eruption of an open international dispute between **India and Sri Lanka** over the guerrilla war being waged by the Tamil minority on the island at the subcontinent's southern tip. And his representative was actively engaged in negotiations involving **Kampuchea and East Timor**, with little sign of progress but some potential.

The big breakthrough for U.N. mediation, however, might just come in the most significant of the disputes in which the Secretary-General has been actively involved: **Afghanistan.** There the terms of settlement under negotiation were virtually agreed. The problem was to locate enough Afghans who, if put in the same room, could produce a coalition government rather than a massacre.

The United Nations and Peacekeeping

U.N. peacekeeping operations historically have arisen from the institution's peacemaking efforts and have served as the most visible mechanism by which dispute-settlement agreements arranged under U.N. auspices can be instituted or preserved. The prospects for future U.N. peacekeeping operations, therefore, depend almost totally on the fruition of peacemaking in Namibia, Western Sahara, or Afghanistan, or of some other mediation in which the Secretary-General is involved.

There have been two major types of peacekeeping operations. One is the **peace force** that interposes itself in bulk between contending armies to avert contacts that could flare from friction to war. The U.N. currently maintains peace forces in Cyprus, on the Golan Heights between Israel and Syria, and in southern Lebanon. The second type of operation involves **unarmed U.N. observers,** of officer rank, who monitor, report, and mediate between local commanders in the field, rather than filling the spaces between combatants. In both cases, the object of the operation is not to resolve the dispute that sparked the outbreak of fighting. Not even the peace forces are equipped to achieve that, and they may fire only in self-defense. Rather, they are effective when they give the parties the excuse to end hostilities—which is often the most that can be achieved.

The **United Nations Interim Force in Lebanon (UNIFIL)**, established in March 1978, was bypassed by Israeli troops during the 1982 invasion. Since then the Israelis have withdrawn to a security zone on the Lebanese side of the frontier, leaving the 5,668-member force unable to fulfill its mandate of patrolling the border. Nevertheless, the force has remained because of the universal assumption that its pullout would doom southern Lebanon to the same chaos that prevailed in Beirut and would create a power vacuum that could generate a direct clash between Israeli and Syrian forces. The Security Council generally renews the UNIFIL mandate for six-month periods, in July and January.

The **financing of peacekeeping operations** has always been a sensitive political issue and a strain on the overall U.N. budget. Over the years, states that object to the peacekeeping operations for various reasons have adopted the practice of withholding operating funds. Such actions have resulted in a deficit of well over $400 million in the various peacekeeping accounts.

UNIFIL's deficit alone was more than $250 million by mid-1987, most of it owed by the Soviet bloc. But the Soviets started paying in 1986—at the same time that the United States began withholding more than half its annual share, which is around $44 million, or 30 percent of the $144 million cost. Most of the burden is borne by the troop-contributing nations, which are reimbursed at a rate lower than their actual costs. The U.S. withholding was mandated by Congress after two touring congressional aides were told by Israeli officials that Israel sees little value in UNIFIL. Israel has since publicly shifted that position, but the congressional curbs still apply [*The Washington Post*, 4/8/87].

The most serious danger UNIFIL faces is the possibility that the radical pro-Iranian Shiite Moslem group, Hizbollah, will target the U.N. troops. So far Hizbollah's anti-UNIFIL stand has been limited to rhetoric. But U.N. officials conceded that the troops could be forced to withdraw if they become unwilling combatants in the area [Interviews with *Issues Before the 42nd General Assembly*].

Two other peace forces continued to operate effectively. The 1,300-member **United Nations Disengagement Observer Force (UNDOF)** has patrolled the Golan buffer zone with no major incidents since June 1974. With the cooperation of the Syrian and Israeli authorities, UNDOF has continued to operate without controversy. Its term was renewed through November 1987 at a cost of about $36 million a year.

The 2,328-member **United Nations Peacekeeping Force in Cyprus (UNFICYP)**, established in 1964, patrols the "green line" between the Greek-Cypriot and Turkish-Cypriot communities, and its mandate runs through December 1987. UNFICYP is financed solely by voluntary contributions at a cost of about $28 million a year and had a deficit of $150 million through mid-1987.

An example of the second type of U.N. peacekeeping operation is the **United Nations Military Observer Group in India and Pakistan (UNMOGIP)**, a small team of observers that has patrolled the line of control in Kashmir agreed between the two countries in 1972. The **United Nations Truce Supervision Organization in Palestine (UNTSO)**, originally established in 1948 to supervise the truce declared by the Security Council after the first Arab-Israeli war, still functions in various capacities in the region. It includes both U.S. and Soviet officers, and some fifty of its members are stationed in Beirut. A small number have been stationed in **Baghdad and Tehran** since June 1984 to verify complaints by Iran and Iraq about attacks on civilian population centers and about the use of poison gas.

The thirty-three-member **Special Committee on Peacekeeping Operations** was established in 1965 to help solve the crisis over peacekeeping finances that threatened to tear the United Nations apart at that time and to draw up guidelines to govern the conduct of all such U.N. operations. The 42nd General Assembly is to consider the committee's report, but no progress toward consensus on peacekeeping theory is expected [A/42/50, item 78].

2. The Middle East and the Persian Gulf

The Iran-Iraq War

After nearly seven years of fighting the Iran-Iraq War continues with **little hope of resolution**. Iraq, which invaded its neighbor in September 1980, has sought to end the conflict since 1982, when Iran drove its armies back to the Iraqi border. But Iran has consistently refused to negotiate until the Iraqi government is overthrown and a successor regime agrees to pay war reparations. In the meantime, the war has inflicted **massive casualties** on both sides, accounting for nearly a million deaths and the injury and dislocation of many millions more [*The Wall Street Journal*, 4/30/87].

The United Nations has attempted to mediate the conflict through several channels. Since 1982, Iraq has repeatedly appealed to the Security Council to negotiate a cease-fire and has agreed to abide by its resolutions. But Iran has refused to cooperate with the Council, which it claims has consistently favored Iraq, but has been willing to work with the Office of the Secretary-General. Recurrent charges by both sides of **chemical warfare, bombardment of civilian populations**, and **mistreatment of prisoners of war** have prompted visits to the front by various U.N. commissions and a tour of the Gulf by the Secretary-General in the spring of 1985. Since June 1984 the U.N. has maintained military observers in Baghdad and Tehran to monitor civilian casualties in both countries. These steps have produced brief respites on some fronts but no framework for peace negotiations.

As hostilities have dragged on, both countries have raised massive armies: Iran currently has some 1.2 million men under arms, many of whom are irregular volunteers, while Iraq has put over half-a-million men into the field. Since 1982, when Iraq assumed a defensive posture, Iran has pressed attacks across the Iraqi border but has been unable to score a decisive breakthrough. Baghdad has built elaborate fortifications, earthworks, and artificial lakes, and has accumulated a formidable arsenal of state-of-the-art weapons systems. Tehran, whose U.S. weapons systems have suffered from shoddy maintenance and a chronic shortage of spare parts since the start of the war, has an indisputable edge in morale and manpower. Over the past five years Iran has launched punishing winter offensives, while staging intermittent probes and feints all year round. These maneuvers have brought small territorial gains at the cost of tens of thousands of lives each year.

Lacking the military and logistic resources to score a decisive victory on the battlefield, Iran has pursued a strategy of attrition, designed to exhaust Iraq's smaller economy and to erode its weaker morale. Every year Iran has mounted a "final offensive," but after weeks of fierce fighting, Iran has broken off its attacks to claim victory and exploit its small gains for propaganda purposes. In the meantime, Iranian leaders continue to announce massive new recruitment drives and to declare their determination to fight on indefinitely.

While a **strategic stalemate** prevails at the front, both Iran and Iraq have struck at each other's ability to export petroleum. On the eve of the war, both belligerents relied on oil for more than 95 percent of their government budgets and foreign exchange, and today the war efforts of Iran and Iraq are critically dependent on oil exports.

At the start of the conflict, Iran was able to cut 80 percent of Iraq's oil exports by destroying Iraqi oil facilities on the Gulf and persuading its ally Syria to cut Iraq's pipeline to the Mediterranean. But in the last three years Iraq has gradually gained the upper hand in the oil war. Baghdad has expanded oil exports by widening its pipelines through Turkey, Saudi Arabia, and Jordan. At the same time, Iraq has reduced Iran's exports by attacking Iran's oil terminals and shipping lanes.

Both countries continue to attack oil facilities and tanker traffic on the Persian Gulf. In 1982, Iraq declared an "exclusionary zone" in the Gulf in which all "enemy vessels" carrying Iranian oil would be subject to Iraqi attack. Two years later, Iraq began to interdict Iranian shipping in earnest, and in 1985 Iraq launched its first successful air raid on Iran's principal Gulf oil terminal at Kharg Island. In the late summer and fall of 1986 Iraqi air strikes at Kharg suspended oil exports for several days, and for the first time Iraqi warplanes began to bomb Iran's transshipment terminal at Sirri Island, four hundred miles southwest of Kharg. By October, Iran's oil exports had dropped to 700,000 barrels a day against a 1985 average of 1.4 million barrels a day (mbd). During the same month, Iran began to ration domestic oil sales. Iraq, on the other hand, was exporting 1.6 mbd in the fall of 1986, up from its wartime low of 0.67 mbd in 1983 [*The Economist* 10/18/86].

The war efforts of both belligerents have been severely taxed by the recent **fall of oil prices**, which dropped from over $20 a barrel in 1985 to a low of $9 a barrel in July 1986. Declining prices and export levels cut Iran's oil revenues by nearly 60 percent in the first half of 1986, reportedly delaying a major fall offensive. For the entire year, Iran earned an estimated $5 billion from petroleum sales, but the war alone cost Tehran at least $7 billion in 1986 [South Syndication Service, 11/28/86].

In the fall of 1986, Iran's flagging fortunes were buoyed by an astonishing windfall: the disclosure in October of secret sales of arms by the United States to Iran. Whatever the final outcome of ongoing investigations in Washington into the arms deal, it is clear that the secret U.S. initiative did not further the negotiation of an "honorable end" to the Gulf war, one of the operation's primary objectives, according to U.S. President Ronald Reagan. On the contrary: by enhancing Iran's arsenal and boosting the morale of its troops, at least temporarily, the arms deal and its disclosure only encouraged the Islamic

Republic to launch yet another "final" offensive, this time personally directed by Speaker of Parliament Hashemi Rafsanjani, who had initiated Iran's secret approach to the United States.

The small amounts of arms sold, valued at $12.2 million by the Pentagon, were not sufficient to alter the strategic balance on the battlefield, even if those arms did address critical Iranian shortages of antitank and air defense weapons. But "Iranscam" surfaced as a spectacular coup that bolstered Tehran's prestige abroad and shook the confidence of Iraqi leaders and their Arab allies. Iran's access to the international arms market was also expanded by the news that Tehran had persuaded the United States to break its own arms embargo, Operation Staunch, which Washington had successfully pressed on many of its allies since 1984.

In December 1986, Iran began its **sixth winter offensive** in as many years. Announcing their intention to "destroy the Iraqi war machine," Iran's leaders directed their principal thrust against the southern Iraqi city of Basra. By January, Iran had thrown 100,000 men into the battle, capturing sixty square miles of Iraqi territory and pushing to within six miles of Basra's suburbs, an area from which Iranian artillery could bombard the city. By mid-January, Iran's drive on Basra had cost 40,000–50,000 Iranian and 10,000–20,000 Iraqi lives, and twice as many casualties, according to Pentagon estimates [*The New York Times*, 1/21/87, 1/27/87]. Iraq responded by stepping up air attacks on Iranian cities, including Tehran, Qum, and Tabriz. After Iran approached U.N. Secretary-General Pérez de Cuéllar, a brief halt on "the war of the cities" was arranged in February, but bombing of civilian targets was soon resumed.

Iran's 1987 winter offensive continued until April, once again without a breakthrough. This time Iran relied less on the "human wave" tactics of past campaigns and deployed a more varied and sophisticated arsenal. Tehran claimed it downed sixty Iraqi planes in January, and Iraqi officials admitted that Iran showed "a distinct efficiency in encountering our planes " [*The New York Times*, 1/26–27/87]. On the ground, Iranian helicopter gunships and antitank missiles were far more evident and effective than in the past. Nevertheless, these improvements in Iranian tactics and weaponry were not decisive.

Iran and Iraq have continued to **escalate the air war** over the Gulf, undeterred by a June 1984 Security Council resolution condemning attacks on commercial shipping in international waters. In 1984 systematic Iraqi interdiction of tankers carrying Iranian oil prompted Iran to retaliate against ships calling on Kuwait and Saudi Arabia, leading to the downing of an Iranian fighter by Saudi warplanes in June 1984. Iran also threatened to suspend Gulf traffic completely by closing the Straits of Hormuz. In the wake of Iran's 1986 winter offensive, the air war accelerated further. By August of 1986, fifty-five tankers had been hit, against forty-six for all of 1985 [*The Economist*, 8/23/86].

In the opening months of 1987, Iran's enhanced arsenal allowed it to commit new weapons to the air war, creating new worries for the Arab countries of the Gulf, the United States, and the Soviet Union. According to U.S. intelligence sources, Iran launched in January its first successful night attacks on Gulf shipping, using Italian-made Sea Killer missiles against three tankers calling on Kuwait. In response, 'a Soviet frigate for the first time escorted Soviet-registered merchant ships bound for Kuwait into the Gulf [*The New York Times*, 1/20/87]. In March, Iran reportedly deployed Chinese-built Silkworm missile batteries near the Straits of Hormuz [*The New York Times*, 3/15/87]. In early April, Iran sent a letter to the U.N. Secretary-General, saying Iran "will spare no effort to prevent the spill-over of the war," and complaining that the United States "has heightened the tension in the region by increasing its military presence in the Persian Gulf area [S/18794]. The U.S. had quietly offered to match the Soviets' protection of Kuwaiti tankers against Iranian attacks in the Gulf, but the issue of the U.S. role there became politically charged in late May after thirty-seven American sailors were killed in a missile attack on the frigate USS *Stark* by an Iraqi warplane. Iraq called the attack an accident. Despite congressional opposition, the Reagan administration vowed to pursue its plan for flying the American flag over Kuwaiti tankers and using U.S. naval escorts to convoy them. Washington hoped that a U.N. resolution demanding a cease-fire in the Gulf would make the reflagging policy more politically acceptable. In a proposal linking the U.N. role with reflagging, Cyrus Vance, chairman of the National Council of UNA-USA, and Elliot Richardson, chairman of the Association, recommended that the United Nations flag fly over the tankers instead [*The New York Times*, 7/8/87].

Responding to both Iranian and Iraqi charges concerning the use of chemical weapons, Secretary-General Pérez de Cuéllar sent an investigative team to the Gulf in late April [PR WS/1332]. The same team had last visited Iran in March 1986, when it found that Iraq had used mustard gas bombs to a far greater extent than it had in 1984. The U.N. Security Council took the occasion to condemn once again Iraq's use of chemical weapons "in clear violation of the Geneva Protocol of 1925" [S/17191, S/18863].

Even if the war should escalate further, a superpower confrontation in the area appears unlikely. Although the United States and the Soviet Union claim neutrality in the conflict, both in fact favor Iraq. In 1984 the United States restored diplomatic ties with Iraq, severed during the Six Day war of 1967, and later removed Baghdad from its list of state sponsors of terrorism, on which Tehran still holds a prominent place. Despite recently disclosed U.S. arms sales to Iran, relations between Washington and Tehran remain acrimonious. The Soviet Union, which signed a twenty-year Treaty of Friendship and Cooperation with Iraq in the 1970s, bitterly criticized Iraq's invasion of Iran; but in 1982, Moscow renewed shipments to Iraq of new-model weapons, accompanied by Soviet economic and military advisers. Relations between Moscow and Tehran have been quite strained ever since, although the Soviet Union has continued to allow its allies to supply Iran with weapons. As recent military moves by both superpowers into the Gulf show, both Washington and

Moscow are anxious to prevent further escalations of the Gulf war.

The conflict between Iraq and Iran is likely to continue as a ruinous war of attrition, as neither side has shown the logistical or military capacity to defeat its adversary in battle. Iraq still has a distinct advantage in matériel, but Baghdad, whose initial invasion of Iran was both costly and ineffective, is in no position to renew an offensive strategy. Nor can Iran's superior morale and manpower compensate for its glaring deficiencies in equipment and logistics.

Tehran clearly hopes that a grueling war of attrition will eventually destroy the morale of the Iraqi Army, forcing it to overthrow the government of Iraqi President Saddam Hussein. Over the past five years Iranian officials have at times expressed their frustration over the tragic waste and futility of the war, only to be overruled by the tenacious Ayatollah Khomeini, who continues to demand that Saddam "commit suicide or flee [his] country" [*The Middle East,* 10/86]. But steady Iraqi pressure on Iranian oil exports, together with the eventual death of the Ayatollah, may yet bring Tehran to the negotiating table.

The United Nations General Assembly has not taken action on the Iran-Iraq War since the 37th Session of 1982–83. The Security Council has passed several resolutions on the war. In its penultimate resolution, in February 1986, the Council called, as usual, for an immediate cease-fire but also deplored "the initial acts which gave rise to the conflict," referring for the first time to Iraq's invasion of Iran [S/Res/582]. This concession to Iran, which fell short of an explicit condemnation of Iraq as the conflict's aggressor, was deemed insufficient by Tehran.

A year later, during Iran's latest winter offensive, Secretary-General Pérez de Cuéllar secretly called the Security Council to address the Gulf war once again. Secret meetings over a period of several months yielded the most recent resolution—a strongly worded demand for an immediate cease-fire and an announcement of the Council's intention to "consider further steps to ensure compliance with this resolution," if necessary. The Council's decision, rendered on July 20, was unanimous [S/Res/598].

The Office of the Secretary-General will continue to play a role in the search for peace in the Gulf. Pérez de Cuéllar has kept in close touch with both Iran and Iraq, and his office has emerged as the only mediator that both parties trust. The July 20 resolution directs the Secretary-General to dispatch a team of U.N. observers to the Gulf "to verify, confirm and supervise the cease-fire and withdrawal"—but this, of course, depends upon the willingness of both combatants to accede to the Security Council's demand. When Iran tires of the Gulf war and its tremendous costs, it may turn to the Office of the Secretary-General for help.

The Arab-Israeli Conflict and the Occupied Territories

Nearly forty years after the establishment of the state of Israel, the Arab-Israeli conflict persists. Hopes of reviving the moribund Middle East "peace process"—for the first time in years—were raised in February 1985, when Palestine

Liberation Organization (PLO) Chairman Yasser Arafat and Jordan's King Hussein signed the **Amman Accord**, which mandated direct negotiations between Israel and a joint Jordanian-Palestinian delegation in the context of an international peace conference.

Israel, Egypt, and the United States responded favorably to the accord, but prospects for peace talks collapsed when the divided leadership of the PLO proved unable or unwilling to commit itself to a negotiating course in cooperation with Jordan. In February 1986, King Hussein publicly abandoned the Amman Accord, bitterly denouncing the PLO's lack of resolve and credibility, and the "peace process" again ground to a halt.

For most of 1986 serious efforts to pursue the elusive Middle Eastern peace process were suspended, although Israeli, Jordanian, and Egyptian leaders occasionally spoke of holding an "international peace conference" as a prelude to further negotiations. In the spring of 1987 the prospect of a diplomatic rapprochement between Israel and the Soviet Union, and the reunion of the PLO at the seventeenth meeting of the Palestine National Council in Algiers, gave Israeli and Jordanian diplomats fresh hope that a vaguely defined "international conference" might be convened. But most observers saw less hope for peace than ever.

The United Nations remains on the margins of the peace process in the Middle East. The General Assembly has reviled Israel relentlessly for its occupation of the West Bank and the Gaza Strip, but Israel has ignored the actions of the General Assembly, protesting the body's strong pro-Arab bias. In the Security Council the United States has continued to veto almost all resolutions critical of Israel, urging its colleagues on the Council to adopt a more "balanced" approach to Middle Eastern issues.

The most intractable problem of the Arab-Israeli conflict remains the **central Palestine question**. Israel has never conceded Palestinian rights to self-determination and continues to treat the PLO as a fundamentally illegitimate "terrorist" organization that operates beyond the bounds of international law and world civilization. The Palestinians, for their part, have refused to recognize the state of Israel without a reciprocal concession from the Israelis, and the PLO continues to claim the right to "armed resistance" within the Occupied Territories and Israel proper.

Israel is willing to negotiate on the basis of U.N. Security Council resolutions 242 and 338, the former conferring legitimacy and "the right to live within secure borders" on "every state in the area" (though many Israeli leaders do not accept the resolution's application to the occupied West Bank). Similarly, the United States will not deal with the PLO until it endorses Security Council resolution 242 and affirms without reservation Israel's right to exist. But the PLO will not accept 242 as the basis for a settlement, since the resolution makes no mention of Palestinian rights and addresses the Palestinians only as a refugee problem. The Arab states, while loudly championing

Palestinian rights, have generally pursued their own interests, when necessary at the expense of the Palestinian people.

The complex issues surrounding the question of an "international peace conference" have divided Arabs and Israelis since the Six Day War of 1967. Arabs have long favored a "comprehensive solution" to the conflict in the Middle East, to be mandated by an international conference that would seat the five permanent members of the Security Council together with all the "frontline" Arab states, Israel, and the PLO. Israel, loath to submit to the collective pressure of the Arabs and the Soviet Union, has preferred to pursue bilateral negotiations with its Arab neighbors, in order to exert maximum bargaining leverage on each and to avoid the Palestinians entirely. The United States, which has brokered several bilateral agreements between Israel and the Arab states since the Yom Kippur War of 1973, has also resisted the idea of an international conference, which would put undue pressure on its ally Israel and might expand Soviet influence in the region.

Both before and after the Amman Accord, Jordan's King Hussein has continued to insist on an international conference, if only as a prelude to direct bilateral negotiations between Israel and a joint Jordanian-Palestinian delegation. This tricky construction was encouraged by Israeli Prime Minister Shimon Peres, who told the United Nations General Assembly in September 1985 that he favored negotiations with a Jordanian-Palestinian delegation that might "be initiated with the support of an international forum, as agreed upon by the negotiating states" [A/40/PV.42, P. 59]. The Prime Minister later indicated that he might sanction an international conference of the kind advocated by King Hussein if the Soviet Union restored diplomatic relations with Israel, severed eighteen years previously during the Six Day War [Newsweek, 11/4/85].

King Hussein's repudiation of the Amman Accord in early 1986 dealt a blow to Peres's plans, but the Israeli Prime Minister pursued the peace process in talks with Morocco's King Hassan and Egyptian President Hosni Mubarak during the summer of 1986. In a surprise visit to Morocco in August, intended as a reprise of Sadat's historic trip to Jerusalem in 1977, Prime Minister Peres conferred for the first time with King Hassan, but the leaders' closing communiqué indicated that they agreed on very little and had no new ideas for peace. Hassan, always an outsider in the Arab-Israeli conflict, found the results of the conference so embarrassing that he quickly resigned as acting president of the Arab League. In September, Prime Minister Peres and Egyptian President Mubarak held a "peace summit" in Alexandria, their third meeting of the year, where the two leaders declared that "1987 will be the year of peace"—a prediction even Egypt's semiofficial press found hard to swallow [Al-Ahram, 9/15/86]. However theatrical and empty, these demarches in the direction of peace were arrested in October, when Prime Minister Peres and Israeli Foreign Minister Yitzhak Shamir exchanged offices, according to a compromise worked out two years previously, when the Israeli Labor and Likud blocs formed a joint ruling coalition following the elections of October 1984. Succeeding Menachem Begin as head of the rightist Likud, Shamir has stridently opposed an international conference of any kind. But as Israel's new foreign minister, Shimon Peres has continued to press his own foreign policy agenda on Arab and American leaders; and in the spring of 1987, Peres began to promote his notion of an international conference as an issue so critical and so divisive within the ruling coalition that it might justify the calling of early parliamentary elections.

In April 1987 the PLO met in Algiers before the convening of the **eighteenth session of the Palestine National Council in Algiers**. Ending almost five years of internecine strife following Israel's invasion of Lebanon and the expulsion of the PLO from Lebanon, the PLO's two largest factions—Yasser Arafat's Fatah and George Habash's Popular Front for the Liberation of Palestine (PFLP)—formally reconciled after Arafat agreed to abrogate the Amman Accord, which had become a dead letter after King Hussein had repudiated it fourteen months previously. Several smaller pro-Syrian factions, including Nayif Hawatimeh's PFLP–General Command, stayed in Damascus, refusing to go to Algiers at all.

The Algiers reunion, which reelected Arafat as PLO chairman, took place in the wake of a gradual **return of PLO cadres and influence to Lebanon,** where a brutal siege of Palestinian refugee camps by the Syrian-backed Shiite Amal had rallied estranged PLO factions around the prestige of Chairman Arafat. In Algiers, PFLP leaders conceded that their faction's strong alliance with Syria had damaged Palestinian unity, while the PLO reunion as a whole resisted pressure from Damascus to cut ties completely with Egypt, which signed a separate peace with Israel at Camp David in 1978 [*Al-Ra'y*, Amman, 4/16/87]. Nevertheless, Cairo reacted to the PLO's strong denunciation of Camp David in Algiers by breaking off diplomatic relations with the organization.

The PLO reunion coincided with new talk in Israel and Jordan of an international peace conference. Jordanian diplomats in Algiers said that in recent trips to Italy and Spain, Foreign Minister Peres had shown far more flexibility than U.S. Secretary of State George Shultz. Jordanians also expressed the hope that differences between Labor and Likud regarding the peace process could be resolved if the Soviet Union restored diplomatic relations with Israel and allowed Soviet Jews to emigrate to Israel [*Jerusalem Post*, 4/22/87]. In March and early April a series of Soviet concessions to Israel, including an informal Soviet promise to allow more than ten thousand Soviet Jews to emigrate via "direct transit" to Israel in 1987 and an official agreement to set up an Israel consular presence in Moscow, seemed to signal a Soviet-Israeli rapprochement [*Le Monde*, 4/3/87].

Nevertheless, prospects for peace in the Middle East seem as grim as ever. The reunion of the PLO at Algiers moved the organization's mainstream away from the kind of peace framework Israel is likely to accept, and there is no consensus in Israel concerning a future peace process. Both the Israeli people and the Israeli parliament remain deeply divided on the merit of an international conference, not to mention the issues such a conference might address. Moreover, Likud's Yitzhak Shamir has so far refused to consider Labor's proposed linkage between Soviet emigration and an international peace conference. Even if the Israeli voters endorse Foreign Minister Peres's foreign policy in new elections, it is doubtful that Peres's formulation would make room for the PLO, which all Arab states have recognized as the sole legitimate representative of the Palestinian people.

Many moderates, both Israeli and Palestinian, feel that peace must be made now before Israel's annexation of the Occupied Territories becomes irreversible, if it is not already so. Israel now controls, directly or indirectly, 50 percent of the West Bank (where more than 140,000 Israelis live in some 110 settlements) and East Jerusalem [*The New York Times*, 1/26/86]. Israel has also confiscated a third of the Gaza Strip, which well-known Israeli demographer Meron Benvenisti has called "the Soweto of the state of Israel." Benvenisti's figures show that the Strip is now as crowded as Hong Kong and may double in population to 900,000 by 1999 [*Jerusalem Post*, 6/7/86]. Meanwhile, mutual hostility and intolerance between Israelis and Palestinians are spreading in Israel and the Occupied Territories, especially among a new generation of Jews and Arabs who have grown up since the Six Day War. Sporadic bombings and attacks by Palestinians, often followed by harsh Israeli reprisals, have further fueled this hatred.

The 41st Session of the General Assembly passed a number of resolutions condemning Israel's occupation of the West Bank and the Gaza Strip. The Assembly's **resolution on "The Situation in the Middle East"** [A/Res/41/162] repeated the body's conviction that "the question of Palestine is at the core of the conflict" and that a just solution to the Arab-Israeli conflict must include the PLO. The resolution demanded "the total and unconditional withdrawal by Israel from all the Palestinian and other Arab lands occupied since 1967, including Jerusalem." It also reaffirmed its call to convene an international peace conference under the auspices of the United Nations.

The 42nd Session of the General Assembly will again address these issues and will no doubt adopt a series of resolutions condemning Israel and its unlawful occupation of Arab lands.

Lebanon

Persistent sectarian strife and public disorder have kept Lebanon in a state of virtual anarchy since the outbreak of the Lebanese civil war in 1975. The situation has deteriorated further since Israel's invasion of Lebanon in 1982. In 1985, Israel's withdrawal from southern Lebanon to a six-mile-wide "security zone" north of the Israeli border raised new hopes that Lebanese internal disputes might be peacefully resolved. But without a functioning central government or a national consensus on how to restore one, Lebanon's many private armies have continued their bloody turf battles.

Syria, which maintains more than 25,000 troops in Lebanon, has not been able to impose peace on its fractious neighbor. Since the Israeli withdrawal, Damascus has brokered numerous "national reconciliation" accords and "security plans," but to no avail. In March 1987 escalating violence between several Lebanese militias and the Shiite Amal, Syria's chief client in Lebanon, threatened to upset the country's precarious balance of power, forcing Syria to occupy West Beirut for the first time since the late 1970s. Syria's move into West Beirut was clearly a last recourse, which put its alliance with Iran in jeopardy (Syrian troops dealt harshly with Iranian-backed militia forces) and expanded Syria's already costly and dangerous involvement in the killing fields of Lebanon.

The United Nations has also been frustrated by its efforts to push war-torn Lebanon toward peace. The mandate of the **United Nations Interim Force in Lebanon (UNIFIL)**, which was sent to restore Lebanese sovereignty in southern Lebanon in 1978 after an Israeli incursion, has been thwarted by Israel's refusal to evacuate its "security zone" and by harassment of local militias, including the Israeli-backed South Lebanon Army (SLA). UNIFIL has also had to contend with the violence of the Shiite Hizbollah, which has not been appeased by Israel's withdrawal from most of southern Lebanon in 1985. U.N. attempts to mediate between Israel and Lebanon broke down in 1985 due to differences between the parties involved. The Security Council has been unable to intervene effectively in Lebanon. Wishing to avoid any association with the larger Arab-Israeli conflict, the Lebanese government has declared Lebanon's civil war "internal," and thus unsuited to consideration by the Council. Differences within the Security Council have further hampered its efforts vis-à-vis Lebanon.

Violence has persisted between the militias of Lebanon's many ethnic and religious communities. In the last year the fiercest fighting has raged in "**the war of the camps**," which started in May 1985 when the Shiite Amal, assisted by elements of the Syrian and Lebanese armies, stormed three Palestinian refugee camps in Beirut and southern Lebanon in an effort to establish Shiite hegemony over the area and forestall the return of PLO guerrillas. This campaign did not drive armed Palestinian defenders from their homes, and Amal has renewed the war of the camps several times in the last two years, culminating in a siege and bombardment of Palestinian camps near Tyre, Sidon, and Beirut that began in October and November of 1986. In Sidon, Palestinian fedayeen fought their way out of their camps and captured the strategic village of Maghdousheh, scoring the PLO's first military victory in Lebanon since the Israeli invasion. In Tyre and Beirut the war of the camps brought Palestinian settlements to the brink of starvation and epidemic by late

February, when Amal began to allow periodic shipments of food and emergency supplies into the Palestinian camps [*Time*, 2/23/87]. The brutal battles between the Shiite Amal and the Palestinians have underscored Amal's fierce determination to control southern Lebanon, moving other factions in the country to oppose Amal's drive for hegemony and to support a revival of PLO power in Lebanon. It was the prospect of a new anti-Amal coalition and a return of the PLO that forced Syria to invade West Beirut.

Turf wars between the Shiite Amal and Druze militias have continued to flare up, most fiercely in February 1987, when a week of fighting in West Beirut left 135 dead and many more wounded [*The New York Times*, 2/20/87]. In late 1986 the Christian Maronite Phalange and the PLO, long bitter enemies, concluded an alliance. In return for a substantial cash payment from the PLO, the Phalange reportedly agreed to help smuggle PLO fighters into Lebanon [*Jerusalem Post*, 1/7/87]. Of the twelve thousand fedayeen who were evacuated in 1982 during the Israeli invasion, up to four thousand had returned to Beirut and south Lebanon by the end of 1986 [*Middle East International*, 12/6/86]. The Christian Phalange, which massacred hundreds of Palestinians in Sabra and Shatila after the PLO evacuation of Beirut in September 1982, now fears the Shiite Amal far more than its old foe, the PLO.

Meanwhile, fighting along Israel's "security zone" continues in the south. The Iranian-backed Shiite fundamentalist organization Hizbollah, whose power and influence has grown rapidly since its formation in the wake of the Israeli invasion, fired Katyusha rockets on settlements in northern Israel and staged raids against Israeli and SLA positions in southern Lebanon, prompting retaliation in force by Israeli warplanes. UNIFIL counted sixty-nine assaults on Israel's security zone in the last five months of 1986, noting that over this period the attacks "became fewer in number but larger in scale" [S/18541].

Lebanon also witnessed a surge in the **abduction of foreign citizens**. While several hostages were released, several dozen more were taken, and about a dozen hostages, mostly American and West European, are still being held captive. In January 1987, Terry Waite, the Anglican envoy who had been negotiating hostage releases for several years, disappeared while on a mission in West Beirut. The abductors of these hostages remain unknown, although they are presumed to be Hizbollah offshoots and radical pro-Palestinian groups.

Another war between Syria and Israel in Lebanon is unlikely. Following allegations that Syria was behind a failed attempt to blow up an Israeli airliner in April 1986, rumors of a new war buffeted the region, but tensions between Syria and Israel quickly subsided. Israel's withdrawal to its security zone in southern Lebanon in 1985 has eased friction between the two countries, restoring Lebanon to the status of a buffer zone separating the Syrian and Israeli armies. At present Israel, Syria, and the Shiite Amal all have an interest in checking the revival of PLO power in Lebanon. Syria's consistent support for Amal's war of the camps, as well as Syrian intervention in West Beirut in March 1987, was activated in part by fears in Damascus that a growing Palestinian armed presence would jeopardize the delicate strategic balance that Israel and Syria have struck.

UNIFIL, which has nearly six thousand troops in southern Lebanon, continues to play a peacekeeping role, although its U.N. mandate proscribes the use of force to stop guerrilla attacks or Israeli countermeasures. According to the Secretary-General, one UNIFIL soldier was killed as a result of Israeli/SLA fire in the second half of 1986, while the force lost five men in an incident involving unnamed "armed groups." In his semiannual report of January 1987, the Secretary-General noted that UNIFIL's finances have continued to deteriorate, owing to the failure of some U.N. members to meet their UNIFIL obligations. In 1986 and 1987, the United States Congress withheld 50 percent of the U.S. assessed share. Although the administration asked Congress for an additional appropriation of $21.6 million to make up part of the shortfall [S/18581], this was not approved.

UNWRA

The United States Relief and Works Agency for Palestine Refugees in the Near East (UNWRA) was created in 1949 to provide humanitarian support for some 700,000 Palestinian refugees. Today the agency extends a wide range of welfare services to more than 2.1 million eligible refugees in the Middle East and provides education to 350,000 Palestinian students in Jordan, Lebanon, Syria, and the Occupied Territories. UNWRA also supplies shelter materials, emergency medical supplies, and food relief for more than 108,000 Palestinians it classes as "special hardship cases."

In 1986, UNWRA's operations were budgeted at $191 million, the largest contributions coming from the United States ($67 million), the European Economic Community ($37 million), and Japan ($11.8 million). The previous year the agency had weathered a severe financial crisis when its proposed budget of $258.2 million faced a sudden and severe shortfall, requiring sharp cuts in education services as well as staff and expenditure reductions across-the-board. The greatest challenge UNWRA now faces is how best to use its severely limited resources to serve its large and quite needy constituency [DPI/NGO/SB/87/4].

As in past years, the anarchy and violence in Lebanon have imperiled both UNWRA clients and personnel, making the agency's work extremely difficult and dangerous. Since June 1982, 26 UNWRA workers have been killed in Lebanon, out of a total staff of 2,300. The agency played a vital role in getting emergency food and medical supplies into the Palestinian refugee camps that the Shiite Amal have besieged since October 1986. Since February 1987,

UNWRA has been permitted to enter many of these camps several times, but the agency's repeated calls to lift the siege have not been heard [PAL 1648, 1649].

3. Africa

Persistent **civil wars** of transnational significance and **deepening poverty** largely resistant to a quarter-century of development efforts continue to tear at an already shredding political fabric on the African continent. The result is an expanding human tragedy that mocks the aspirations of Africa's first generation of nationalist leaders.

Foremost among the issues facing the continent—and scheduled to dominate the agenda of the 42nd General Assembly, as they did the 41st—are the crisis of Southern Africa and of the African economy. In their magnitude and complexity these particular problems overshadow other issues such as the fates of the Western Sahara and Chad, refugees, and, potentially, the Horn of Africa. But as more and more of these issues are seen as manifestations of the same syndrome of deteriorating political institutions and economic performance, they are being considered less and less in isolation from one another on the agendas of the General Assembly. It is for this reason too that in matters relating to Southern Africa and the continent's economic recovery the United Nations has increasingly explored the opportunities for cooperating with the **Organization of African Unity**, the body that represents the continent as a whole. The **Southern Africa Development Coordination Conference (SADCC)** has also begun to play a similar, if lesser, regional role.

Southern Africa

In the year between the 41st and 42nd General Assemblies several important developments have influenced the prospects for change in Southern Africa. The **economic sanctions** on South Africa passed by the U.S. Congress over the veto of President Reagan gave new momentum to the movement to bring such pressures on Pretoria. The European Economic Community has also imposed sanctions, though to date they are somewhat milder. And in June the Reverend Leon Sullivan, author of racial equity guidelines for multinational firms operating in South Africa, announced his judgment that economic sanctions and not just equitable business behavior were necessary.

Such pressure has posed the question of how to mitigate the adverse effects on South Africa's neighbors of the Botha regime's response to an increase in sanctions. The strong showing by the Botha government in the May 1987 whites-only election for the white parliamentary chamber has undermined the hypothesis that fissures on the left and right in the white community of South Africa have destroyed the present government's political base. The U.S.

government's open support for the **National Union for the Total Independence of Angola** (**UNITA**) in the Angolan civil war has rendered the war's resolution a more distant prospect; and this in turn has made less likely further international agreement on independence for **Namibia**, which South Africa—with Reagan administration support—has linked to the withdrawal of the Cuban troops who are defending the Angolan government against UNITA. The death of Mozambique's President Samora Machel in a plane crash, under suspicious circumstances, drew international attention to the country's dire economic situation, which many attribute to Machel's policies and to South Africa's support for Renamo, the guerrilla force bent on overthrowing Mozambique's present regime. South African raids on Botswana, Zimbabwe, and Zambia dramatized the Botha government's commitment to destabilizing neighboring regimes as a means of ensuring its own survival.

For a long time now and with near-unanimity the General Assembly has made clear its support for comprehensive and mandatory sanctions leading to an end to apartheid in all its manifestations in South Africa and to the establishment of majority rule, to independence for Namibia on the basis of internationally supervised free elections, and to an end to South African attempts to destabilize the governments of neighboring countries. The General Assembly has also indicated its support for both collective and national efforts to address the problems of relief and development to lift the peoples of Africa out of poverty. The real issue before the 42nd and subsequent General Assemblies is to consider additional strategies for implementing these objectives that will generate more rapid progress than has been seen in the past.

South Africa. Major international conferences to build on resolutions of earlier sessions and to mobilize support against apartheid have been a prelude to the 42nd General Assembly. Their implicit purpose has been to rain down upon South Africa ever-heavier torrents of world opinion and to increase pressure on the Pretoria regime. In mid-June 1986, at the UNESCO headquarters in Paris, came the World Conference on Sanctions against Racist South Africa, a cooperative effort of the United Nations, the Organization of African Unity, and the Non-Aligned Movement initiated by the 40th General Assembly. Its tasks were to review recent developments in South Africa and antiapartheid measures taken by governments and international organizations, and to determine what additional measures might be taken to speed apartheid's demise. Of particular concern were implementing comprehensive and mandatory sanctions, preventing breaches of the arms embargo against South Africa, imposing an oil embargo, and offsetting the impact of sanctions against neighboring frontline states. Invitations were sent to all members of the United Nations, some nonmember states, institutions within the U.N. system, liberation movements, and other organizations working to end apartheid. Noteworthy by their absence as either participants or observers were the

United States, the United Kingdom, West Germany, and the more conservative African states, such as Malawi and the Ivory Coast.

Stating as its broad goals a democratic South Africa and an end to apartheid, independence for Namibia, and peace in the region as a whole, the conference followed the General Assembly in urging mandatory and comprehensive sanctions, judged the U.S. policy of "constructive engagement" a failure, and urged an end to any form of collaboration with the South African regime. It also urged an end to all military trade with and support for South Africa, with particular reference to curbing the regime's nuclear capacity; proposed an intergovernmental agency to monitor compliance with the oil embargo and efforts to discourage banks from rescheduling South African debts; and urged the prohibition of technology transfer and the termination of air and shipping links as well as imports of South African agricultural products. At the same time, the conference commended the Southern African liberation movements for their commitment to justice for all peoples of the region notwithstanding their persecution at the hands of the South African government.

Building on the 38th Assembly's declaration of the **Second Decade to Combat Racism and Racial Discrimination**, the Commission on Human Rights convened in Yaounde, Cameroon, a seminar on International Assistance to Peoples and Movements Struggling against Colonialism, Racism, Racial Discrimination, and Apartheid (April 28–May 9). The seminar called upon nongovernmental institutions, private organizations, and individuals to continue and to increase support for the Trust Fund for the Second Decade and sought support for SADCC as a vehicle for assisting Southern African liberation movements and for reducing their collective economic dependence upon South Africia. It also appealed to transnational corporations still doing business in South Africa and Namibia to cooperate in supporting liberation movements as well as sanctions intended to put an end to apartheid—and attempted to add teeth to the appeal by requesting U.N. member states to take punitive measures against recalcitrant individuals and institutions.

The mobilization of international public opinion and resources against apartheid also gained impetus from Zimbabwe's accession to the presidency of the Non-Aligned Movement. The movement pledged its support for the African Solidarity Fund, intended to assist the cause of liberation movements in the region.

U.S. sanctions banning all new investment by Americans in South African businesses, prohibiting importation of such products as coal and steel from South Africa, and cancelling U.S. landing rights for South African airlines added strength to the international sanctions movement, but estimates were that no more than 10 percent of South Africa's trade with the United States would be affected. Whatever the President's domestic reasons for appointing a black American, Edward J. Perkins, as ambassador to South Africa at this time, the appointment seemed yet another herald of a new U.S. posture toward South Africa. Shortly afterward, major U.S. corporations began to announce their withdrawal from South Africa, among them IBM, General Motors, Honeywell, and Eastman Kodak. But these dramatic moves did not hide the fact that many large corporations continue in South Africa, and the issue remains a divisive one in universities and in debates over the investment of pension funds. How effective such withdrawals prove to be in the long run will depend upon how the many and complex component issues are resolved.

The imposition of **new sanctions** has been spotty worldwide. The governments of Japan, West Germany, and the United Kingdom, for example, have yet to take major steps, although individual companies, such as Barclays of Britain and the Dutch-based multinational SHV, have moved to divest (the latter after numerous arson attacks on its facilities in the Netherlands). In March 1987, Sweden moved to ban all trade with South Africa, Norway and Denmark having taken this step a year earlier. Of even greater potential significance, however, was Israel's action in the same month to ban further military sales contracts—a decision that appears to have been taken at least partly in response to pressure from the United States. One reason for Israel's previous reluctance was its concern for the status and well-being of the more than 120,000 Jews in South Africa.

Reinforcing the resolutions of the Paris Conference of 1986 as well as those of previous General Assemblies, the 41st General Assembly again called for mandatory and comprehensive sanctions; appealed for assistance to liberation movements that offer resistance to apartheid and destabilization campaigns in the region; condemned Israeli arms trade with South Africa; urged further support for the oil embargo and nonfraternization with South Africa in sports and cultural events; and supported the work of the special committee in sponsoring conferences and seminars to highlight the problem of apartheid and to mobilize support for its elimination.

As had been the case in previous years, such resolutions passed overwhelmingly over the opposition or abstentions of the United States, several European countries, Israel, and the more conservative countries of Latin America and Africa. The most dependable opponent in the last category was the Ivory Coast, joined by Malawi on such issues as the oil embargo.

The **central issues before the General Assembly** and all other institutions that subscribe to the objectives it has proclaimed for the region are: (1) What works? (2) What have been the effects in the region of the measures that have been taken? (3) What additional measures can be taken to increase the salutary effects and diminish the unwanted ones? The most persistent argument against sanctions has been that they will not move the South African regime, that these "hostile" external initiatives may enable it to rally broader support than it otherwise could, and that they may be counterproductive for other countries of the region. Against these arguments, supporters of sanctions have noted that the leaders of the oppressed peoples of the region have accepted the costs of sanctions in the cause of bringing down apartheid, while they have appealed to friendly governments and organizations to support the groups most likely to be affected by a South African backlash.

The Botha regime has shown itself prepared to magnify, intensify, and extend its pattern of repression to secure its hold on power domestically and regionally, while maneuvering to blunt the short- and long-term effects of increased economic sanctions. Most recently, emboldened by its electoral success, the regime moved to reinstate emergency measures. The effects of such increased repression have been apparent in the regime's measures to carry out the state of emergency: arrests, detentions, torture, and killings; political trials and forced resettlement of whole black communities; increased repression of a broadening array of domestically based groups, such as labor and students, which demonstrate their opposition to apartheid; and aggressive action to destabilize the governments of neighboring countries.

The South African regime imposed a nationwide state of emergency in June 1986 in direct response to a planned ten-day boycott of white-owned businesses, coordinated by the United Democratic Front (UDF), the Congress of South African Trade Unions (COSATU), and the South African Council of Churches, on the tenth anniversary of the Soweto uprising. It was a prelude to a year of escalating violent struggles against apartheid, each topped by an increase of official repression. A central feature of the emergency regulations has been tighter **restrictions against reporting by journalists** on the struggles within the country, the effects of which are to limit external coverage of antiapartheid protests and government crackdowns and to make the South African Bureau of Information the sole source of "legitimate" information on strikes, boycotts, schools, and local organizations within the townships. Reporting of "subversive statements" (defined as any form of opposition to a Cabinet official), of opposition to conscription by young whites, of forced removals of black communities, and of any protests against restrictions on press freedom is now also illegal.

The enforcement of the emergency regulations has resulted in heavy, around-the-clock patrolling of townships by the army as well as the police and in violence against blacks, resulting in the deaths of an estimated 2,300 and the detention of more than 20,000. Armed personnel sit in black classrooms; they have attacked peaceful demonstrations in churches, schools, and at funerals; and they have raided the headquarters of COSATU.

To enforce these measures in the townships the government has recruited special black constables, who rule with the assistance of both police and army units. Vigilante groups, with the encouragement and support of the regime, have warred against antiapartheid groups in these areas. Some of the vigilante groups have been associated with **Inkatha**, the party of **Kwa Zulu Chief Minister Gatsha Buthelezi**, who leads a significant constituency seeking to negotiate with rather than overthrow the Botha regime. Civil rights workers, UDF officials, and others testify to killings, beatings, and torture by these units as part of their effort to maintain their authority within the townships. Children have suffered arrest and even death, and some have been sent to special camps for "reorientation" to the realities of white minority rule. Reacting to public pressure, the government claimed to have released most of these children as of mid-May 1987. Noteworthy too has been the extension of such repression to a growing number of dissident whites. Police may ban any gathering at any time for any reason.

Although many have been held without trial, the regime has conducted extensive trials of some others. Here the main purpose appears to be to undermine resistance rather than to convict—the evidence for which is a relatively low rate of convictions. Those held without trial have been confined to overcrowded detention centers whose conditions are deplorable and where beatings, torture, and killings are commonplace, according to reports from those who have been released.

Demographic patterns have increasingly undermined even the paper viability of the government's **homeland strategy,** which is to perpetuate these areas' economic dependence upon the South African regime while obliging them to receive all blacks not wanted in the white areas. Industrial development in some homelands has been insufficient to permit the maintenance of this delicate balance, and this fact is responsible for the rapid population growth in the unplanned squatter communities on the fringes of white-dominated cities. The government is unable or unprepared to provide for emigration of such magnitude, while failure to do so offers a continual challenge—even a threat —to political stability. Despite an earlier promise to discontinue the leveling of these urban settlements and the involuntary relocation of these "homeland" citizens, such forced relocation continues and more is in prospect. Increasingly, the process is carried out through intimidation and coercion.

The **African National Congress** (ANC) has campaigned to make South Africa ungovernable until apartheid is ended and true democracy realized, and it is in the townships that African communities have sought to substitute the authority of their own establishment for that of the Botha regime. Here "people power" has been practiced, the basic units of which have been the **street committees,** often the special targets of the South African government. A high percentage of the regime's detainees have been members of these committees [Special Committee Against Apartheid, *Recent Developments in South Africa,* 1/87]. Street committees have been composed of teachers, factory workers, clerics, and unemployed youth, and have provided grass roots coordination or resistance to the regime.

Increasingly, the war between the regime and people power has become a fight for the minds and souls of the young—that is, in the schools and in the churches. School boycotts organized by the committees and school closings ordered by the regime have been the major weapons in the battle over what the youth of the country should be taught about its history. For example, will the work and the writings of Nelson Mandela, Walter and Albertina Sisula, and other black nationalist leaders by included? White youth have increasingly rebelled at conscription campaigns made necessary by the government's determination to suppress manifestations of people power. Even elements of the Dutch Reformed Church have spoken out against the imprisonment and treatment of detainees.

Unions as well as the major political parties have linked grass roots and national campaigns for fundamental political change. The Congress of South African Trade Unions (COSATU) has supported the parties in their campaigns for an end to the emergency, apartheid, and detentions, including that of Nelson Mandela, while waging economic war with the regime over wages and workers' health and safety, especially in the mines. At the same time, new trade union federations—the Council of Unions of South Africa and the Azanian Confederation of Trade Unions—have emerged, representing degrees of difference with COSATU over affiliation with political parties and perhaps over the extent of worker control. Under the umbrella of common abhorrence of apartheid, differences over political strategy separate the major political parties. These are: the ANC, the Azanian People's Organization, the United Democratic Front, the South African Communist Party, and especially Inkatha, led by Buthelezi [Tom Lodge, *Black Politics in South Africa Since 1945* (London, New York: Longman, 1983)]. The position of Inkatha, the most conciliatory of these parties, was undermined greatly when, in December 1986, the South African regime rejected a proposed multiracial constitution in Natal, which Inkatha had backed.

In this growing civil war, the 42nd General Assembly faces the issues both of how to promote unity behind its campaign for comprehensive and mandatory sanctions and of how to implement those sanctions so as to maximize their favorable and minimize their unfavorable consequences. On the one hand, despite growing turmoil in South Africa, the Security Council again in April 1987 failed to approve such sanctions because of U.S. and U.K. vetoes, reinforced by West Germany's negative vote and the abstentions of France, Italy, and Japan. On the other hand, early commentaries on the impact of sanctions have warned that the effects may include strengthening corporate power in South Africa and enriching the few who control it, perhaps making it less rather than more responsive to pressures for political change [*The New York Times*, 12/31/86; *Forbes*, 3/9/87].

The Southern Africa Region.   South Africa continues to seek to defend its own apartheid system by rendering wholly dependent those of its neighbors it can control and keeping chronically destablized those it would like to control, thereby creating a region of buffer states to insulate itself from external pressures. South Africa was instrumental in effecting a military coup in Lesotho in 1985 because its cautious and conservative leader, the late Chief Jonathan Leabua, had failed to be sufficiently pliant. It has raided Zimbabwe, Zambia, and Botswana for allegedly harboring ANC exiles bent on guerrilla action against the regime. It openly supports civil wars against the governments of Mozambique and Angola, and it relentlessly holds on to its illegal de facto colony, Namibia. Alone among its neighbors, Swaziland appears to have escaped the wrath of the Botha regime to date. In addition, there is evidence that South Africa has passed along to its neighbors some of the effects of economic sanctions against apartheid through inter alia cancellation of employment contracts. Sanctions backlash provides a backdrop for consideration by the 42nd General Assembly of three particular regional crisis areas: Namibia, Mozambique, and Botswana.

Namibia. At the urging of the **United Nations Council for Namibia**, the General Assembly met in special session on the subject of Namibia in September 1986. The session took place on the twentieth anniversary of the General Assembly's decision to terminate South Africa's mandate over the territory. Despite off-and-on-again negotiations between South Africa and the Western Contact Group, and some progress on the issue of supervision of free elections as a prelude to independence for Namibia, South Africa's illegal occupation continues and has intensified. The regime has effectively nullified negotiations by linking them to Cuban withdrawal from Angola, with the acquiescence of the Reagan administration and the reluctant concurrence of other members of the Contact Group. In June the Reagan administration reaffirmed its support of South Africa's position that Cuban troops defending the Angola government from the National Union for the Total Independence of Angola (UNITA), supported by both the U.S. and South Africa, must be withdrawn before it will agree to further steps toward independence for Namibia. The Reagan administration did resume dialogue with Angola, however, broken off earlier.

The months preceding the Special Session were marked by increasing intransigence on the part of South Africa, which installed an "interim government" that proceeded to draw up a draft constitution for a "republic of Namibia." The government has imposed military rule on its illegal colony reminiscent of that practiced at home—for example, in its attempts to suppress the Ai-Gams (the Nama name for the capital, Windhoek) conference of churches, political organizations, and others that have declared both the interim government and its "constitution" unacceptable. The holding of the conference itself reflects a rising tide of opposition to illegal consolidation pressed not only by the **South West Africa People's Organization (SWAPO)** but by other organizations as well. SWAPO had sought, without success, to make

1986 the "Year of Decisive Action" for achievement of independence and majority rule.

The Special Session demanded South Africa's unconditional and complete withdrawal from Namibia, an interim adminstration to be established by the United Nations Council for Namibia, rejection of all constitution–formation initiatives by South Africa with respect to Namibia, reaffirmation of support for SWAPO as the legitimate representative of the people of Namibia, endorsement of armed as well as peaceful struggle to achieve Namibian independence, rejection of the "constructive engagement" strategy of the Reagan administration and of "linkage" of the Namibian and Angolan problems, and the extension of comprehensive and mandatory sanctions to Namibia.

The 42nd General Assembly will confront the fact that the South African government responded by proceeding with the draft constitution and the interim government, unmoved by the resolutions of the Special Session.

Mozambique.   The death of President Samora Machel in a plane crash under mysterious circumstances drew attention to the related phenomena of the country's ongoing civil war, its grinding poverty, its recent attempts to change development strategies to strengthen its economy and mitigate deplorable living conditions, its complex and unsatisfactory relationship with South Africa, and its strategic importance to the region.

Claiming unprovoked attacks on its soldiers, South Africa abandoned the Nkomati accords struck with the late president, an agreement that stipulated that neither country would support those seeking the overthrow of the other. South Africa continues to support the MNR, or Renamo, which for the first decade of Mozambique's independence has perpetuated the civil war that marked the fifteen preceding years. The major international famine relief efforts needed to support Mozambique have directly reflected its inability to develop in the face of civil war. War and poverty have continued to undermine the authority of the Frelimo government as they did the earlier Portuguese colonial administration. They have obstructed the government's efforts to rethink its policies, including greater receptivity to Western approaches to development. While seeking to overthrow the Frelimo regime, the Botha government has also sought to negotiate with it, not least because its port of Beira is an important potential instrument for sanctions-busting. It is also important to the country's landlocked neighbor and ally, Zimbabwe, whose rail link to the port of Beira is the major alternative to shipments of goods through South Africa. The rail link has been a major target of Renamo guerrilla attacks. Massive rehabilitation is required if it is to be serviceable to both countries, necessitating major support from international development financiers. To this end Zimbabwe, Tanzania, and Malawi have committed troops to assist in clearing the port facility. Work is also under way in clearing the port of

Nakala to further reduce Mozambique's shipping dependence on South Africa. Meanwhile, the heads of state of Mozambique, Zaire, Zambia, and Angola met and agreed in principle on April 30 to begin rehabilitation of the Benguela railway, another potential trade corridor not under the control of South Africa. Even UNITA leader Jonas Savimbi promised to allow all nonmilitary material shipped on the railway to pass without hindrance through the zones his movement controls.

Despite its port facilities, Mozambique remains heavily dependent on South Africa not only for trade outlets and employment but for essential services such as electric power. Meanwhile, its neighbor Malawi has been accused by both Zimbabwe and Mozambique of harboring Renamo guerrillas. However, in mid-1987 Malawi made clear to its neighbors that it would no longer tolerate Renamo partisans on its soil. In the Mozambique situation, therefore, solutions to aggravated underdevelopment, internal political weakness and instability, and the South African problem are all joined.

While the regional political struggle continues, a desperate struggle for survival goes on for an estimated 670,000 displaced persons in Angola and at least 3.5 million people in Mozambique, victims of the combined and interrelated ravages of war, drought, and famine. Under United Nations auspices, a donors conference in Geneva pledged $255 million for the relief of endangered people in Mozambique, while $210 million had been raised for Angolan refugees as of June 1987. The major difficulties in both theaters have been finding the means of reaching people at risk who are trapped in war zones and persuading donors to provide resources to help regenerate development as well as to relieve immediate food and health emergencies.

Botswana. Since its independence Botswana has been nearly universally recognized as a model of stable, multiparty democracy, interracial harmony, and moderately successful development. Its two postindependence leaders, the late Sir Seretse Khama and Quett Masire, have been recognized as men of vision and statesmanship, successfully walking the tightrope between economic dependence on South Africa and the nation's own political independence, especially with respect to apartheid.

In addition to making raids on Botswana, along with Zimbabwe and Zambia, for its alleged harboring of ANC guerrilla warriors, South Africa attempted in late 1986 and early 1987 to force de facto recognition by Botswana of the neighboring "homeland" of Bophuthatswana by insisting that those in transit between Botswana and South Africa, including rail employees, secure Bophuthatswana visas.

The African Development Crisis

The 13th Special Session of the General Assembly, convened in May 1986, was the first such session ever to address comprehensively a crisis enveloping an entire continent. It was also the first session in the five-year "dialogue" between African countries and representatives of donor countries to be held on the basis of African proposals for the continent's economic recovery.

Earlier, African governments and the World Bank had been at cross-purposes over the relative contributions to their plight of international and domestic economic failures, the relative importance of South-South as against North-South trade in producing recovery, the relative importance of food self-sufficiency and export promotion, the relative importance of agriculture in national development strategies and of small producers within the agricultural sector, and especially the suitability of World Bank and International Monetary Fund (IMF) processes for demanding policy reform of African countries. Multilateral and bilateral donors have come to recognize their own contributions to the crisis, the necessity of their greater financial support for the needed reforms, and the efforts of African countries to undertake reforms on their own initiative instead of under threat of external economic coercion.

For their part, African governments appeared to appreciate the importance of policy reform, of shifting domestic development priorities, and of renewed domestic effort in the quest for economic recovery. These themes were reflected in the plan presented to the Special Session by the Organization of African Unity.

The Special Session marked both achievements and continued barriers to international cooperation in promoting African economic recovery. On the one hand, intensive negotiations produced broad agreement on the substantive measures necessary for renewed African economic development with the cooperation and assistance of international and bilateral development agencies. These measures were incorporated in the **United Nations Programme of Action for African Economic Recovery and Development 1986-90.**

The U.N. program placed primary emphasis upon the revitalization of the agricultural sector, especially upon women farmers, who are also predominantly quite small-scale farmers; preparation for and early warning of food shortfalls occasioned by drought and/or pestilence; and a variety of medium-to long-term measures to increase agricultural productivity. Significantly, the emphasis was upon increased food production, with relatively little emphasis upon the export promotion stressed by bilateral donors and by the World Bank and the IMF. Livestock development, long the poor relation in rural development strategies, was given high priority. Reforestation of a once richly covered and now rapidly balding continent and attendant measures to control desertification and to develop firewood schemes also claimed a high priority. The Special Session agreed that agricultural recovery depends upon parallel measures to build capacity for producing agricultural equipment, spare parts, and other agricultural inputs; strengthened transport and communications facilities; improved marketing and distribution channels; price incentives for producers; and improved capacity for project design and implementation. The session recognized the importance of improved management capacity and popular participation in development. It drew attention to the need for more and better family planning, to the requirements of refugees and displaced persons, and to the role of women in development processes.

The Special Session was less successful in reaching agreement on the forms that international commitment should take in promoting African economic recovery. The key sentence in the report of the Special Session stated that "The international community recognizes that the African countries need additional external resources" [Resolutions and Decisions Adopted by General Assembly at its Thirteenth Special Session, 5/27/86–6/1/86, p. 15]. But the major bilateral donors present at the Special Session refused to commit themselves to the specific external finance goal of $128.1 billion over five years set by the African countries, or to turn the session into what some referred to as a "pledging conference." Further, although the session recognized the negative impact of the debt burden on African development, the donor countries differed among themselves over the manner and extent of debt forgiveness and/or rescheduling. The delegates did agree on a variety of mechanisms to streamline cooperation and efficiency in the provision of external assistance, and they agreed that measures to promote noninflationary growth and elimination of protectionism would be key external factors facilitating African recovery. They further agreed that no bilateral donor should become a net recipient of capital flows from African countries as a result of structural adjustment during the life of the U.N. program, 1986–90.

To emphasize the U.N. commitment to effective and full implementation of the Special Session's recommendations, Secretary-General Pérez de Cuéllar appointed Ambassador Stephen Lewis of Canada, a major figure in helping participating countries reconcile their differences in order to arrive at the plan, as his special adviser on the plan's implementation. He also established a steering committee to oversee the United Nations' activities in support of implementation of the program. Composed of the heads of major U.N. bodies with development responsibilities, the committee is to work through the Economic Commission for Africa at the regional level and through U.N. resident coordinators/U.N. Development Programme resident representatives. He also designated a committee of experts, under the chairmanship of Sir Douglas Wass of the United Kingdom, to seek means of improving the financial position of heavily indebted countries undertaking structural adjustment in search of renewed development.

The 42nd General Assembly is to prepare for a review and appraisal of the five-year program, which is to occur near its midpoint during the 43rd Session in 1988. Although it is still too early to determine what, if any, changes in the African economic situations are incipient as a consequence of U.N. endorsement of the OAU-sponsored recovery program, certain preliminary trends appear to be emerging that are likely to influence General Assembly deliberations in the 42nd and subsequent sessions.

First, many countries of the continent are still in no position to participate in the initiatives endorsed by the U.N. program as they struggle to recover from famines induced by drought and civil wars. Thus, General Assembly resolutions center more on relief than on development. These resolutions address the plight of refugees in Africa; assistance to countries in Southern Africa affected by sanctions backlash; emergency food aid to Ethiopia; emergency assistance to Mozambique, Chad, Uganda, and the frontline states as a group; and measures to counteract a new infestation of locusts and grasshoppers over much of the continent.

Second, a sense of national identity and determination to preserve the reality of political independence survives in African countries even when political structures are too weak to institutionalize it or when governments misrepresent it in their excesses. While the World Bank and the IMF have voiced cautious optimism and given their recognition to African governments' efforts to undertake policy reforms, many African governments regard World Bank and IMF demands for policy reform as assaults on their national integrity. Ethiopia's leader, Colonel Mengistu, deals with these lenders only through ministers who have little authority to negotiate on their own. Although it is one of the African countries most open to Western influences, Kenya bridles at and deflects the impact of World Bank and IMF demands. Tanzania has gradually come to accept the Bank's demands but has resisted the pace demanded of it, viewing it as a ticket to political suicide. In Nigeria the Babangida government was unable to accommodate the Bank's requirements for structural adjustment in the face of widespread opposition based on the belief that these requirements involved surrender of national sovereignty. Nigeria's suspension of negotiations with the IMF is believed to have forestalled a coup attempt against the Babangida regime based on the belief that it was "too soft on the IMF" [*Africa Report*, 11-12/86].

In short, the challenges to the 42nd and succeeding General Assemblies are two. On the one hand, there is a need to break the cycle of destitution and political decay that stands in the way of implementing the U.N. program. On the other hand, international dialogue to promote development reform must take due account of African nations' undiminished sense of national identity and their requirements for deliberations with the international development community on the basis of mutual respect and understanding of each other's political as well as economic circumstances.

Chad and Western Sahara

Among the other important issues meriting the continued attention of the General Assembly, but pushed to one side by the magnitude and complexity of the Southern African and continental development crises, are the war over Western Sahara and the civil war in Chad.

The Western Saharan conflict erupted in 1975, when both Mauritania and Morocco attempted to annex the uranium-rich region as Spain prepared to bestow political independence upon it. Mauritania withdrew from the conflict in 1979. Nearly torn apart by the issue, the OAU Heads of State meeting in 1983 eventually hammered out a plan that called for a cease-fire and a referendum on the region's future under U.N. auspices, to be preceded by direct negotiations between **Morocco and the Frente Polisario**, the independence/resistance movement. But Morocco withdrew from the OAU because of its seating of the Polisario as a full member.

The 41st General Assembly endorsed the OAU plan. Acting initially on the basis of General Assembly resolution 40/50, the Secretary-General sought to promote talks between Morocco and the Frente Polisario over the future of Western Sahara, and he has continued to be active in that effort. Morocco's position has been complicated by its close relationship with the United States, which the Polisario believes has reinforced Moroccan unwillingness to negotiate. Meanwhile, a low-level war of attrition continues, which has propelled as many as 165,000 Sahrawi (Saharan) refugees into temporary camps across the border in Algeria, where they depend heavily on approximately $4 million in relief assistance per year from the United Nations High Commissioner for Refugees.

Chad has requested that the 42nd General Assembly consider aggression against and occupation of its country by Libyan forces at a time when Chad appears to have gained the upper hand militarily. Libya entered the Chadian civil war at the request and in support of former Chadian President Goukouni Oueddei in 1983, though the nations later broke with each other over the level of support provided. Goukouni has been at large first in Libya and, after his break with Libya, in Algeria. Meanwhile, Nigeria, the Ivory Coast, Gabon, and the Republic of the Congo have actively sought to reconcile Goukouni and his successor, Chad President Hissene Habré, on the basis of a common desire to end civil war and preserve Chad's political integrity. Such diplomatic activity has so far failed to bring the two sides together. Within Chad itself, however, the rival factions have largely united to fight the Libyans, now supported within the country by only a very small coterie. Substantial French and U.S. assistance has helped the government of Hissene Habré to modernize its forces, while the Libyan armies appear to be dispirited in fighting a war over which there has been much grumbling at home—factors not compensated for by the quality of their Soviet arms. Distrustful of Libyan intentions, Chad seeks the U.N.'s good offices to seal the permanent withdrawal of Libyan forces from its soil. A possible military solution, or a diplomatic one, will return the focus of attention to the underlying causes of the Chadian conflict—the fragile basis for a common policy among the many, often ethnically based factions almost continuously at war with each other since the country's independence in 1960.

4. Central America

From November 1986 through the spring and summer of 1987 the American domestic political crisis known as the **Iran/contra affair** mesmerized the nation and, in one of its many ironies, totally overshadowed the ongoing crises from which it arose—those in the Persian Gulf and Central America. As the United States focused on what had happened in Central America—the illegal funding of the Nicaraguan rebels, or contras, from profits generated by secret U.S. arms sales to Iran—less attention was paid to what was happening there, or to what might happen later. **Fighting intensified** in both Nicaragua and El Salvador. **U.S. citizens** allied to both camps were beginning to die, albeit in small numbers. Peacemaking attempts were being devised, were being thwarted, and were withering. The U.S. Congress faced a critical choice, along with the administration, about whether to continue funding the Nicaraguan contras for the 1988 fiscal year, beginning in October 1987, and if not, what the nation's alternative objective and tactic should be.

Virtually all the organs of the United Nations family—the Security Council, General Assembly, World Court, Secretary-General, Human Rights Commission, and even the World Bank and the International Monetary Fund—became **political battlegrounds** in this struggle. But most of the events played out in these forums were peripheral skirmishes. The essence of the war was being fought out in Washington.

The ultimate issue was whether the United States had the right, the need, or the ability to stem forcibly the spread of "pro-Soviet" regimes in the region and whether the effort could lead to the use of U.S. soldiers in combat in Central America. Just two days before the opening of marathon televised hearings into the Iran/contra scandal, President Reagan launched his campaign for the renewal of U.S. military aid to the rebels [*The Washington Post*, 5/4/87]. He argued that they offered the only road to democracy in Nicaragua and warned that without their pressure the Sandinista government would bring in the Soviets, threaten to destabilize El Salvador, and pose a threat to U.S. national interests. Few congressional opponents of the administration policy defended the Nicaraguan government, but they questioned the Sandinistas' capacity to export their revolution. They also questioned the abilities and intentions of the rebels, whose leaders range from disaffected Sandinistas to officers who served under Anastasio Somoza Debayle, the right-wing dictator overthrown by the 1979 revolution. The alternative offered to the Reagan policy was a resort to a negotiated agreement that would require the restoration of democracy in Nicaragua.

U.S. military support for the guerrilla groups—covert but legal—had been cut off as of 1984 by the **Boland Amendment,** which made it illegal to provide military funding, facilities, or training. A legal gray area was whether the

President or his aides could personally solicit military support for the contras from foreign governments or private American citizens. During the two-year period that the Boland Amendment was in effect, various administration officials, including the President, openly encouraged support for the contras. Some privately became involved in soliciting citizen contributions, aid from governments such as Israel, Saudi Arabia, and Brunei, and surreptitious official support for various contra projects, such as a secret airfield located in Costa Rica. Some sources said the total amount the contras received from these sources in 1985 was $32 million. The 1986 figure was not known [*The Washington Post*, 5/4/87]. The degree to which President Reagan knew of or participated in these efforts was a matter of dispute, but the White House denied that he authorized any of the illegal actions.

By the time the uproar over these acts began in November 1986, Congress had acted to restore **contra funding,** approving $100 million for fiscal 1987, including $70 million in military aid, and lifting many of the legal restrictions. In March 1987 the Senate voted down (52 to 48) an attempt to withhold the last $40 million of that appropriation [*The New York Times*, 3/19/87], but the closeness of the vote indicated the difficulty Reagan would face in winning approval of his $105 million request for 1988.

Support for the contras was also hurt by the disarray within their political umbrella group, the **United Nicaraguan Opposition (UNO).** The two respected and moderate members of the triumvirate that unified the anti-Sandinista factions—Arturo José Cruz and Alfonso Robelo—resigned in March and April 1986 respectively to protest their irreconcilable differences with the conservative Adolfo Calero, who heads the largest military unit, the ten thousand-man-strong **Nicaraguan Democratic Force (FDN).** The FDN, with operations in the northern part of the country and several smaller units in the south totaling about a thousand fighters, were the main contra forces in the field. Their effectiveness, with the weapons provided through legal U.S. funding, has been increasing—including more hits against government helicopter gunships and the ability to sustain continuous operations inside Nicaragua—but they remain limited in their capacity to pose a long-range military threat to the Sandinista regime. So too has been their popularity in Nicaragua and on Capitol Hill due to charges of human rights abuses to match those of the Sandinistas and attacks on civilian targets. The Sandinista military establishment, equipped with modern Soviet-made helicopter gunships, outnumbered that of the rebels by about six to one. The Sandinistas were most vulnerable to criticism for their limitations on press freedom, imposition of other state-of-emergency restrictions, their feud with the Catholic Church hierarchy, and their administrative and political blunders. A typical misstep was the staging of a large-scale raid against contra troops in Honduras on the eve of a Capitol Hill vote.

The Sandinista **incursions into Honduras**—and clashes with Honduran troops—were frequent but for the most part unpublicized. Friction with Costa Rica has diminished. The danger of a widening of the war was ever-present but still remote.

Americans have died in Nicaragua while helping both sides. In October 1986 a supply plane ferrying arms to the contras was shot down, killing the crewmen. One of the Americans aboard, Eugene Hasenfus, survived and was convicted of terrorism by a revolutionary court. He was freed in December. Benjamin Linder, a volunteer engineer working on a water project in a Nicaraguan village, was killed by the contras in April 1987. The previous month saw the first American military adviser killed in combat in the civil war in neighboring El Salvador, Staff Sergeant Gregory Fronius.

Apart from such incidents, the international spotlight has veered away from **El Salvador**, even though the seven-year civil war between leftist guerrillas of the **Farabundo Martí National Liberation Front** and the government of **Christian Democratic President José Napoleón Duarte** intensified in the months preceding the 42nd Assembly. The rebels have targeted both civilians and the Salvadoran economy, seeking control of rural populations and the weakening of the Duarte government. Peace talks between the two sides, launched in 1985, have petered out. Human rights groups, such as the New York–based Lawyers Committee for Human Rights in a March 1987 report, credit the government with limiting abuses by security forces but called for more strenuous prosecution of offenders.

On the diplomatic front, the **Contadora Group** (Panama, Mexico, Venezuela, and Colombia), named for the island off the Panamanian coast where the four first gathered to mediate the disputes in Central America, ground to a stalemate in its four-year effort to draft a regional peace treaty. The four were bolstered by a **"support group"** of Argentina, Brazil, Peru, and Uruguay in the effort to achieve a meeting of the minds among the five Central American nations (El Salvador, Nicaragua, Guatemala, Costa Rica, and Honduras). But the reality was that the political gap lay between Washington and Managua, not among the regional disputants—and that was an abyss no piece of paper could bridge. In December 1986 the Secretaries-General of the United Nations and the Organization of American States (OAS), Javier Pérez de Cuéllar and João Clemente Baena Soares, launched their own initiative to revitalize the Contadora process by calling in all the parties and enumerating the potential "technical services" that the two international organizations could provide for the cause of making peace. Among these were the capacity to monitor borders, supervise withdrawal of military forces, dismantle military bases, investigate arms trafficking, protect refugees, and verify the departure of foreign military advisers. The object was to reassure the Central American governments that the objections raised about the viability of the Contadora draft peace treaty could be answered in part by these technical services [*The New York Times*, 12/21/86]. The two men visited Central America to reinforce their offer in January, but the results, though instructive, were not fruitful. "I found no desire on the part of each country to make sacrifices in its position to find a solution," said Pérez de Cuéllar [*The New York Times*, 1/22/87].

An alternative diplomatic effort was launched in February 1987 by **Costa Rican President Oscar Arias Sánchez,** who put forward a **ten-point plan,** to be considered by the other four Central American presidents at a meeting in Esquipulas, Guatemala, in June. The Arias plan [A/42/130] was endorsed by the U.S. Senate in a nonbinding 97-1 vote in March, but reservations were expressed by both the Reagan administration and Nicaragua. It calls for an immediate cease-fire throughout Central America, an end to foreign military assistance for rebel groups, and a ban on governments' allowing havens for the guerrillas fighting their neighbors. It would also require negotiations between each government and its domestic opposition, and it would set precise deadlines for restoration of press and other freedoms, and for open elections involving U.N. and OAS monitoring. U.S. officials objected to provisions that would end U.S aid to the contras without barring Soviet aid to the Sandinistas and would limit the rebels' ability to function in tangible terms, while requiring intangibles from the Sandinistas, to be delivered at a later date [*The New York Times*, 4/25/87]. Costa Rican officials have charged Americans, including National Security Adviser Frank Carlucci, with trying to strong-arm Arias into amending the plan to favor U.S. needs. U.S. officials have expressed fears that Nicaragua might abruptly accept the Arias plan as written, putting U.S. allies such as El Salvador and Honduras in a diplomatic bind. But Arias feared that his plan, like the Contadora blueprint before it, would be placed on a pedestal, there to wither and die. A meeting of the Central American presidents in Guatemala to consider the Arias plan was scheduled for June 1987 but postponed until August at Duarte's request. It was to be preceded by consultations at the ministerial level in Honduras and El Salvador.

At the United Nations, the Security Council was convened on several occasions by Nicaragua, but the U.S. veto prevented it from taking any action. On July 31, 1986, the United States vetoed a Nicaraguan resolution under which the Council would have urged "full compliance" with a ruling by the International Court of Justice at The Hague (also known as the World Court) the previous month demanding an end to U.S. support for the contras. The week-long debate gave Nicaraguan President Daniel Ortega Saavedra an opportunity to reap extensive and favorable media exposure with his denunciation of President Reagan's "immoral policy of state terrorism." But it failed to isolate the United States from its allies on the issue, as France, the United Kingdom, and Thailand abstained in the voting [*The Washington Post*, 7/29, 8/1/86]. Other Council debates—such as one that followed the downing of the Hasenfus plane—proved inconclusive as well.

The **General Assembly** held four separate debates related to Central America. One in the Plenary adopted a consensus resolution [A/Res/41/37] blessing the efforts of the Contadora Group. Another Plenary resolution called for compliance with the World Court decision [A/Res/41/31; vote: 94–3, with 47 abstentions]. The Economic (Second) Committee adopted a resolution [A/Res/41/164; vote: 83–2, with 44 abstentions] deploring the U.S. trade embargo against Nicaragua, and the Humanitarian (Third) Committee adopted resolutions on human rights in El Salvador [A/Res/41/157; vote:110–0, with 40 abstentions] and Guatemala [A/Res/41/156; vote:134–0, with 21 abstentions]. For the first time, the United States joined in support of both texts, which praised the improved conditions in the two countries. All four items remain on the agenda of the 42nd Assembly.

5. Afghanistan

The most significant dispute in which the Secretary-General and his aides played a vital mediating role was clearly **the Soviet occupation of Afghanistan,** which had for nearly eight years blocked improved relationships between Moscow and both Washington and Beijing, and which remained a major irritant in Soviet dealings with most Third World nations. For five years Under-Secretary Diego Cordovez had acted as the energetic interlocutor in "**proximity talks**" between Pakistan and the Soviet-backed Kabul government on the terms for withdrawing the 118,000 remaining Soviet troops, an end to outside interference in Afghanistan, and the return of some 4 million refugees. On an informal level, he became the intermediary between Moscow and Washington as well, and kept both China and Iran informed of progress.

By the end of 1986 only two issues remained to be resolved. One was the length of time that Soviet troops would be given to withdraw. The second went beyond the scope of the periodic U.N.-sponsored negotiations in Geneva. There was a need to shape a government in Kabul that could survive the Soviet departure, remaining on good terms with Moscow while satisfying the leading factions of the splintered rebel movement, the *mojahedin.* Diplomats close to the negotiating process cautioned that the difficulty of piecing together such an arrangement should not be underestimated, even with an assumption of goodwill on the part of the superpowers and Afghanistan's neighbors [Interviews with *Issues Before the 42nd General Assembly*].

The most obvious candidate for a figurehead around which Afghan factions could rally was the **former king, Zahir Shah,** who was deposed in 1973 and lives in Rome. He said in an April 1987 interview in the German magazine *Der Speigel* that he would be available to play such a role. One idea being considered was a "**transitional council**" that might also include one or more former prime ministers, now in exile, who would be acceptable to several of the *mojahedin* field commanders and some of the seven Islamic leaders based in

Peshawar, Pakistan. The Afghan Communist Party would retain a role in the transitional regime as well. The seven Peshawar factions were said to be split over the plan, with three supporting the ex-king, two on the fence, and two adamantly opposed. The two opponents, Gulbudin and Sayaf, the hard-line Islamic fundamentalists, could split from the seven-part coalition on this issue, diplomats said. The assumption of all parties appeared to be that Najibullah, the Afghan leader installed in Kabul after Babrak Karmal was abruptly deposed in May 1986, would have to be replaced for a transition government to be viable. The process by which such a coalition might take shape involved nebulous discussions and feelers by Soviet and Pakistani officials among Afghan communities in Europe, Pakistan, and Afghanistan itself.

While this amorphous process was under way, the formal negotiations were treading water. The talks involve four documents: **an Afghan-Pakistani agreement on noninterference**; **a U.S.-Soviet guarantee** of Afghan security; an Afghan-Pakistani agreement on the **return of the refugees**; and a paper linking **Soviet troop withdrawal** to the other three undertakings, providing for monitoring of the accords and adjudication of possible violations. The rounds of proximity talks in May, July, and August 1986 (during which Cordovez shuttled between the Afghan and Pakistani delegations in Geneva) completed agreement on the wording of the texts, except for the details of monitoring and the withdrawal timetable.

During visits to Kabul and Islamabad in November, Cordovez resolved the monitoring arrangements that had been demanded by Washington, winning agreement that U.N. units involving dozens of monitors would supplement satellite surveillance and would have free range of movement on both sides of the border—in Afghanistan and Pakistan—to ensure that Soviet troops were in fact withdrawing and that the United States and Pakistan were living up to their pledges to cut off all cross-border weapons flows and (within reasonable limits) guerrilla movements. Monitors would be headquartered on each side of the border and would have the power to determine how violations would be rectified.

In February 1987 the gap on the withdrawal timetable was narrowed significantly, as Pakistan demanded that the pullout be complete in seven months and Moscow insisted that it stretch to eighteen months. (The earlier positions had been four months and four years, respectively.) It was clear that a compromise of around one year was within reach, but both sides apparently decided to stop short of final agreement to let discussions on a new Kabul government catch up to the pace of the U.N. talks.

There had been initial skepticism that Soviet leader Mikhail Gorbachev was sincere in his apparent shift of policy on Afghanistan and in his determination to negotiate a withdrawal of the troops that occupied the country in December 1979. But British Prime Minister Margaret Thatcher pronounced herself convinced of his sincerity on that score after her visit to Moscow in early

1987, and Washington officials were beginning to take the prospect of an agreement more seriously.

In Washington, strong differences remained between the State Department, which viewed Soviet pressures on Pakistan as a significant long-range threat and supported a compromise solution in Afghanistan, and the Pentagon, which believed that military pressure on the Soviets in Afghanistan could be sustained and intensified, leading to more favorable settlement terms than those being discussed—in particular, an Afghan government free of pro-Soviet influences. There was also strong pressure from Congress to bar any deal that might constitute a "sellout" of the *mojahedin*. A nonbinding congressional resolution opposed any withdrawal timetable longer than four months. A complicating factor was opposition from liberals on Capitol Hill to the **$4 billion aid package proposed for Pakistan** by the Reagan administration, on the ground that the regime of President Mohammed Zia ul-Haq is adamant in its pursuit of **nuclear capability**. Once the dispute over the aid package is resolved (thought to be no later than October 1987), Pakistan is expected to assert itself on behalf of a settlement in Afghanistan, which would make the probable peace terms more salable in the White House, despite residual opposition in Congress and at the Pentagon.

The domestic political pressure and external military **pressure on Pakistan** increased throughout 1987.

Fighting spilled over the Pakistani border, Zia's opponents criticized him for demanding too much of Moscow, and the Pakistani residents of border and refugee areas grew increasingly resentful of the Afghan military camps and refugees in their midst. **Air strikes** in the border zone killed some 150 Afghan and Pakistani villagers in March 1987. The Pakistanis claimed that they downed one Afghan military plane in the border region (Afghanistan called it a civilian airliner) and admitted losing one of its U.S.-made F-16 fighters in a border skirmish.

The fighting inside Afghanistan continued with undiminished ferocity on both sides. *Mojahedin* claimed that they had crossed the Soviet border to inflict casualties and to dynamite support-base targets within the Soviet Union proper. In retaliation, Soviet planes carpet-bombed Afghan border towns and villages. A **cease-fire offer** announced in January by the Najibullah government was rejected by the guerrillas, but there were signs that hard-line factions within the Afghan Communist Party felt Najibullah had gone too far [*The Washington Post*, 4/28/87].

In May 1987, Karmal was removed to Moscow for "medical treatment"—a hint that he may have been seeking to regain control of the government. Soviet Deputy Foreign Minister Yuri Vorontsov visited Kabul in mid-May 1987 to press the regime to accept the inevitability of a coalition government.

The **flow of arms** to the *mojahedin* increased in late 1986 and 1987, according to U.S. sources [Associated Press, 3/31/87]. Effective Stinger ground-to-air missiles began arriving in large numbers late in 1986, enabling the *mojahedin* to challenge Soviet air power—in particular the deadly helicopter gunships— for the first time. The Americans claimed that an average of one aircraft a day was downed in the first weeks after the Stingers arrived. Subsequently, the Soviets were forced to adopt the tactic of shielding each transport with eight helicopters as it arrived at Kabul airport. U.S. reports claimed that Soviet casualties through the end of 1986 totaled some 35,000 troops and more than a thousand aircraft. The aid flow for the *mojahedin* was estimated at $3 billion since 1980, and the 1986 figure alone was put in excess of $600 million from all sources (including Saudi Arabia, Egypt, Israel, China, and Iran). But more than half the total never reached the fighters in the field—another reason why powerful elements in Peshawar would prefer to see the fighting continue and were reluctant to participate in any settlement that might cut the arms traffic.

The international community has kept the pressure on Moscow by adopting annual resolutions calling for the immediate withdrawal of all foreign troops from Afghanistan. The Pakistani-sponsored text was adopted by the 41st General Assembly on November 5 by a vote of 122–20, with 11 abstentions. The issue remains on the agenda of the 42nd Assembly [A/42/50, item 31]. Both the Assembly and the U.N. Human Rights Commission also adopted strongly worded resolutions condemning massive human rights violations by Soviet troops and the Afghan government. The U.N.'s special rapporteur on the situation, Felix Ermacora of Austria, was invited to visit Afghanistan for the first time in 1987.

6. Indochina

After several years in which the **struggle between guerrilla groups and Vietnamese occupation forces in Democratic Kampuchea** (Cambodia) was stalemated on the ground and in the political arena, a series of changes in the internal politics of the regional powers and in the interrelationships among them have opened the **possibility of movement** for the first time since Hanoi's December 1978 invasion.

Vietnam itself has undergone political upheaval. In February it experienced a major government shakeout, two months before parliamentary elections. A new prime minister (Pham Hung) and a new head of state (Voch I Tong) were designated by the national assembly in June. While this political process went on, Vietnamese foreign policy was paralyzed. Some observers expressed fears that the ultimate selection of two members of the older generation as the new leaders indicated that policy toward Kampuchea was unlikely to change significantly. There was one sign of thaw, which came before the elections with the adoption of a more pragmatic economic policy, designed to encourage outside investment from the West, Japan, and even

Vietnam's apprehensive neighbors in the **Association of South East Asian Nations (ASEAN)**, which is composed of Brunei, Indonesia, Malaysia, the Philippines, Singapore, and Thailand [Interviews with *Issues Before the 42nd General Assembly*].

That tendency was encouraged by a major **shift in Asian policy by the Soviet Union**, Vietnam's chief ally. Moscow signaled its willingness to improve relations with China and to include Kampuchea on the agenda of their talks for the first time. Foreign Minister Eduard Shevardnadze toured Vietnam, Indonesia, Laos, Kampuchea, and Australia and stopped over in Thailand, expressing the Kremlin's desire for a solution on Kampuchea and better relations with ASEAN. Thailand's foreign minister, Air Chief Marshal Siddhi Savetsila, responded with a visit to Moscow in May, and he was followed to the Soviet capital by Hanoi's new party chief Nguyen Van Linh and Foreign Minister Nguyen Co Thach.

The United States signaled its willingness to improve relations with Vietnam by announcing the appointment of retired Army General John W. Vessey as a **special presidential envoy** to Hanoi to foster joint efforts to account for the 2,416 American servicemen still listed as **missing in action in Indochina** during the war that ended in 1975. The Vessey mission was agreed to in principle in talks at the U.N. in October 1986 [*Far Eastern Economic Review*, 4/30/87]. In preparation for the mission National Security Council aide Richard Childress visited Hanoi May 26-28, 1987, but reported that "more work needs to be done" prior to General Vessey's departure. The U.S. position remains that relations with Vietnam cannot be normalized until the MIA issue is resolved and Vietnam withdraws its 140,000 troops from Kampuchea.

The Vietnamese invasion easily ousted the **Khmer Rouge regime of Pol Pot**, which the international community recognizes as responsible for the deaths of some 2 million Cambodians from 1975 through 1978. Hanoi installed in Phnom Penh the **People's Republic of Kampuchea (PRK)**, headed by Heng Samrin and Hun Sen, but it has not won broad recognition, and the country's U.N. seat remains occupied by the **Coalition Government of Democratic Kampuchea (CGDK)**, an amalgam of three resistance groups. These are the Khmer Rouge; the **Khmer People's National Liberation Front (KPNLF)**, headed by former Prime Minister Son Sann; and the **Sihanoukist National Army (SNA)**, a smaller group led by Prince Norodom Sihanouk, the former hereditary ruler of Kampuchea, who serves as titular president of the coalition and remains a respected figure within the country and the international community. The status of the coalition eroded in May, when Sihanouk took what he called a "leave of absence" from its presidency, apparently to protest Khmer Rouge attacks on his troops inside Kampuchea and to signal Beijing that its tough pro-Khmer Rouge stance should be modified.

These strange bedfellows are backed by the United States and China as well as by ASEAN—and by most members of the Non-Aligned Movement, who view the occupation of any small nation by its larger neighbor as a potential threat to each of them.

In the field the most effective of these guerrilla groups remains the Khmer Rouge, equipped by China. The Sihanoukists also claim to engage in some military operations inside Kampuchea. The KPNLF remains an ineffective fighting force and is hampered by an ongoing leadership struggle. It was singled out for criticism in February 1987 by the New York–based Lawyers' Committee for Human Rights, which charged that its leaders abused Cambodian refugee groups under their control in camps located in Thailand. Khmer Rouge leaders such as the notorious Ta Mok—accused of personal involvement in the genocidal atrocities of the 1970s—were also fingered by U.N. officials for abusing refugees in the Thai camps [The New York Times, 2/15/87, 2/19/87]. Control over refugee populations is the prime means by which the guerrilla groups recruit their forces. U.N. officials claimed, however, that the United Nations Border Relief Operation had been successful in separating civilians and combatants in the camps and in establishing an international presence in most camps to help protect civilian refugees from abuse by various warlords or by Thai troops [A/41/707].

The military value of the camps for the guerrilla groups diminished when the Vietnamese succeeded during the 1985 dry season offensive in pushing the refugee concentrations out of Kampuchean territory and away from the border zone. Since then, the level of fighting on the Thai border has remained low. The various guerrilla groups claim to be active in fighting and recruiting deeper inside Kampuchea, but there has been no diplomatic or journalistic corroboration of their numbers or their claims. The few diplomats in Phnom Penh are limited in their travels and report a continuing low level of minor security breaches in the vicinity of the capital.

On the **diplomatic front,** the ASEAN nations have signaled their willingness to compromise by hinting that an eventual coalition of the various Kampuchean factions could exclude Pol Pot and the most egregious of the Khmer Rouge war criminals while incorporating other Khmer Rouge elements. This is a step toward the Vietnamese demand that the as yet undefined "Pol Pot clique" must not participate in any ultimate all-Cambodian coalition. The Chinese have thus far shown no sign of abandoning their Khmer Rouge allies, but Chinese Foreign Minister Wu stated that China "would not like to see any single group monopolize power in Kampuchea" [A/41/PV.8, pp. 46-47] and China has endorsed the CGDK eight-point proposal, which calls for national reconciliation, leading to a "quadripartite" government, including the Phnom Penh regime.

The U.N. role has been to monitor developments, feeling out the moment when mediation by Secretary-General Javier Pérez de Cuéllar or his representative, Under-Secretary Rafeeuddin Ahmed, might be fruitful. Mr. Ahmed visited Hanoi in February 1987, and the Secretary-General discussed the matter during his visit to China and Japan in May.

The **General Assembly** has remained a forum for maintaining the **diplomatic pressure** on Hanoi to withdraw from Kampuchea. Its annual vote on the issue helps to sustain the unspoken embargo by the West against aid flows and significant trade with Vietnam, despite the potential oil reserves and export markets that Indochina offers. Thanks to intense lobbying by ASEAN and the Chinese, the majority for the Kampuchea resolution continued to grow during the 41st Assembly [A/Res/41/6; vote: 115–21, with 13 abstentions]. Hanoi submits its own rival item each year, entitled "Question of Peace, Stability, and Cooperation in South-East Asia" [A/42/50, item 42], but it has never had sufficient backing to put any resolution to the vote, nor has it challenged the credentials of the CGDK delegation since 1982.

7. Cyprus

The window of opportunity for an agreement to end the twenty-three-year-long dispute between the **Greek and Turkish communities on Cyprus** appeared to be closing in the months preceding the 42nd General Assembly. Secretary-General Javier Pérez de Cuéllar, who for years has been the sole mediating mechanism between the two sides, made two overt efforts to break the deadlock that solidified in June 1986, but neither was successful.

"We are thus at an impasse," said Pérez de Cuéllar in his June 1987 report to the Security Council [S/18880]. "A deadlock exists at present in my efforts to restart effective negotiations," he continued, citing several elements that give "increasing cause for concern," among them: "Distrust between the leaderships of the two communities remains deep," and a "potentially dangerous military buildup is taking place on the island."

The reasons for the entrenchment of the status quo were varied. The dispute between Greece and Turkey, the two patrons of the Cypriot communities, shifted in March 1987 away from the Cyprus issue to the question of oil exploration and sovereignty in the Aegean Sea. But both sides backed away from a confrontation—like any flareup on Cyprus—that could have shattered the southern flank of the North Atlantic Treaty Organization (NATO). Tensions on Cyprus itself eased after a hot July in 1986 that included a controversial visit to the Turkish Cypriot sector by Turkey's prime minister, Turgut Özal; Greek Cypriot demonstrations to protest the move; and a week-long Turkish Cypriot closure of the border crossings along the "green line" that separates the two communities. The closure had temporarily cut off supplies for some one thousand non-Turkish residents of the zone, which the Turkish Cypriot community had declared the **Turkish Republic of Northern Cyprus** in 1983 but which is not recognized by any nation other than Turkey. Some 650 Danish and Austrian soldiers in the 2,300-member **United Nations**

Peacekeeping Force in Cyprus (UNFICYP) were also cut off. Shortly after that reminder of military dominance by Turkey's occupation force, which has controlled the northern 37 percent of the island since its 1974 invasion, U.N. officials began to notice that the size of the Turkish garrison had increased by about 4,000 to some 28,000 over several months. The Greek Cypriots responded by increasing their military establishment [Interviews with *Issues Before the 42nd General Assembly*]. Despite a relatively stagnant economy and lack of progress toward international recognition, the Turkish Cypriot community appeared satisfied by its sense of physical security, and no pressures to speed the negotiating process were evident.

On the Greek Cypriot side, where about four-fifths of the 800,000 Cypriots live, the boom economy continued to put the area controlled by the internationally recognized **Republic of Cyprus** on a par with most of industrialized Western Europe, and far above the standard of living in Greece [*The New York Times*, 7/22/86]. Unemployment remained at a low of about 3.3 percent, and inflation was far below European norms. This prosperity appeared to have defused the political pressures to resolve the problems of refugees from the 1974 invasion. The hard line taken by the government of President Spyros Kyprianou, with the support of Greek Prime Minister Andreas Papandreou, won a vote of confidence in the December 1985 elections. New presidential elections were scheduled for February 1988, and because the campaign had effectively begun by the fall of 1987, diplomatic observers believed it would be difficult for the Greek Cypriot side to give the appearance of making concessions. The successful domestic line taken by Kyprianou has been that Cyprus is a problem of invasion and occupation rather than a dispute between two communities—and so the focus must be on the Turkish troop pullout, which must be solved through an international conference.

The international consensus that had existed to bolster the **Secretary-General's mediation efforts** softened somewhat in the wake of the negotiating deadlock. Western governments gave Cyprus a lower priority as the threat to NATO shifted to the Aegean dispute, and the Soviet Union, as one manifestation of its general international activism, changed policy on Cyprus, seeking a larger role for itself in the negotiation of a solution through the convening of an **international conference under U.N. auspices to settle the international aspects of the Cyprus problem** [A/41/96 of 1/21/86]. The Soviet policy change also produced a weakening of support for the Secretary-General's negotiating process by the influential Greek Cypriot Communist Party.

The two communities had been close to an agreement in early 1985, but a summit meeting between Kyprianou and Turkish-Cypriot leader Rauf Denktash failed. A refined version of the Secretary-General's "draft framework agreement" was presented to the two sides on March 29, 1986. Denktash accepted it, but—as was the case the previous year—Kyprianou raised objections. The text [S/18102/Add.1/Annex II of 6/11/86] envisages a **bizonal federation** with a

Greek-Cypriot president and a Turkish-Cypriot vice president; a bicameral legislature in which one house would be equally divided and the other would provide the Greek Cypriots with a 70–30 ratio; a cabinet with the same ratio; and a constitutional court with a non-Cypriot member holding the balance. Each community would have both executive and legislative veto power, but there would be complex deadlock-breaking mechanisms to prevent government from coming to a grinding halt. Each state or province would exercise control over local matters, but the federal government would deal with elements such as foreign affairs, defense, and finance. The Turkish Cypriots would give back some of the territory they now occupy, retaining 29 percent of the island.

A transitional regime would be established only after final agreement on all elements of the pact, including three key unresolved issues: the timetable for the withdrawal of the Turkish troops, the nature of international guarantees, and the degree to which Cypriots from one community would be able to travel, own property, and reside in the other.

The Greek Cypriots maintain that these "**three freedoms**" must be absolute, that all Turkish troops (and Turkish settlers who have come since 1974) must leave, and that Turkey can no longer serve as a guarantor because that would provide it with an excuse for a renewed occupation if the Turkish Cypriots tie up the government with their veto powers.

The Turkish Cypriots fear they will be overrun by the majority unless some limits are placed on the "three freedoms." The same fear leads them to demand a continuing Turkish military presence and a renewed Turkish role (with Greece and the United Kingdom) as guarantor.

In his reply to the "draft framework agreement," Kyprianou said he could comment on the text only after agreement had been reached on the three key unresolved issues. His point was that he would lose leverage on the three outstanding issues if he were to agree in advance to the constitutional guarantees desired by the Turkish Cypriots. He proposed either a **new summit meeting** between himself and Denktash to resolve the three major remaining issues before Pérez de Cuéllar's text is adopted or, preferably, that an **international conference** tackle the issues of troop withdrawal and guarantees—the procedure initially proposed by the Soviet Union. Denktash made clear that neither the summit meeting nor the international conference (at which the Turkish Cypriot side would be at a disadvantage) would be acceptable to him until the Secretary-General's draft has been accepted as the basis for negotiation.

The Secretary-General's first attempt to break this impasse came in November 1986, when Under-Secretary Marrack Goulding went to Cyprus to sound out the idea of an **open-ended agenda** for talks between the two communities. Neither side would agree. The Turkish Cypriots said they wanted the Secretary-General's text to be the basis for such talks; the Greek

Cypriots insisted on "priority" in any discussion for the three unresolved issues and stressed the desirability of the international conference.

Goulding made another trip to Cyprus in February 1987, offering to keep the Pérez de Cuéllar text "on the table" while holding separate "**noncommitting and informal" discussions with each side** to see whether the talks might generate new positions that might break the ice by "clarifying" each side's stand. This vague formulation was accepted by the Greek Cypriots, while Denktash said he could not accept it unless the Greek Cypriots accept the March 1986 document.

Since intercommunal fighting erupted in 1964, the peace on Cyprus has been kept by UNFICYP, which patrols a 180-mile buffer zone. But as of June 1987, the force, which is financed solely by voluntary contributions, was more than **$150 million in the red**. This placed the financial burden on the troop-contributing countries (Austria, Canada, Denmark, Finland, Ireland, Sweden, and the United Kingdom). The last payment they received for the services of their troops covered June 1979. Sweden announced that it would withdraw its 350-member contingent at the end of 1987, citing costs as a prime reason. The Secretary-General suggested to the Security Council and General Assembly that they consider shifting the financing of the force to some form of assessed contributions, the funding method used for the other U.N. peacekeeping operations [S/18491 of 12/2/86]. However, after long consultations, Pérez de Cuéllar conceded that "the necessary agreement does not at present exist for such a change" [S/18880/Add. 1 of 6/11/87]. The Council has routinely authorized the continuation of UNFICYP each June and December and has continued to encourage the Secretary-General's mediation efforts [S/Res/597 of 6/12/87; vote: 15–0].

The "**Question of Cyprus**" is a perennial item on the Assembly agenda [A/42/50, item 46], but it has remained undebated since May 1983. In May 1987 the Greek Cypriot government announced its intention of pressing a debate on the Cyprus question at the 42nd Assembly, where the Republic of Cyprus, as a member in good standing of the **Non-Aligned Movement**, can count on a clear majority. The object would be to use such a resolution as leverage to promote the convening of an international conference and to increase pressure on Turkey to withdraw its occupying force. One sign of the Greek Cypriot objective was a strong resolution, critical of the continuing Turkish occupation, adopted at the March 1987 session of the **U.N. Human Rights Commission**. The resolution opposed settlement by Turkish immigrants and called for the restoration of the "three freedoms" [U.N. press release, HR/3080]. What had caused the Greek Cypriots to hesitate before seeking Assembly action in the past was their reluctance to lose Western support for an unbalanced resolution, which could make it even more difficult for the Secretary-General to mediate a way out of the negotiating deadlock.

8. Other Colonial and Sovereignty Issues

One of the United Nations' historic achievements has been to stimulate the **transition from colonialism to independence** of almost half its present members, and this has virtually completed the task of decolonization. Aside from Namibia and territories such as East Timor and Western Sahara, which, rather than gaining independence, have been annexed, most of the remaining handful of non-self-governing territories appear to be too small to be viable on their own.

The U.N. maintains a decolonization committee, formally entitled the Special Committee on the Situation with Regard to the Implementation of the Declaration on the Granting of Independence to Colonial Countries and Peoples, but informally known as the **Committee of 24**. This body monitors the status of the remaining territories and reports annually to the Assembly. In recent years (including 1987) the committee has debated and adopted a resolution on **Puerto Rico**, despite the U.S. contention that the commonwealth attained self-governing status long ago, that it is a part of the United States, and thus it is not a U.N. issue.

The 41st Assembly adopted resolutions on **six British territories** (Anguilla, Bermuda, the British Virgin Islands, the Cayman Islands, Montserrat, and the Turks and Caicos Islands), **three U.S. possessions** (American Samoa, the U.S. Virgin Islands, and Guam), and **Tokelau**, which is administered by New Zealand. The resolutions generally assumed that independence would be the preferred destiny of the indigenous peoples and urged the colonial powers to pave the way for that future.

A new colonial controversy arose when the Assembly, prompted by the nations of the **South Pacific Forum**, decided [A/Res/41/41A; vote: 89–24, with 34 abstentions] to restore **New Caledonia** to the U.N.'s official list of non-self-governing territories, which means that under **Article 73 of the Charter**, France, the administering power, is obliged to provide the U.N. with information each year on social, economic, and political developments in the territory. France, which had declared New Caledonia an overseas province in 1946, opposed U.N. reconsideration of the issue. But the Pacific island nations called for independence for the territory, in which political unrest had been escalating. More substantive debates on New Caledonia were scheduled in the Committee of 24 in the summer of 1987 and anticipated in the Assembly discussion of the committee's annual report [A/42/23].

There were two other colonial disputes involving France. One is a claim by Madagascar to the islands of **Juan de Nova, Europa, Bassas da India, and Glorieuses**. Paris claims they were never part of Madagascar. No action was taken by the 41st Assembly, but the issue is on the agenda of the 42nd [A/42/50, item 81]. The other deals with **Mayotte**, the fourth of the **Comorian Islands,** three of which achieved independence in 1975. The Christian residents of Mayotte, however, objected to linkage with the other three Muslim islands. The 41st Assembly adopted a resolution in November [A/Res/41/30; vote 122–1, with 22 abstentions] reaffirming the sovereignty of the Islamic Federal Republic of the Comoros over the island of Mayotte and urging France to speed negotiations. The item remains before the 42nd Assembly [A/42/50, item 29].

A political stalemate has also continued between the United Kingdom and Argentina over the **Falkland Islands, or Malvinas,** in the South Atlantic, over which the two sides fought a brief but bloody war in 1982, claiming the lives of 712 Argentines and 256 Britons. London has ruled the islands for some 150 years, and the current inhabitants, virtually all of British descent, want its continued protection. Argentina's claim, never abandoned, has been on the U.N. agenda since 1965. Since the fighting the two countries have never formally ended hostilities or reestablished normal relations. The dispute was exacerbated when the United Kingdom imposed a **two-hundred mile conservation zone** in the rich fishing grounds around the islands, and required anyone wanting to fish within 150 miles to obtain a license before February 1, 1987. The United Kingdom rejected Argentina's offer of a formal end to hostilities in exchange for a lifting of the 150-mile "military protection zone" [*The New York Times,* 11/19/86]. A mildly worded resolution adopted on November 25 [A/Res/41/40; vote: 116–4, with 34 abstentions] made no reference to the new fisheries dispute, and attracted nine more votes than a similar text had the previous year. The Argentine resolution called for negotiations on all aspects of the dispute and urged the Secretary-General to help mediate. But the United Kingdom remained opposed to any discussion of the sovereignty issue with Argentina and objected to the resolution's omission of a guarantee that the islanders' wishes would be taken into account. Pérez de Cuéllar did his share by prodding both parties, and there was some hope that the fisheries dispute might be dealt with separately. Otherwise, there appeared to be no movement toward a broader accommodation between Buenos Aires and London.

Representatives from Portugal and Indonesia continued their quiet discussions at the U.N. in the months before the 42nd Assembly on the **question of East Timor** [A/42/50, item 114]. Civil war broke out in the Portuguese territory in 1975 between a faction seeking independence, the **Frente Revolucionaria de Timor Leste Independente (FRETILIN),** and one seeking integration with Indonesia. Indonesia annexed the territory in 1976, and over the years the backing for the FRETILIN insurgency has waned, despite continuing reports of massive human rights violations, famine, and disease. In late 1986 and early 1987 some progress was made on the humanitarian concerns, with increased access to the island by foreigners, including diplomats and the media. There was a permanent presence of some voluntary agencies and the **U.N. Children's Fund (UNICEF);** and periodic visits by representatives of the **International**

Committee of the Red Cross had resumed. The issue has not been the subject of an Assembly debate or resolution since 1982. The half-dozen negotiating sessions, held in the presence of U.N. Under-Secretary Rafeeuddin Ahmed, dealt with prospects for a U.N.-supervised referendum of some sort on the territory's final status, but both sides maintained their positions. Portugal wants the voters to be given an alternative to remaining a part of Indonesia, but the Indonesians want to limit the exercise to an internationally observed confirmation of the status quo, without consideration of other options. Both want the U.N.-mediated talks to continue.

The U.N. initially established a separate category, the **trust territory**, and a **Trusteeship Council** to supervise the eleven areas involved. That system is now down to its final client, the **Trust Territory of the Pacific Islands**, also known as **Micronesia**, administered by the United States. The vast area of 2,100 islands has 168,000 inhabitants, divided into four distinct districts: Palau, the Marshall Islands, the Federated States of Micronesia, and the Northern Marianas. The first three have chosen a "compact of free association" with the United States, which gives them autonomy but cedes defense arrangements to Washington. The Marianas opted in 1975 for commonwealth status.

President Reagan signed a proclamation on November 3, 1986, implementing the arrangements with the Marshalls, the Federated States, and the Marianas. Action on Palau—a potential site for a major U.S. naval base—remains stalemated by a provision in Palau's constitution banning nuclear weapons from its territory, a provision that can be overridden only by a 75 percent vote in a plebiscite. Four U.N.-observed plebiscites, the last one held on June 30, 1987, failed to attain the 75 percent mark. Although the most recent vote, with 67.6 percent approving the compact, was up about 2 percent from the previous vote on December 2, 1986, it still did not reach the necessary 75 percent. But even after the constitutional issue is resolved by the 15,000 Palauans, the final decision on severing the U.N. link to Micronesia—the only "strategic trust" that was created—belongs to the Security Council, rather than to the General Assembly, and there it could be blocked by a Soviet veto.

II
Arms Control and Disarmament

The year 1987 may well be remembered as one in which all things seemed possible. Unprecedented opportunities for arms control arose at the same time that serious disputes threatened to undermine the basis for international cooperation on security matters. On the one hand, both superpowers demonstrated renewed willingness to negotiate a major agreement. European leaders began an intense debate over the requirements of their security. China remains in the process of demobilizing 1 million soldiers, a task that it began in 1985, and became more assertive in international security and disarmament affairs. On the other hand, both superpowers pursued policies that endangered existing treaties. New voices questioned the idea of disarmament. Third World arms races showed no signs of slowing, and regional warfare continued unabated.

The 42nd General Assembly will thus open its deliberations on arms control and disarmament with a legacy of deep ambivalence. The world is entering a new diplomatic era governed by new rules. The bitter confrontation of the early 1980s has subsided—not to anything like the détente of the early 1970s, but to a security environment of which even experts have only a hazy understanding.

The United Nations is poorly suited to cope with this dynamic situation. The General Assembly is not an institution known for its flexibility. Its strength is consistency rather than facile innovation. If momentum is allowed to determine the General Assembly's actions, the Assembly will continue to emphasize the kinds of resolutions it has passed for years. By repeating tired formulas, it will doubtless become even less relevant to the swiftly changing international situation. Only with strong leadership and imaginative responses can the General Assembly overcome its disarmament inertia.

The General Assembly cannot be accused of inactivity. At its 41st regular session in 1986, the First Committee (Political and Security) passed sixty-seven disarmament resolutions. As usual, this was one more than the year before. The enormous size of the First Committee's agenda reflects its role as the chief disarmament body in the United Nations system. While actual negotiations take place primarily in the forty-nation Conference on Disarmament in Geneva, the First Committee is one place where all 159 members of the United

Nations can address disarmament issues.

An increasing number of delegations agree that the United Nations' disarmament agenda has grown too unwieldy and that the number of resolutions tends to diminish their significance. It is widely believed that the First Committee must reduce the size of its opus if it is to become more influential, but this is a very difficult task.

The large number of resolutions is partly caused by the Assembly's inability to agree on basic issues. Last year twenty-two resolutions were passed by consensus (another record) but often at the cost of avoiding important issues. Where consensus is impossible, the Assembly often passes several parallel resolutions on a single agenda item, each sponsored by a different voting bloc—usually socialist, Western, or Non-Aligned. Contradictions among such resolutions are not uncommon. A related problem is the tendency to adopt the same resolutions year after year. Few delegations are willing to foreclose any proposal that could facilitate disarmament or to admit that a particular cause is lost.

As a result, the Assembly disarmament agenda is highly ritualized. This year's debate should be dominated by reactions to the **United Nations Conference on Disarmament and Development,** held in New York August 24–September 11, and by preparations for the Third Special Session on Disarmament to be scheduled for some time prior to the 43rd General Assembly. But most items under discussion will closely resemble those of previous years. The most reliable guide to this year's disarmament agenda is often last year's. New items are usually introduced cautiously. Rather than take imprudent action, the Assembly is inclined to request reports from the Secretary-General. Preparing these reports is a major responsibility of the **United Nations Department for Disarmament Affairs.**

After eight years under the leadership of Under-Secretary-General Jan Martenson, the Department for Disarmament Affairs has a new director, Under-Secretary-General Yasushi Akashi. He arrives at a moment when U.N. disarmament studies are coming under increasing scrutiny from the General Assembly [A/Res/41/86C]. The **United Nations Institute for Disarmament Research (UNIDIR)** confronts a different problem. Its director, Liviu Bota of Romania, is being held in his country under suspicion of espionage. Efforts by Secretary-General Pérez de Cuéllar and Western delegations to secure his release continue.

The U.N. approach to restraining armaments is shaped above all by the delegations. Historically, most members feel uncomfortable with the limited goals of arms control as practiced by the superpowers, tending to favor an unambiguous commitment to outright disarmament. There is also a cynical side to disarmament diplomacy: as practiced in the General Assembly, disarmament commonly means disarming one's adversary. The Soviet Union and its supporters routinely present proposals designed to embarrass or divide the NATO allies. Proposals from the United States have a way of placing their greatest burdens on Moscow. The nonaligned often seem more interested in restraining the great powers or their local adversaries than in disarming themselves.

Most delegations will support any well-written disarmament resolution. The superpowers themselves set the extremes. Moscow takes pride in the fact that it cast no negative votes in the First Committee last year (although it abstained eight times). China was only a little less agreeable. Washington shows its antipathy to the U.N. disarmament process by casting more negative ballots than anyone else. On seven resolutions passed by the First Committee in 1986 the United States gave the only negative vote. France and the United Kingdom were often the only governments to join the United States in dissenting.

Besides such internal factors, U.N. disarmament deliberations also reflect outside forces. The First Committee usually grows quieter when superpower summits are in the offing. With a Reagan-Gorbachev meeting likely by the spring of 1988, the Assembly is likely to adopt a wait-and-see attitude. Other factors may constrain the 42nd Assembly. Many of its disarmament leaders face distracting domestic problems and declining government authority. For various reasons, prominent middle and small powers like India, Mexico, Romania, Sri Lanka, and Sweden are less able to assert themselves this year than they have been in the past.

The 42nd Session should witness a sharp increase in European influence. With important exceptions, European delegations will strive to bridge the gap between Moscow and Washington. The result could be an unusually low-keyed session distinguished by hard diplomatic efforts to build consensus.

1. Strategic Weapons

Since the signing of the SALT II Treaty in 1979, Soviet and U.S. officials have been unable to conclude any major nuclear weapons accord. Political disputes, technological change, and differing perceptions have all stood in the way. To some, the arms control process appeared to have degenerated into a cynical propaganda show by the early 1980s. At one point it broke down completely, when Moscow withdrew its delegation from the Geneva negotiations in 1983 to protest NATO intermediate-range missile deployments. The Geneva negotiations resumed in early 1985. Known formally as the **Nuclear and Space Arms Talks (NST)**, they focus on three separate negotiations: offensive strategic wapons, such as land- and sea-based missiles and bombers; defensive weapons, such as antiballistic missile systems and other types of space-related weaponry; and intermediate-range forces in Europe.

Only in the last year has frustration yielded to serious hope for a major new agreement. For policymakers in Moscow and Washington, the next few months will be decisive. Although Soviet Communist Party General Secretary Mikhail Gorbachev and President Ronald Reagan are both under pressure to conclude an agreement, only the outlines of a new strategic weapons treaty have been established and many painful questions remain to be resolved. In the meantime, each government is wary of the other.

In many cases, it seems that the impetus for new agreements has come from Gorbachev. Under his leadership, Soviet diplomacy has become more active than at any time since the fall of Khrushchev more than twenty years ago. While he has not abandoned the foreign policies of his predecessors, Gorbachev has implemented them with greater imagination. In January 1986 he presented a sweeping proposal for complete nuclear disarmament in fifteen years. Independent observers noted that the Gorbachev plan only integrated previous Soviet initiatives, but it nevertheless set the tone for the peace offensive that followed. Since then, Moscow has deluged the world with at least twenty-six formal arms control proposals.

By seizing the arms control initiative, Gorbachev has assumed an international posture that complements his domestic role as an energetic leader bent on change. Of the two, it is his domestic policy that is most controversial at home. Opposition to **glasnost** (openness) and to Gorbachev's economic reforms is becoming increasingly outspoken and organized. Gorbachev no doubt recalls the fate of the last reform-minded General Secretary of the Soviet Union, Nikita Khrushchev, who was ousted at least in part because of his attempts to liberalize the Soviet system. Gorbachev himself must worry about adversaries in the ruling Politburo, the military, and the bureaucracy. To fortify his domestic policy he needs to demonstrate success in foreign policy. A major arms control agreement would do much to consolidate his position.

In contrast to Moscow's dynamism is Washington's increasingly reactive approach to arms control. After dominating the strategic arms control agenda for decades, the United States has allowed the Kremlin to take the leading role in negotiations. After six years in office, the Reagan administration appears to have lost the energy and conviction of its early years; President Ronald Reagan, Secretary of State George Shultz, and Secretary of Defense Caspar Weinberger seem less assertive in general. The disclosure of the Iran/contra scandal in November and the subsequent congressional investigations have weakened the President's foreign policy mandate. Many of the administration's brightest mid-level officials are leaving, while the Republican Party has lost control of the U.S. Senate. As a result, Reagan finds himself in much the same position as Secretary Gorbachev, hoping that an arms control agreement will bolster his authority and prestige.

The confluence of their needs was dramatically illustrated at their meeting in Reykjavik in October 1986. Although it was planned as a glorified tête-à-tête, the meeting swiftly evolved into a full summit. To some, the outcome was a diplomatic fiasco. Others saw it as promising evidence of the potential for consensus. The two leaders agreed to strive to reduce their strategic arsenals to 1,600 launchers with no more than 6,000 nuclear weapons for each side. This would amount to a reduction of approximately one-third, although the exact numbers depend on accounting rules yet to be agreed upon. The Soviets sought a commitment from the United States to adhere to the 1972 Anti-Ballistic Missile Treaty (ABM), but the President refused to compromise his Strategic Defense Initiative (SDI). Reagan did indicate his willingness to act upon his 1981 proposal to cut intermediate-range nuclear forces in Europe to zero. Officials on both sides of the Atlantic were shocked when the two leaders announced that all ballistic missiles would be eliminated within ten years. In the following weeks the White House acknowledged that mistakes were made at the meeting, and it gradually retreated from the positions taken there. All that remains is the lingering image of two leaders who want an agreement but cannot make the concessions it requires.

There are many areas for agreement outside the strategic realm. Recent events have shown that the superpowers can make important progress on nuclear testing, proliferation, accidents at sea, hot-line modernization, and even intermediate-range nuclear weapons. An agreement concluded this year at the Stockholm Conference on Confidence- and Security-Building Measures and Disarmament in Europe to improve mutual confidence and to reduce the risk of surprise attack is described below. One outcome of the negotiations at Geneva has been a new agreement to establish a joint U.S.-Soviet crisis-management center. Strategic nuclear weapons, however, remain the most important element of nuclear arsenals. The specific difficulties of controlling strategic weapons deserve special scrutiny.

Offensive weapons pose the most immediate concern. Both superpowers rely on a mix of intercontinental ballistic missiles (ICBMs), ballistic-missile submarines, and cruise-missile-armed bombers to deter attack. The 1972 SALT I Treaty and the still unratified 1979 SALT II Treaty have stabilized these strategic arsenals. SALT I limits the number of delivery systems, while SALT II restrains the freedom to increase the number of warheads or air-launched cruise missiles. Although the superpowers have generally adhered to both treaties, recent developments threaten their long-term viability.

The Soviet Union and the United States both continue to modernize their forces. The Soviets are replacing aging fixed-silo ICBMs with new road-mobile SS-25s. According to the Pentagon, deployment of the rail-mobile SS-24 is scheduled to begin in 1987. A new fleet of Typhoon ballistic missile submarines is being commissioned, while cruise-missile-armed Bear-H bombers are in production. A new Tupolev strategic bomber is in flight-test. In the United States, the B-1 bomber finally became operational in November 1986 after seventeen years of controversy. The first of fifty MX missiles were deployed the following month. At sea, the U.S. Navy continues to commission Ohio-class submarines, soon to be armed with Trident II missiles capable of destroying hard targets on land.

All these modernization activities are legal within the existing treaty regime. More worrisome are activities that threaten the credibility of those arrangements. Washington accuses the Soviet Union of systematically violating the SALT treaties. Among its allegations are charges of excess numbers of bombers, encryption of missile-test data, and development of two new types of ICBMs, when the SALT II Treaty permits only one. The most important and persuasive U.S. allegation concerns the Soviet radar at Krasnoyarsk (or Abalakova). There is a growing consensus that the radar, because of its location, orientation, and inclination, violates the 1972 ABM Treaty. In response, the United States has deliberately surpassed SALT II limitations by deploying additional cruise-missile-armed bombers. This "proportional response" is intended to show resolve. So far Moscow has chosen not to react to the U.S. challenges, confining itself to countercharges of U.S. violations—principally the modernization of early warning radars in Greenland and the United Kingdom—that it has voiced in earlier years.

At the same time that existing treaties are in danger of disintegrating, there is no consensus on what a new treaty should try to accomplish. Outright nuclear disarmament is only a distant goal, rhetoric aside. Simple formulas for 50 percent reductions must be clarified to specify particular delivery systems, numbers of warheads, throwweights, and so forth. The problems are complicated by the differences between Soviet and U.S. forces. Different types of nuclear weaponry with different capabilities make direct comparison between the two difficult. Lesser problems stalled completion of the SALT II Treaty for almost five years.

The United Nations has always been ambivalent about superpower arms control. The General Assembly welcomes bilateral negotiations and encourages progress toward new treaties [A/Res/41/86A]. The Assembly maintains that the superpowers have a special responsibility to lead nuclear disarmament and insists that other nations cannot begin to disarm until the superpowers drastically reduce their arsenals [A/Res/41/56P]. But most delegations are dissatisfied with the existing SALT regime. Many contend that the extant treaties only legitimate the superpowers' nuclear forces, and they argue that a justifiable agreement must cut superpower forces to the lowest possible level. This approach conflicts with the conclusion of many arms control analysts, who have often observed that the most ambitious agreements are the most difficult to negotiate and who point to the lack of precedent for drastic reductions. But for other security specialists, recent developments in theatre and strategic weapons suggest that it may be possible to break these historic patterns.

The Assembly continues to emphasize resolutions advocating a **nuclear freeze.** Calls for the immediate cessation of the production and deployment of all nuclear weapons entered the popular debate through the peace movement of the early 1980s and they have since become a permanent part of the U.N. disarmament repertoire [A/Res/41/60E, 60I, and 86F]. The Assembly has yet to resolve basic problems with the freeze approach. For example, it is commonly claimed that existing weapons such as multiple-warhead ICBMs in fixed silos are themselves destabilizing, and arms control advocates argue that stability would be greatly improved by replacing these weapons with new systems such as mobile ICBMs and single-warhead missiles. The Assembly is also coming to recognize that it must address the question of deterrence, and to this end a resolution was passed last year to initiate a study on the nature of deterrence [A/Res/41/86R].

One specific arms control issue that has caught the Assembly's attention is **treaty compliance and verification.** With the exception of the Krasnoyarsk radar, White House accusations of Soviet cheating have not won many converts in the General Assembly. Nevertheless, most delegations agree that verification problems must be overcome. Resolutions have been passed urging Moscow to make more information available and calling for all nations to adhere to the letter of their treaty commitments [A/Res/41/59J and 86Q].

Defensive weapons were of comparatively little interest to the United Nations until President Reagan initiated the Strategic Defense Initiative in his 1983 speech. Previously the issue seemed to have been settled by the 1972 ABM Treaty. As later amended, this treaty limits each superpower to a single ground-based interceptor missile installation. Only the Soviet Union maintains such a system, a defensive ring surrounding Moscow, currently undergoing extensive modernization.

Space-based missile defenses still lie in the future, but they already weigh heavily in superpower negotiations and in the General Assembly. In theory, successful space-based defenses could alter the foundation of superpower security. Instead of relying on offensive forces to deter through threat of retaliation against cities, nations could maintain security by defending against attack. The actual capabilities and implications of such defenses are impossible to assess; the technology is still too primitive and the doctrines too inchoate. Both superpowers have large research programs, and Moscow has funded a significant program since the late 1950s [Sayre Stevens, "The BMP Program," Asdon B. Carter and David N. Schwartz, eds., *Ballistic Missile Defense* (Washington, D.C.: The Brookings Institution, 1984), p. 191]. Most analysts believe that the United States has gained a commanding lead since the White House tripled funding for research and development under SDI.

U.S. support for SDI is not uncritical. White House officials and administration advisers believe that a skeletal system could be put in place by 1992.

Others say the White House predictions are hopelessly optimistic. The technical problems, they argue, grow more daunting as more is learned about the requirements of the system. The Congress is wary and has already cut funding by almost 40 percent.

As the public has begun to question SDI, the program's enthusiasts within the Reagan administration and their congressional supporters are increasingly anxious to begin early deployments of strategic defenses. Efforts in this direction have precipitated a bitter debate over the **legality of the SDI under the ABM Treaty.** To accelerate the program, the White House wants to test components of a potential system in space. The ABM Treaty is usually interpreted to prohibit such activities. Under the traditional "narrow" interpretation, advanced testing would necessitate renegotiation or abrogation of the treaty.

A new "broad" interpretation by State Department legal adviser Abraham Sofaer states the exact opposite: that the treaty does permit such testing in space. The broad interpretation has been welcomed by howls of protest from administration critics. Former Senator J. William Fulbright summed up the opposition when he said, "the administration has the right under the treaty to propose amendments or to withdraw. . . . It does not have the right to perform radical surgery by tortured reinterpretation" [*International Herald Tribune*, 3/13/87]. After examining the secret negotiating record of the ABM Treaty, Senator Sam Nunn presented a highly influential refutation of the broad interpretation, accusing Sofaer of "a complete and total misrepresentation." The controversy persists, and as long as the White House pursues space-based defenses it cannot be considered settled.

Another school of thought maintains that, with or without SDI, the ABM Treaty must be amended. Technological change is undermining the foundation of the 1972 treaty. For example, to prevent either side from acquiring the battle-management capabilities needed to predict the specific targets of individual warheads, the ABM Treaty imposed restrictions on the location and orientation of early-warning radars. But advances in technology have transformed battle-management from a radar location problem into a computer software problem. With sophisticated computer software, radar operating from most any location will be able to predict the exact destination of nuclear warheads. This development will not only further complicate compliance with the goals of the ABM Treaty but is likely to propel a new form of arms competition, the development of **maneuverable reentry vehicles (MARVs).** MARV development could lead to new requirements for testing weapons that, in turn, could become another obstacle to nuclear testing accords. Another gray area surrounds **antisatellite (ASAT)** weapons, which could be developed into effective ABM weapons. These ambiguities cannot readily be resolved under the existing treaty. It is not enough to uphold agreements; they must also be adapted to changes in their environment.

Little progress has been made on these issues in the ongoing Geneva negotiations. Moscow insists on extending the principles of the ABM Treaty to prohibit all work on space-based defenses. Washington takes the opposite position and refuses to consider any limitations on SDI research. At the Reykjavik meeting Secretary Gorbachev indicated that the Soviet Union would be willing to accept laboratory research only—where verification of a prohibition is virtually impossible—and only in exchange for a renewed U.S. commitment to uphold the ABM Treaty. Earlier Soviet statements seemed to indicate that they might consider some off-laboratory research.

The General Assembly has not tried to break the deadlock in the Geneva negotiations. Instead, its efforts have concentrated on establishing the principle of "preventing the militarization of outer space." For the last two years the First Committee has been able to winnow down several alternative resolutions into a single authoritative document. At the 41st Session it was possible to accommodate all nations, except the United States, which abstained [A/Res/41/53]. The resolution called upon the Conference on Disarmament to intensify its work on the topic and urged all nations to respect extant treaties such as the ABM Treaty.

2. European Security

Offering a contrast to the frustrations of offensive and defensive weapons is the third area of East-West negotiation, European security, which holds some promise for a major breakthrough. After years of fruitless efforts, Moscow and Washington have adopted comparable positions on **intermediate-range nuclear forces (INF)**. Serious problems remain, especially for European leaders, but the momentum for an agreement is unmistakable. Consequently, it would be especially tragic if this opportunity were lost to inertia and timidity.

Europe remains the focal point of superpower confrontation as the nexus of strategy-making and force-planning and the justification for many of the most consequential decisions of the nuclear era. Despite the superpowers' global outlook, European concerns still rank highest on their security agendas. The North Atlantic Treaty Organization (NATO), with sixteen members, has more than 2 million troops in Europe. The Warsaw Treaty Organization (WTO) has seven members fielding more than 2.5 million troops. It is in Europe that an outbreak of hostilities is expected to escalate quickly to nuclear warfare between the Soviet Union and the United States. Nowhere else are the stakes so high and so immediate.

Arms control agreements can play an essential role in the preservation of European security. But the elements involved in a successful European agreement are manifold and almost impossible to coordinate. Secretary Gorbachev's proposal of February 28, 1987, on intermediate-range nuclear forces

(INF) potentially revolutionized the situation by cutting through the tangled factors that previously inhibited agreement. Many difficult problems remain to be resolved before his offer can lead to an actual treaty, but nowhere else is the outlook as promising.

Gorbachev's proposal to eliminate intermediate-range nuclear forces in Europe reiterates a formula almost as old as the issue itself. In the mid-1970s, European officials grew alarmed at Soviet deployments of Backfire bombers and SS-20 intermediate-range missiles. With these systems it was feared that the WTO could potentially weaken U.S. guarantees to defend Western Europe. These systems could be used to target all of Western Europe at a time when U.S. retaliation could only come from forces based in North America. European officials questioned the United States' guarantee to risk its own cities to retaliate against a Soviet attack on its European allies.

Concerned about the danger that Europeon security was being decoupled from that of the United States, West German Chancellor Helmut Schmidt called for counterdeployments of intermediate-range systems in Western Europe. Able to hit Soviet territory from Europe, these systems would restore the credibility of the United States' extended deterrent. In the formal twin-track decision of 1979, NATO agreed to deploy 108 Pershing II missiles and 472 ground-launched cruise missiles and simultaneously to make an effort to negotiate a solution to the problem.

In 1981, President Reagan presented his **zero option**. NATO would deploy no INF systems if Moscow would dismantle its inventory of SS-20s. This proposal made no progress at the time, nor did efforts to strike a compromise. NATO deployments started in November 1983, ending a grueling political battle for the indecisive governments involved. At the Reykjavik meeting in 1986, Gorbachev and Reagan agreed in principle to eliminate their respective intermediate nuclear forces. Each side would retain a hundred INF warheads (thirty-three Soviet SS-20s with three warheads each and a hundred U.S. ground-launched cruise missiles) outside of Europe. But nothing came of this until Gorbachev's February 1987 proposal, repeating the Reagan zero option and the Reykjavik formula and introducing several essential concessions. Moscow agreed to ignore U.S. nuclear-capable aircraft based in Europe or at sea; British and French independent nuclear forces would not have to be restrained, as the Soviets had previously insisted; Moscow dropped earlier demands that progress in INF be accompanied by U.S. concessions on SDI; and it agreed to on-site inspection.

These are tremendous concessions for the Kremlin. To the White House, hungry for a deal, the situation looks outstanding. European governments are less enthusiastic. Having endured the trauma of INF deployment, they are not overjoyed to see the missile go. Many fear that in its haste to conclude an agreement, the White House will compromise the security guarantees it originally sought to reinforce. Some officials on both sides of the Atlantic would prefer to see INF reduced but not eliminated, thereby maintaining the U.S. security umbrella.

A major debate has developed over the question of **short-range missiles in Europe**. In response, the USSR has agreed to include these weapons in an INF deal, but European anxieties persist. It is argued by some that NATO is yielding the battlefield to the WTO's overwhelming superiority in these systems. Others are concerned about the adequacy of NATO's conventional forces, which may have to be expanded to compensate—a costly alternative. Some European spokesmen believe that their nations will lose regardless of what happens.

These are painful issues, and the General Assembly will not have an easy time with them. European delegations will doubtless remind their colleagues that disarmament can actually weaken security if it is not managed carefully.

Lesser agreements have come more easily. On September 22, 1986, the thirty-five-nation **Stockholm Conference on Confidence- and Security-Building Measures and Disarmament in Europe** ended two-and-a-half years of negotiation with an accord that greatly improved the confidence-building measures of the 1975 Helsinki Final Act. It reduces the risk of surprise attack by calling for prior notification and observation of all major military exercises from the Atlantic to the Ural mountains, and it is supported by strong verification provisions. The agreement has won the General Assembly's encomium and is already being adhered to [A/Res/41/86L].

The Stockholm agreement benefited from having modest goals, which facilitated the negotiating process. The **Vienna negotiations on Mutual and Balanced Force Reductions** (MBFR) enjoy no such advantage. This thirteen-year-old negotiation was intended to complement nuclear arms control by stabilizing the conventional military environment. Over the years it has made real progress, but there is very little hope for a final agreement soon, or even at all. Despite the vigorous support of the General Assembly, there are too many hurdles to overcome. Some participants—especially France—are opposed to the very idea of reducing conventional forces. Others, like West Germany, are more concerned with the problem of keeping their forces up to strength at a time when the number of eligible conscripts is declining. A persistent data discrepancy concerning the number of WTO troops inhibits essential agreement. Some Western governments, as well as security and arms control experts, hope the MBFR talks will politely disappear. Others, led by Denmark, believe that the basic idea of conventional arms control can be promoted through the United Nations [A/Res/41/59C].

3. Nuclear Proliferation and the Nuclear Test Ban

The General Assembly has trouble dealing with the issue of **the spread of nuclear weapons to the Third World**. Its Third World majority maintains that the severest problems confronting international peace and security are the nuclear arsenals of the nuclear weapon states: the United Kingdom, France, China, the United States, and the Soviet Union. Many Third World leaders insist that the spread of nuclear weapons to additional countries (horizontal proliferation) is secondary to the control of the growth of existing nuclear inventories (vertical proliferation). As a result of these divisions, the Assembly avoids straightforward statements of support for the nonproliferation regime. With regard to the **Treaty on the Non-Proliferation of Nuclear Weapons** (**NPT**) and its monitoring agency, the **International Atomic Energy Agency** (**IAEA**), the General Assembly tends to emphasize the duties of the states with nuclear weapons over the responsibilities of the nonnuclear weapons majority.

Recent disclosures in the press show just how difficult it is becoming to prevent the spread of nuclear weapons. On October 5, 1986, *The Sunday Times* (London) printed an article based on claims by a former Israeli physicist that Israel has assembled at least a hundred nuclear weapons and can manufacture ten per year. On March 8, 1987, *The Observer* (London) quoted Pakistan's chief nuclear scientist, Abdel Qader Khan, as saying that his country can produce a bomb at will, a claim that was subsequently confirmed by President Zia ul-Haq in an interview in *Time* magazine [3/30/87]. India tested a "peaceful nuclear device" in 1974 and is now debating whether to build a stockpile of actual weapons. Brazil, South Africa, and South Korea are widely thought to have surreptitious nuclear weapons programs. Libya contines to try to procure nuclear weapons or components from friendly governments or on the black market.

Time will only increase the likelihood of further proliferation. The basic technology needed to build a nuclear weapon is over forty years old. Newcomers benefit from an immense published literature and the availability of powerful computers. Experience with civilian nuclear power generation provides much of the essential knowledge and facilities. Even in countries without civilian facilities, the costs present no major obstacle, since a reactor, uranium fuel, and reprocessing and manufacturing facilities can all be acquired for about $200 million. For many countries, the question of proliferation is becoming a purely political one, with neither technology nor costs standing in the way.

At the center of these issues is the NPT itself, which continues to gain signatories. The most recent of these was Spain, which in March 1987 announced its intention to sign the nineteen-year-old document, joining more than 130 states that have signed already. Notably absent from their ranks are many of the countries most likely to extend proliferation: Argentina, Brazil, India, Israel, Pakistan, and South Africa.

Although there are more than a few likely proliferators, the General Assembly has focused its interest exclusively on Israel and South Africa. Both are criticized for refusing to cooperate with IAEA inspections and safeguards to ensure that their nuclear facilities are not used for military purposes [A/Res/41/55A and 93]. Other potential proliferators oppose safeguards or restrict IAEA inspection to selected facilities. But it is highly improbable that the Assembly will call attention to their noncompliance.

The Assembly is expected to emphasize the demands of nonaligned countries for easier access to civilian nuclear technology. Many Third World nations have retained their enthusiasm for nuclear power. Article IV of the NPT and the IAEA Charter assure the nonnuclear weapon states access to civilian nuclear technology in exchange for safeguarding their facilities. The nonaligned routinely condemn export restrictions that hinder their nuclear programs. Supplier restraint, however, is essential if proliferation is to be inhibited. After India's nuclear detonation in 1974, a multilateral organization, the London Nuclear Suppliers' Group, was established to monitor exports of nuclear technology. The organization is surrounded by controversy. Efforts by the United States to extend the group's authority to all elements of nuclear technology have met with opposition from leading nuclear exporters such as Belgium, Switzerland, and West Germany; and nuclear importers have denounced the organization as an illegal cartel violating the spirit of Article IV.

A small success for nonproliferation was announced in April 1987, with the establishment of an **International Missile Technology Regime.** Including among its members most of the Western leaders in missile- and space-launch technology, this regime will control the export of missile technology, making it difficult for would-be proliferators to develop long-range delivery systems. The nonaligned will probably react to it in much the same way they have reacted to the London Group.

The United Nations prefers to approach the proliferation issue through the general question of a **Comprehensive Nuclear Test Ban (CTB).** The CTB enjoys widespread support in the General Assembly, where it is seen as a way of inhibiting the entire nuclear arms race. A CTB would place identical restrictions on the nuclear powers and potential proliferators. Advocates argue that a test ban would erode confidence in nuclear weapons and hinder modernization. It would also create difficulties for nations trying to develop new nuclear arsenals. Currently, nuclear testing is restrained by the (atmospheric) 1963 Partial Test Ban Treaty and the unratified Threshold Test Ban Treaty of 1974. The proposed CTB has been negotiated in several forums, most recently in the Geneva Conference on Disarmament.

Moscow attempted to draw Washington into a CTB through its nineteenth month moratorium on nuclear testing, which ended in February 1987. The United States declined to join the Soviet Union for the same reason it opposes a CTB: the difficulty of verifying compliance and the need to ensure the reliability of the U.S. stockpile.

Washington's protestations have not prevented the CTB issue from becoming a favorite of the General Assembly. What the Assembly lacks is consensus on how to achieve a CTB. The 41st Session passed five CTB resolutions, and the 42nd Session will face stiff barriers to developing a single position. A popular but highly politicized approach urges that all nuclear testing simply cease [A/Res/41/46A and 54]; another would prohibit the production of fissionable materials [A/Res/41/59L]; and yet others aim at the negotiating process, urging the creation of an international seismic monitoring system to assure proper verification [A/Res/41/47] or that the existing Partial Test Ban be expanded into a genuine CTB [A/Res/41/46B]. A more immediate concern of the General Assembly may be the final ratification of the 1974 **Threshold Test Ban Treaty**. This agreement, banning nuclear tests over 150 kilotons, has not been ratified by Washington because of concern over verification.

Another way to restrain the spread of nuclear weapons is through the creation of **Nuclear Weapons Free Zones (NWFZs)**. NWFZ treaties already in effect cover Antarctica, the ocean floors, the moon, and outer space, but extending the concept to inhabited areas has proved more difficult. The only current example is the Treaty of Tlatelolco, which aims to establish a Latin American NWFZ; but this treaty is not adhered to by the Latin American nations that are among the most likely proliferators: Argentina, Brazil, Chile, and Cuba. Another problem arises when an outside power has—or reserves the right to have—nuclear weapons in the region. In the case of Tlatelolco, the General Assembly has pointed out the problem posed by France, which reserves the right to base nuclear weapons in its territories in the region [A/Res/41/45].

France has its hands full in the South Pacific, where Australia, New Zealand, and six small island states have signed the 1985 Treaty of Rarotonga. The new treaty would establish a South Pacific NWFZ intended primarily to halt French nuclear testing at Mururoa Atoll, three thousand miles northeast of New Zealand. France refuses to halt its tests lest its independent deterrent weaken, and General Assembly recommendations [A/Res/41/59N] have had little effect on its resolve. But after eighty-four nuclear tests in twelve years, Mururoa is in danger of a serious radiation leak. France is looking for a new test site, although the most likely choice is another South Pacific island.

Two other NWFZ proposals among the ranks of perennial General Assembly resolutions would establish Middle Eastern and South Asian NWFZs [A/Res/41/48 and 49]. The South Asian proposal is opposed, however, by a regional power that refuses to relinquish the nuclear option, India, while Israel and the Arab states have submitted differing proposals on a Middle Eastern NWFZ. African denuclearization is blocked by South Africa's refusal to open its nuclear facilities to IAEA inspection [A/Res/41/55A].

4. Conventional and Chemical Weapons

The General Assembly has repeatedly reaffirmed its conviction that the first priority for disarmament must be nuclear weapons. In the opinion of most member states, only nuclear weapons endanger the existence of civilization. Some nonaligned delegations routinely criticize proposals to examine conventional military issues, arguing that these distract the international community from the more important job of nuclear disarmament.

Nevertheless, the United Nations is beginning to give more attention to conventional arms control. It is becoming increasingly difficult to ignore the weapons that have caused virtually all military casualties since 1945 and that account for over 80 percent of global military spending. U.N. consideration of conventional disarmament concentrates on the inventories of the major powers and of the superpowers in particular [A/39/348]. Although resolutions endorsing broader consideration of conventional disarmament have received only lukewarm support from the Assembly [A/Res/41/59C], they have led to greater awareness of the MBFR process in Vienna and in the Stockholm negotiations, described above. Many nonaligned delegations question the significance of these negotiations and display little enthusiasm for future initiatives.

China is increasingly active on conventional military issues. Following its decision to discharge a million soldiers—primarily for economic reasons—Beijing has sought reciprocal action. The Soviet Union responded with token reductions of its forces in Mongolia. China brought its case to the General Assembly, winning approval of a resolution urging "the countries with the largest military arsenals . . . to continue negotiations on conventional disarmament in earnest" [A/Res/41/59G].

Naval armaments constitute the aspect of the conventional military balance that concerns the Assembly most. Navies remain a basic tool of diplomacy and foreign intervention. Their significance is seen continuously in naval exercises and in events like the 1982 South Atlantic War between Argentina and the United Kingdom and U.S. naval activity off the coasts of Lebanon and Libya in recent years. A study of the naval race by the United Nations Department of Disarmament Affairs was well received by the General Assembly last year [U.N. Fact Sheet No. 44, 4/86], and its diverse recommendations will provide the basis for further U.N. consideration [A/Res/41/59K]. A new issue may emerge as the Soviet Union completes its first large aircraft carrier at its Black Sea shipyards. Operation of the vessel may violate the 1936 Montreux Convention, which prohibits aircraft carriers from passing through the Bosporus.

Arms transfers to the Third World dominate public discussion of the conventional arms race. Yet this issue is an extremely sensitive one in the General Assembly. The Third World majority resents efforts to control the arms trade, efforts seen as paternalistic meddling by some and as a deliberate attempt to weaken the Third World by others. Only in the case of South Africa has the Assembly acted forthrightly to restrain arms sales, passing embargoes in 1963 and 1977. In recent years, however, Peru has won support for a toothless proposal encouraging regional disarmament [A/Res/41/59M].

The outlook for a ban on **chemical weapons** is much brighter. Negotiations in the Conference on Disarmament in Geneva have continued for eighteen years, seeking to finish the job started by the 1925 Geneva Protocol. The Protocol, with 118 signatories, is the oldest multilateral arms control agreement in effect. It prohibits the use of chemical weapons in war, although it does not ban their manufacture. It is buttressed by the 1972 Convention banning biological weapons. Compliance with both agreements is voluntary; they have no verification mechanisms and rely on good faith and enlightened self-interest to assure compliance. Rather than rely on the goodwill of their adversaries, many nations continue to prepare for chemical and biological warfare (CBW). France, the Soviet Union, and the United States maintain significant stockpiles of chemical weapons. Official U.S. estimates claim that at least a dozen other nations have stockpiles as well.

The CBW issue has been kept controversial through a series of recent events. The United States has charged Moscow and its allies with using toxic "yellow rain" in Afghanistan, Kampuchea, and Laos. Studies by the U.N. Secretary-General have been unable to confirm or deny the allegations. The Soviet Union maintains that the United States is escalating the arms race by preparing to manufacture a new class of "binary" chemical munitions. Washington says the program is intended exclusively to enhance peacetime safety. The superpowers have also charged each other with violations of the **1972 biological weapons convention.** Washington maintains that an anthrax epidemic in the Soviet city of Sverdlovsk in 1979 resulted from biological warfare experiments; the Soviet press has accused the United States of creating the disease AIDS in a biological warfare experiment at Fort Detrick, Maryland. Moscow has bitterly denounced the U.S. allegation, while former U.S. Ambassador to Moscow Arthur Hartman dismissed the Soviet AIDS claim as "a repugnant attempt to sow hatred and fear" [*International Herald Tribune*, 4/8/87].

Chemical weapons can be fabricated by virtually any nation willing to make the investment. This was demonstrated in the spring of 1984, when the world learned that Iraq was using chemical weapons in its war with Iran. Iraq is believed to have used civilian fertilizer factories purchased from West Germany to produce mustard gas. By using civilian technology to violate the 1925 Geneva Protocol, Iraq exemplifies the need for a comprehensive ban and the difficulty of verifying one.

The verification issue has been the major stumbling block to progress in Geneva. A shift in the Soviet position on this issue may make possible an outright ban on the production of chemical weapons. On-site inspection is the key to any such agreement. Soviet negotiators have indicated that Moscow would be amenable to an international inspection agency similar in principle to the IAEA. This agency would be empowered to conduct inspections of military and civilian chemical facilities to assure that chemical weapons are not being manufactured. Working out the details of this arrangement could still take years, but there is reason to hope that such an agreement might be reached in the not too distant future.

The General Assembly takes great interest in the CBW issue but lacks consensus on it. The 41st Session passed four CBW resolutions dealing with implementation of the 1972 biological weapons convention and with encouraging the negotiations on chemical weapons in the Conference on Disarmament [A/Res/41/58A and 58D]. The Assembly was seriously divided by an East German resolution to prohibit CBW, interpreted by Western and some nonaligned delegations as a political swipe [A/Res/41/58B]. A French resolution urging compliance with existing agreements won stronger support [A/Res/41/58C].

5. Comprehensive Disarmament

Although the General Assembly's disarmament agenda is far more ambitious than the arms control priorities of the major powers, it is not ambitious enough for the majority of delegations. Their aspirations are manifested in vigorous support for comprehensive disarmament. Although there is no chance that comprehensive disarmament can be achieved in the foreseeable future, it is kept on the agenda as a long-range goal.

The best known of these proposals, **General and Complete Disarmament**, has been under consideration since 1959, when it was introduced by Soviet Premier Khrushchev. Today it serves exclusively as a miscellaneous category for hard-to-classify resolutions on topics like radiological weapons and the role of specialized agencies [A/Res/41/59A-0]. More emphasis is placed on the reduction of military budgets [A/Res/41/57]. Before much can be accomplished in this area it will be necessary to know how much nations invest in their security. Many Warsaw Pact and nonaligned governments refuse to cooperate with resolutions requesting detailed data [A/Res/41/59B]. The Assembly has generated greater support for studies of military research and development and of the economic and social consequences of military spending [A/Res/41/59H and 86I].

The United Nations Conference on Disarmament and Development will be convened in New York, August 24 to September 11, 1987. The conference will be the most impressive manifestation yet seen at the U.N. of the belief that military spending hinders economic development by squandering scarce resources. Washington blocked previous attempts to convene such a meeting, arguing that disarmament and development are both worthwhile objectives but denying there is a relationship between the two. The United States is not alone in its position. Some Third World defense analysts, led by India's K. Subrahmanyam, hold that defense spending accelerates industrial development. Such views may be irrelevant in New York if the deliberations focus exclusively on Northern disarmament and Southern development. The United States declared that it would not participate in the conference.

Another major conference mandated by the 41st General Assembly is the **Third Special Session on Disarmament (SSOD III)** scheduled for 1988

[A/Res/41/60G]. The Special Session will attempt to accomplish what its predecessors in 1978 and 1982 could not—the promulgation of an integrated international statement on disarmament. Although the previous Special Sessions helped to publicize disarmament, they were deadlocked on many substantive issues. Their principal accomplishments—a restructuring of U.N. disarmament forums, the United Nations World Disarmament Campaign, Disarmament Week, and the United Nations Disarmament Fellowships—seem small compared with the effort put into organizing them. Indeed, the Special Sessions have grown controversial over time and may suffer from future budget cuts [A/Res/41/60A, 60B, 60H, 86D, and 86O]. Another product of the Second Special Session—the United Nations Regional Disarmament Centres in Africa and Latin America—are being established, although their role remains to be refined [A/Res/41/60D and 60J]. Some observers are skeptical that another Special Session can do much more, and it has been suggested that the Special Session be delayed at least until 1989, when a new U.S. president will assume office.

If and when the international climate changes to permit complete disarmament, the United Nations hopes to be ready. The Ad Hoc Committee on the World Disarmament Conference continues preparations for the first such meeting since the disastrous disarmament conference of 1932–34 [A/Res/41/61]. The Assembly also supports continued work on the elaboration of a Comprehensive Program of Disarmament, under consideration in the Conference on Disarmament [decision of the 41st Assembly taken without a vote]. This work is more important as a statement of intention than as a practical measure. It leaves no doubt about the kind of world the Assembly envisions.

III
Economics and Development

1. The World Economy in 1987

In 1987 the world economy entered its fifth year of recovery from the global recession of the early 1980s. The expansion, however, has been slow, unevenly distributed among countries, and plagued by nagging problems in the areas of trade and finance. The Third World debt crisis hangs over world economic prosperity like an avalanche waiting to happen. Volatile currency exchange rates play havoc with investor choices. Trade imbalances persist and commodity prices have fallen to their lowest real value in the postwar period [International Monetary Fund, *World Economic Outlook*, 4/87, p. 93]. On the brighter side, the advanced industrial countries attempted to coordinate their macroeconomic policies, and work began on a new round of multilateral trade negotiations. Nevertheless, this cooperation is fragile and does not guarantee that key industrial countries will seek to rely more heavily on international organizations in economic matters next year.

Recent global economic performance suggests that the next few years may be troubled. In 1986 the rate of income growth among industrial countries continued to decline from a 1984 peak of 4.7 percent. Industrial-country income grew 3.0 percent in 1985, 2.4 percent in 1986, and is predicted to grow only 2.3 percent in 1987 [IMF, *WEO*, 4/87, table A–2]. The United States' rapid recovery after the 1980–82 recession failed to ignite substantial growth in the other industrial countries. Indeed, the sharp fall of the U.S. income growth rate in 1984–85 was the main cause of the slowdown in 1985–86 relative to 1984. Real income growth in Japan, the only other country that maintained high growth rates in 1984–85, slowed to a moderate level in 1986 of 2.5 percent. European growth in 1986 remained about the same as in the previous two years, at 2.4 percent. With foreign demand for Japanese exports responsible for much of Japan's growth in 1984–85, the slow growth rates of domestic demand in both Japan and Europe have become a source of conflict. Rapid growth in the United States, combined with anemic domestic demand in other industrial countries, has been partly responsible for the global trade imbalances that now plague the global economy. In seeking greater economic coordination, the industrial countries are likely to pay particular attention in 1987 to the need to stimulate Japanese and West German growth rates.

These concerns are aggravated by perceptions that the recovery from the 1980–83 global recession was unusually weak and by fears that one of the longest postwar recoveries cannot be sustained indefinitely. Except for the United States, industrial countries experienced peak-of-recovery growth rates far below normal and, in most cases, below the growth rate averages in the 1970s. Industrial country unemployment remains high at 8.0 percent [*Ibid.*, table A–4]. IMF projections for the future indicate growth will get worse before it gets better, with predicted growth rates for 1989–95 slower than the average rates for 1986–88 [*Journal of Commerce*, 4/24/87]. These same predictions flatly reject as overly optimistic U.S. government projections for U.S. Gross National Product (GNP) growth through 1992. With stocks and bonds in their fifth year of a vigorous bull market, most analysts predict that the steam of the recovery may well be spent [*The Economist*, 1/3/87]. Even long-ignored long-cycle wave theories—which predict depressions of massive proportions within the next ten years—have gained new adherents in recent years [*The Economist* 4/18/87].

Industrial countries continued to pursue anti-inflationary policies in 1986. The United States led the way, cutting inflation to 2.6 percent from 3.3 percent in 1985. Overall industrial-country inflation was reduced to 3.4 percent in 1986, down from 9.3 percent in the prerecessionary peak of 1980. How long this trend will last, however, is not at all certain. Up until now, a largely inexplicable increase in domestic money velocity has offset what should have been a more inflationary U.S. monetary policy. Despite the Gramm-Rudman-Hollings budgetary resolution, the U.S. budget deficit is likely to fall only slightly, as both the Reagan administration and Congress have proposed budgetary targets with deficits in excess of last year's novel budgetary device. Finally, the rapid depreciation of the dollar is raising import prices dramatically. Japan and West Germany are also considering expansionary policies to fulfill the macroeconomic policy coordination goals of the major industrial countries. Still, the IMF expects inflation to ease in 1987 before climbing again in 1988 [IMF, *WEO*, table A–8].

The **slide of the dollar** from its peak value in March 1985 continued through July 1986. After stabilizing in the second half of 1986, the dollar again began to depreciate in early 1987—a trend that the Louvre Accord of February 22, 1987, which enhanced policy coordination among the major industrial countries, gave renewed vigor. By the end of February 1987 the dollar had declined by 32 percent from its peak in early 1985 [IMF, *International Financial Statistics*, 3/87]. The sharp appreciation of the yen relative to the dollar has placed tremendous political pressure on the Japanese government because of its negative impact upon export competitiveness. In the United States, exchange rates currently remain the major policy tool to correct the trade deficit. Both the former Federal Reserve Board Chairman Paul Volcker and former Chairman of the Council of Economic Advisers Martin Feldstein have expressed concern that the unusually rapid dollar decline may be hard to stop. If the decline continues, it could trigger an interest-rate jump that might push the economy into recession [*The Wall Street Journal*, 2/20/86; *The Washington Post*, 1/19/87]. In addition to these developments, economists have become aware of the importance of exchange rates in newly industrializing countries (NICs)—rates that have not appreciated against the dollar during the recent dollar slide [*The AMEX Bank Review*, 9/29/86]. Meanwhile, the "J-curve" effect—higher import prices preceding reduced import demand by many months or even years—has resulted in an enormous U.S. trade deficit ($170 billion in 1986). Consequently, protectionist sentiment has increased in both the United States and its industrial-country competitors.

Efforts by the major industrial countries to coordinate policy yielded one of the most strongly worded summit declarations at the end of the Tokyo summit in May 1986. The summit gave trade talks strong momentum, which carried through to a successful conclusion of the Punta del Este conference launching the new trade round. Furthermore, the issue of agricultural policies received the direct attention that was necessary to keep it as a high-priority item on the agenda of the new round. However, macroeconomic policy coordination proved elusive, and the second half of 1986 was characterized by drift. Only the Louvre Accord of February 1987 put these efforts back on track, with the United States renewing pledges of budgetary stringency and Japan and West Germany pledging expansionary policies, in contrast to their traditional anti-inflationary bias. These efforts yielded a further pledge by the Japanese government to recycle its trade surplus as investment capital for debtor countries. While the **Venice summit**, held in June 1987, yielded only a weakly worded communiqué, most analysts expect close coordination to continue at the ministerial level [*The Wall Street Journal*, 6/9/87]. In sum, the policy divergences of the early 1980s have been narrowed dramatically over the last twelve to eighteen months [WEO, p. 26].

Developing countries continued to experience relatively slow growth in 1986. Sharp commodity price declines, and continued limitations on external finance, kept developing-country income growth to 3.5 percent in 1986. This was up from 3.2 percent in 1985 but still substantially below the 6.1 percent average annual growth in 1969–78 [WEO, table A–5]. Adjustment reforms and anti-inflationary policies met with some success in reducing inflation (from 41 percent in 1985 to 29 percent in 1986) and increasing incentives for exports. The terms of trade, however, moved against most developing countries, and investment was crimped by the unavailability of external sources of finance.

Although conditions for exports of manufactures improved in 1986, most such exporters remain troubled by debt service problems and severely limited commercial lending. The economies of countries with recent debt-servicing problems grew 3.2 percent in 1986 compared with 2.7 percent in 1985, but this was still far below the 5.1 percent growth in 1986 experienced by countries without debt-servicing problems and below the 5–6 percent average growth rates experienced by all developing countries in the 1970s.

With a 0.7 percent income decline in 1986, **oil exporters** suffered from the dramatic fall in oil prices. By mid-1986 the decline was roughly 60 percent from November 1985. Since July 1986 prices have recovered to the $18–$22 a barrel range, still a substantial drop from the $27–$31 range in 1985. The collapse of OPEC production controls was partly responsible for the decline of oil prices, though the continuing entrance of new, non-OPEC sources of oil on the markets served as another major factor.

At the same time, the decline of oil prices contributed to growth increases among developing countries that must import oil. Despite worsening terms of trade, both agricultural and mineral exporters grew substantially faster in 1986, with rates up from 4.6 percent in 1985 to 5.4 percent.

Real growth in the developing countries varies greatly from region to region, reflecting the varying impact of commodity prices, debt-servicing problems, and business cycles. Debt problems continued to beset the **newly industrializing countries** (**NICs**) in Latin America. Those in Asia experienced moderate growth in 1986—down from the rapid growth years of 1983–84. Overall, developing countries in Asia grew 5.7 percent, in Latin America 4.0 percent, and in sub-Saharan Africa 4.0 percent. The Middle East experienced no income growth in 1986.

Centrally planned economies in Eastern Europe posted substantial income gains (an estimated 4.3 percent) in 1986 [WEO, table A–1]. Rumblings of reform in the Soviet Union raise the possibility of new opportunities for trade with the COMECON nations. It is too early to predict the full extent of these reforms, but many Sovietologists doubt that Soviet leader Mikhail Gorbachev can engineer significant change in the Soviet economy.

In sum, the global economic outlook remains mixed. Industrial-country income growth slowed, while oil-importing developing countries grew more rapidly, largely at the expense of the oil-exporting nations. The year 1987 is expected to bring slower growth for industrial countries, developing countries, and centrally planned economies alike. Numerous indicators point to a significant slowdown or even recession in 1987–88.

2. Trade

The interlinkages between trade and finance are strong and complex, and the lines that divide them seem increasingly artificial and blurred. The three most important macroeconomic events of 1986 underline this trend. The management of exchange rates is an issue of extreme salience for world trade because of the impact of currency values on short-term trade competitiveness and trade balances. The Third World debt crisis continues to hamper international trade and threatens to enter a new phase as debtor countries find import-compression unsustainable. Finally, the new round of trade negotiations includes significant efforts to liberalize services trade, such as investment and finance.

Global imbalances in the area of trade continued to be a major problem for industrial as well as developing countries in 1986. The U.S. trade deficit hit a record high, amounting to 3.3 percent of U.S. GNP. This was mirrored by trade surpluses exceeding 4.0 percent of GNP in both Japan and West Germany. Developing-country exports increased in volume terms, but fell in value terms because of sliding prices. Third World imports grew slightly, although they remain below the 1980 level. Consequently, the developing countries experienced a $38 billion reduction in their trade surplus. This surplus was swamped by the services deficit—mostly interest on debt. Thus, the developing-country current account deficit grew to roughly the 1981 level, when the debt crisis first emerged.

World trade volume grew by 4.9 percent in 1986, but whether world trade value grew or contracted in 1986 depends upon which currency is used to compute it. Because of the decline in the value of the dollar, global trade value grew by nearly 10 percent in dollar terms. However, in terms of special drawing rights (SDRs)—the IMF unit of currency, based upon a weighted group of major industrial country currencies—world trade value actually contracted. The moderate growth of world trade volume in 1986 was caused by the sluggish nature of income growth, the ongoing debt crisis, and rising levels of protectionism, especially in the form of nontariff barriers. The effect of the debt crisis on industrial-country exports received more attention in 1986 as debtors were forced into a new round of import compression. Imports by countries with recent debt-servicing problems fell by 5.2 percent in volume terms in 1986 (compared with growth of 2.7 percent by countries without such severe problems) [WEO, tables A–20 and A–25]. Predictions for 1987 foresee a slackening in trade volume growth to about 2.5 percent [Financial Times, 3/27/87].

The use of trade for political purposes took a new turn in 1986, as key nations took action to loosen their trade and financial ties with South Africa. After much debate, the Commonwealth nations, the United States, Canada, and Japan introduced or strengthened trade sanctions against South Africa in order to pressure that country's government to abolish apartheid [South, 1/87]. Though the measures have received mixed reviews from the economic point of view, the sanctions reinforce the global trend of employing trade for political, rather than economic, goals.

GATT and the Uruguay Round

The member states of the **General Agreement on Tariffs and Trade (GATT)** overcame significant differences of opinion regarding trade liberalization in services and agricultural trade in order to launch a new round of global trade negotiations. With a number of industrial countries dragging their feet on agricultural trade and several developing countries expressing reservations about the expansion of GATT into services trade, the preparatory committee meetings came to a standstill in the spring of 1986. When the United States threatened to break with tradition and seek a vote (rather than consensus) on launching the round, the contracting parties averted disaster by creating new mechanisms for negotiations. At Punta del Este, Uruguay, in September, ministers adopted a complex and ambitious two-track program of negotiations covering both goods and services trade.

The **Uruguay Round**, as it is titled, still faces large obstacles to success. The round did not formally begin on schedule in January 1987 because of disagreement over the powers of a monitoring body (to ensure that the standstill and rollback provisions of the Punta del Este declaration are observed). Since the resolution of this issue, GATT has been able to establish negotiating groups on fourteen goods trade topics and set a schedule for fulfilling the negotiation goal of completion within four years. In the area of services, the talks have proceeded much more slowly, raising doubts as to how the parallel sets of talks will be brought together into one package in the end.

The key issues for the world trading system in 1987 do not lend themselves to traditional bloc negotiating stances. Because of the nontariff nature of the Uruguay Round, many countries are finding alliances that cross North-South lines as useful as traditional intraregional alliances. The Tokyo Round (September 1973 to November 1979) put to rest most tariff-related issues, and recent policy trends involve nontariff measures. Of particular importance to this round are talks on **quantitative restrictions**, such as orderly marketing agreements and voluntary export restrictions. In dealing with adjustment pressures, industrial countries have resorted to these measures with increasing frequency to restrict trade without violating previous agreements. Quantitative restrictions are also preferred by developing countries undergoing balance of payments crises, often caused by debt problems. Issues such as safeguards and subsidies, frequently used by governments intervening to soften the blow of recession, will be highly contentious, but they strike at the heart of the way in which the trading system works. Another difficult issue will be agriculture.

Newer issues, such as trade in services, trade-related investment, intellectual property rights, and high-technology trade, provide a full agenda for the round. Although no consensus exists on how to proceed in any one of these areas, their inclusion gives key industrial countries an incentive to support GATT efforts for trade liberalization. The industrial countries are more likely to concede on issues the Group of 77 consider vital if they see the possibility of agreeable compromises over the newer issues. The Uruguay Round promises to include the developing-countries' concerns more fully than at any previous round, but success still hinges on agreement among the key industrial countries, especially in the area of agricultural trade.

The number of countries that jostled to gain admittance to GATT in 1986 highlights the importance of this round for world trade. Among the contenders, Mexico (which became a member in 1986) and China (which is still negotiating on membership concessions) are the most important. In addition, the Soviet Union began in 1986 to test the ground for its own entrance into GATT; and though most industrial countries have expressed reservations about the inclusion of such a large centrally planned economy, the GATT secretariat remains open to the idea. The United States is likely to oppose Soviet membership, at least for the duration of the Uruguay Round, on political and economic grounds.

Primary Commodities

Overproduction and price declines for most commodities cut deeply into developing-country earnings again in 1986, aggravating balance of payments problems. The completion of trade negotiations will happen much too late to affect the disequilibria now existing in commodity markets. Many producers will be forced to cut production dramatically in 1987 and 1988. Partly for these reasons both the World Bank and the InterAmerican Development Bank chose in 1986 to focus their annual assessments of development upon **global agricultural trade.**

The costs of maintaining high domestic price supports for industrial-country farmers reached a new peak in 1985–86, leading to greater willingness on the part of industrial-country governments to negotiate agricultural trade liberalization in the Uruguay Round. With producer subsidy equivalents ranging up to 70 percent, the talks will be difficult but necessary [U.S. Department of Agriculture, *Government Intervention in Agriculture*, 1/87]. The cost of subsidization in the United States hit an all-time record high in 1986, causing alarm about budgetary priorities. Although there is strong public sentiment to increase export subsidies to save Northern farmers from the self-generated glut, budgetary pressures provide an opportunity for governments to reduce the subsidies before the round concludes, since increased consumption is unlikely to remedy the situation soon. Global food production has outstripped consumption consistently since the food scares of 1973–74, and global food stocks continue to rise rapidly [Food and Agriculture Organization, *Production Yearbook*].

The situation of cash crops is equally distressing. Quantitative restrictions on imports in industrial countries and overproduction in developing countries combined to produce severe price falls in all except the beverage commodities. Food prices in 1986 were down 34.1 percent compared to 1980. Agricultural raw materials have declined 21 percent over the same period [IMF, *International Financial Statistics*, 1986 yearbook and 3/87 monthly edition].

Demand for metals has experienced a dramatic secular downturn. Industrial-country consumption of minerals, ores, and metals grew at rates much slower than GNP growth in the period between 1971–73 and 1981–83. In many cases, consumption of these commodities actually fell over that period, in marked contrast to industrial-country consumption in the decade prior to 1971–73 [UNCTAD *Bulletin*, No. 229, 2/87, p. 9]. In 1986 metal prices slid another 6 percent, to a total decline of 34.5 percent since 1980 [IMF, *IFS*].

Oil prices tumbled 55 percent in 1986, when Saudi Arabia no longer agreed to act as OPEC's swing producer and began instead to recapture its world market share. The shock of the fall in prices had the effect of stimulating reassessment within OPEC regarding its oil production quotas, which were already becoming meaningless in 1985. Toward the end of 1986 oil prices began to rebound with the prospect of renewed discipline on the part of OPEC. It is doubtful, however, that prices will rise again soon to the range prevalent in the period 1983–85, especially if the industrial countries enter a recession in the next two years.

The prospects for near-term stabilization and policy coordination of **international commodity markets** remain dim. Essentially, either the United States or the Soviet Union must ratify the **Common Fund for commodities** if it is to come into force, but neither is likely to do so. OPEC unity has been sorely tested in recent years and is shaky at best. The Compensatory Financing Facility of the IMF is now acting as a procyclical force in commodity markets, because of the long-term nature of price declines and the short-term repayment requirements of the facility.

Individual international commodity agreements ran into severe trouble in the wake of the collapse of the International Tin Agreement in 1985–86. Natural rubber negotiations failed. Even with coffee, which fared well in 1985–86, the suspension of quotas because of high prices has led to disagreement among suppliers and producers about renewal of the agreement. However, new agreements over cocoa, olive oil, and olives, plus the beginning of operations of the International Tropical Timber Agreement, may be viewed as hopeful. For the UNCTAD VII meeting in July 1987, negotiations on commodities will be pivotal—both in an institutional sense, as eight years of efforts on the Integrated Program for Commodities have not forestalled a commodity crisis in the eighties, and on a practical level, as the commodities regime seems on the verge of a collapse.

Manufactures and Services

Despite positive developments centered around the start of the new trade round, a number of countries took **restrictive trade actions** in 1986, and several **trade disputes** emerged in full force at the beginning of 1987. Meanwhile, U.S. efforts to seek bilateral and regional trade improvements met with general failure. By April of 1987 the near-term trade picture for the United States looked bleak enough for Congress to move rapidly toward a sweeping overhaul of U.S. trade laws that will make it easier for industry to acquire relief from what it considers unfair trade practices. These efforts are intended to back up U.S. negotiators as they seek to gain greater U.S. access to foreign markets.

In August 1986 yet another "temporary" restraint on textile trade was negotiated when the **Multi-Fiber Arrangement (MFA)** was renewed with a number of restrictive modifications. While some of the least-developed countries may profit from the new MFA, the expansion of the coverage to more fibers can only have a negative impact on overall trade and on Third World incomes.

The United States announced it would pursue voluntary export restraint agreements with major machine tool manufacturers in the summer of 1986. This affects Japan and the NICs primarily. The measure represented a weak and largely futile attempt to avert rising protectionist sentiment in the U.S. Congress. The fundamental macroeconomic policies (undervalued currencies) that created the NIC trade surpluses remained unaffected throughout the year.

Analyses of the U.S. Caribbean Basin Initiative, which aimed to bolster development efforts in the Caribbean and Central America, indicate rather minimal effects in its first three years of operation [Stuart K. Tucker, "The Caribbean Basin Initiative: Elevated Expectations and Limited Means," unpublished manuscript]. Meanwhile, talks to establish a free trade area between Canada and the United States nearly floundered before they began and still remain adrift.

In the hope of diffusing congressional ire over the U.S. trade deficit, the Reagan administration in early 1987 brought the EEC-U.S. dispute over agricultural trade and over entrance of Spain and Portugal into the European Common Market to the brink of a trade war before resolving the situation. Similar concerns led to the imposition of special 100 percent levies on selected Japanese products when the United States became dissatisfied with progress on semiconductor trade. On the other hand, Brazil managed to ward off U.S. threats to retaliate against Brazilian trade barriers, especially in the computer sector, by exploiting U.S. concern with the debt crisis and its impact on Brazilian politics. There is little chance that such piecemeal efforts will continue to appease Congress, given the persistent U.S. trade deficit; and a U.S. trade bill will probably pass in 1987, with stormy international trade relations likely to follow.

3. Money and Finance

Dominating international financial news in 1986 were the **Third World debt crisis** and cooperative international efforts to manage **exchange rates**, especially the value of the dollar. Related as it was to both of these issues, the movement of the United States into the position of the world's biggest net debtor placed new pressures on financial markets.

Off the front page, **financial markets** continued to change at a revolutionary pace. Technological change and financial liberalization in the 1980s have ushered in a new era for the international financial system. The explosive spread of computer networks and telecommunications equipment has greatly improved financial communications. The push for services trade liberalization has been assisted by bilateral and unilateral efforts to relax rules regarding foreign banking activities, especially in the formerly closed Asian markets. The "Big Bang"—the move by London markets to twenty-four-hour operations in the autumn of 1986—illustrates the globalization of finance that has taken place in the 1980s. Coming at a time of sluggish world economic activity, this trend presents problems as well as opportunities, since financial regulations have not adapted to these changes as fast as the markets have themselves changed.

The Debt Crisis

With the announcement of the **Baker Plan** in Seoul in 1985, the debt crisis entered a new phase. Though the plan still called upon the debtor countries to undertake domestic reform, it recognized that the debt will not be serviced without faster economic growth. To stimulate such growth, the plan envisioned a stronger role for the World Bank and pleaded for new injections of commercial bank finance. This approach represented the industrial countries' first admission that the traditional short-term IMF austerity prescriptions were not working to solve the balance of payments crises of debtors.

By the spring of 1987 little of the Baker Plan had actually been implemented, but the plan had stimulated debate on the nature of the debt crisis. Earlier conclusions that the problem was a short-term liquidity crisis were discarded, and a myriad of debt relief schemes surfaced as Barber Conable became the new World Bank president. The plan of U.S. Senator Bill Bradley to forgive some of the debt gradually and to reduce interest rates charged to debtors drew the most attention and led to new discussions about the true value of the debt. While debt-equity swaps are being used in some cases, investment-related schemes have only a limited potential, given the sheer size of the debt burden compared with what could conceivably be bought in the Third World without stirring up sovereignty concerns.

Commercial banks generally used 1985–86 to retrench and reduce their exposure to future losses on the debt. Some banks, led by Citicorp, moved toward writing off the debt when they shifted it to the liability column in their 1986 accounting. As a result, U.S. Treasury officials and others now refer to a "menu of options," from new lending to debt write-offs, as a part of the Baker Plan. Secondary markets allowed banks to sell their debt claims at extreme discounts—in the range of 70 percent of face value for the major debtors and as low as 10 percent of face value for Bolivian debt. Unfortunately for debtors, these debts remain full obligations. Net lending turned negative for many market borrowers. In 1986, developing-country interest and principal payments on long-term debt surpassed new lending by about $30 billion. The IMF joined the exodus by draining $5 billion of its resources (net of lending) from the Third World [Statement by Richard E. Feinberg before the Subcommittee on International Finance, Trade, and Monetary Policy of the Banking Committee, U.S. House of Representatives, 3/3/87].

In early 1987, Japan, in a move timed to defray international anger over its trade surpluses, announced its willingness to recycle large sums of money into the debtor economies. With the United States building up large foreign debts of its own and facing severe budgetary pressures, Japanese capital is the most likely source for new lending. In a hopeful twist, several plans for making use of the Japanese surpluses call for a discounting facility tied to the World Bank or the IMF that would buy up the debt claims of reluctantly involved commerical banks. Such a facility would do what secondary markets have not done—reduce the payments burden on debtor countries [World Institute for Development Economics Research, "Mobilizing International Surpluses for World Development: A W I D E R Plan for a Japanese Initiative," 5/87].

In early 1987, Brazilian officials unilaterally announced their decision to postpone all debt payments for an indefinite period, sparking short-lived fears that other key Latin debtor countries would unite behind Brazil in a debtor's cartel. Once again, however, the debtors chose to go their separate ways in dealing with creditors. Most debt service delays in 1987 relate to the fall in oil prices. The unified actions envisioned by the Cartagena Group have not materialized because, in the view of some observers, the group's members underestimate their bargaining power.

International Cooperation and the International Institutions

The dramatic increase in commercial lending and international trade flows in the 1970s dwarfed trends in both multilateral and bilateral **official development assistance (ODA)**. Although the IMF still played a leading role in debt negotiations, the role of international financial institutions relative to private banks and central banks decreased until the mid-1980s. As commercial banks retrench in the late 1980s, multilateral development banks are becoming more crucial to the Third World. Macroeconomic and exchange rate policies of industrial countries, however, no longer fall into the IMF's domain. Now more than ever international coordination is necessary, yet much of it is being done by key finance ministers along bilateral or exclusionary multilateral channels. All of these shifts leave the Bretton Woods institutions in a state of turmoil about their current role in the international financial system. The arrivals in

1986–87 of Michel Camdessus to head the IMF and Barber Conable to lead the World Bank may allow for a future redefinition of roles, but may also involve considerable transition time as the leaders attempt to establish themselves within their institutions.

Aid to the low-income developing countries received a boost in December 1986, when thirty-three donor nations agreed to a $12.8 billion three-year replenishment of the **International Development Association (IDA)**, the World Bank's soft loan agency. About half of IDA loans are expected to go to sub-Saharan Africa this year, compared with 36 percent in 1986. Though the United States has agreed to provide about $958 million each year, many observers are skeptical, since the United States is in arrears on its past pledges to the IDA, as well as to the African Development Bank and the International Finance Corporation [The Washington Times, 4/22/87]. Moreover, the "militarization" of the U.S. foreign aid budget in recent years threatens to undermine congressional support for foreign aid, risking further arrearages.

Coordination of monetary policy to effect a depreciation of the dollar continued to be a top priority for industrial-country finance ministers in 1986. Exchange rates fluctuated rapidly and without apparent direction well into the second half of 1986. Efforts to reduce the value of the dollar began to show progress in February 1987 with the Louvre Accord. But domestic political pressures in Japan are building as the yen rises. Additionally, American concerns over dollar-induced inflation seem to indicate that finance ministers may seek an end to the dollar slide sometime in 1987. It was thought that this might be an issue for the Venice summit, but conflict in the Persian Gulf diverted the participants' attention. Earlier, in April, the IMF Interim Committee had applauded coordination efforts but noted that exchange rates in newly industrializing countries would also have to adjust if global trade imbalances are to be addressed [IMF Survey, 4/20/87].

4. Transnational Corporations, Science, and Technology

Overview

The global image of **transnational corporations** (TNCs) is rapidly evolving, and a new look is beginning to emerge. Over the past few years the United Nations and its member states have moved toward a greater acceptance of the role of these corporations in the world economy. At the same time, efforts to liberalize the regulation and management of TNCs have helped to alter the attitude of the TNCs themselves toward host countries. The decidedly less confrontational tone adopted by the U.N. agencies and activities most concerned TNCs, including the IMF, the GATT, the U.N. Centre on Transnational Corporations, and the U.N. Conference on Science and Technology for Development, reflects the cumulative effect of these changes.

These U.N. agencies now openly acknowledge the **new climate for cooperation** with transnational corporations, although this shift may put them on an uncertain footing with some of the members that had supported them in the past. Early in the decade, developing countries had unequivocally denounced TNCs, claiming that the corporations were impeding development and competing unfairly on a global basis. In contrast, TNCs today tend to be seen as agents of the investment, trade, and technology transfer required for development, and individual U.N. member countries are increasingly engaged in a global competition to attract direct foreign investment. Host countries have come to a much more sophisticated awareness of the growth that can be achieved through the involvement of TNCs in national economies, while TNCs are now much more likely to compete with one another to secure relationships in developing-country markets.

In addition to increased competition both by and for TNCs, the past year has seen a dramatic adjustment in the global balance of economic power. Some major changes include the sharp decline of the dollar, the lower cost of oil, lower interest rates, greater flexibility in the rescheduling of debt and in debt-for-equity exchanges, and new direct foreign investment. TNCs are also no longer the exclusive property of developed nations. As the economic power of the newly industrializing countries has grown, the number of TNCs based in these countries has risen. Furthermore, the decline in the economic significance of the oil-exporting countries has increased the relative importance in world markets of oil-importing developing countries. Most economic estimates suggest that 1987 will see these countries importing goods and services at levels 4 to 5 percent higher than in 1986 and exporting at even higher rates.

This new strength has led to **greater bilateralism in negotiations with TNCs**. Even the least-developed countries are able to do business with TNCs on a more equal footing than in the past, and the demand for corporate regulation within the U.N. context is noticeably less strident than it was even a few years ago. One exception to the trend toward bilateral negotiations is the crisis many developing countries face in meeting their obligations to multinational banks and other lending institutions. As the net indebtedness of these countries now exceeds $1 trillion, with annual interest payments of $50 billion, both the banks and the governments seem to be moving toward multilateral solutions.

Another development that will influence the way in which the United Nations and its agencies are likely to address TNCs and the issue of technology transfer this year has been the fragmentation of traditional interest groups within the U.N., including OPEC, the OECD countries, the Group of 7, and the Group of 77.

In this changed atmosphere, new issues have arisen. There is a greater focus on trade barriers and trade imbalances between nations, regardless of whether or not TNCs are involved. Certain technology transfer issues are becoming inextricably linked to national security concerns. Developed countries, in particular, see the role of services in multinational trade as deserving more focused attention than it has been given to date either in discussions of TNCs or in the GATT. Developed countries, especially the United States, are also demanding the protection of intellectual property, including trademarks, copyrights, and patents, as a precondition for trade or investment. Finally, there is progress toward the creation of the equivalent of a global accounting standard for transnational business enterprises.

It is perhaps surprising that these concerns have outweighed the international impact of the three great industrial accidents that took place at Bhopal, Chernobyl, and Basel. Two new international treaties were negotiated under the International Atomic Energy Agency that require notification in the case of nuclear accidents and provide accident assistance when requested. Negotiations on a similar accord to cover chemical accidents are under way at the U.N. Environment Programme. Despite the initial outcry following these accidents and the European Community's continuing concern about environmental quality, it appears unlikely that any significant multilateral agreements will be reached with regard to the international management of technology.

These environmental disasters highlight two deeply rooted problems that governments face in dealing with transnational enterprise. First, because countries must compete for direct foreign investment if they are to secure local economic benefits, they find themselves under pressure to accept higher risk technologies that they may not be able to monitor properly. Second, questions of legality and responsibility become very complex across national borders. TNCs are increasingly adept at seeming to conform to the letter of host country law, while in fact using other legal environments to get around local legislation.

New loopholes that enable TNCs to evade regulation—indirect investment and the use of secondary agents are examples—have prompted the U.N. Centre for Transnational Corporations to devote a much greater portion of its work to legal issues than in the past, especially with regard to **South Africa**. Over the last year TNCs have managed to dodge some of the perennial concerns about corporate links to South Africa through disinvestment. In many cases, however, the TNCs have simply turned their multinational holdings into subsidiaries of South African enterprises or sold their local operations to management, who continue to act as their agents. These practices have not escaped the notice of the United Nations Economic and Social Council, which stated:

The shift on the part of many transnational corporations from equity to non-equity links to the South African economy raises questions about the impact of disinvestment on apartheid. Although disinvestment is likely to reduce the inflow of new capital into South Africa, it does little to stem the flow of products and technology through non-equity links [E/C.10/1987/9†].

In this case, news headlines have painted a much more rosy picture than the reality perceived by the Centre for Transnational Corporations, which is shifting its efforts to a much more difficult phase of the struggle to prevent the transfer of funds and technology to the South African government.

Regulatory Environments and Codes of Conduct

Three major **codes of conduct** are currently under review at the United Nations. With deliberations now in their thirteenth year, the most advanced of these is the work of the U.N. Centre on Transnational Corporations. A review of the center's involvement in developing countries' investment projects confirms the observation that **relations between developing countries and TNCs have become more pragmatic in recent years.** According to the center, the more flexible attitude adopted by many developing countries is largely a response to the disadvantageous conditions they have faced in global markets. Under the impact of adverse market conditions, governments and companies alike have been obliged to get rid of much of the ideological lumber that had hindered their relationships in the past [E/C.10/1987/9].

In large part, TNCs have come to be seen as a major source of development capital and one to which developing countries are turning with greater frequency as the availability of new development funds from commercial and international agency lending sources continues to dwindle. Joint ventures between domestic entities and TNCs have become especially popular, creating difficult legal questions as the difference between the domestic and the foreign enterprise becomes buried in a maze of issues, such as transfer pricing, transborder data flows, and licensing agreements.

Host countries seem to have shifted toward a view of TNCs as a manageable risk. How realistic these perceptions are remains to be seen. At the same time that the legal and technical complexities of foreign investment are increasing, the economic pressures on many developing countries may encourage them to cut too many safeguards in an effort to attract capital from abroad. For these reasons, helping member states to devise policies that encourage investment while taking potential risks into account has become a major part of the center's work. As the center noted in early 1987:

> The past ten years have proved to be a learning experience through which developing countries and TNCs have come to understand better one another's

objectives, requirements, and constraints. Intense discussions in international forums of transnational corporations have added to this growth of mutual understanding. The parties are now able to approach commercial transactions with much more confidence and pragmatism [E/C.10/1987/9].

Some credit for the improved relations between TNCs and developing countries must go to the center. Its efforts to collate bilateral agreements and host country laws have generated the kind of information that has permitted host countries to adopt more liberal policies. Although in the 1970s the U.N. had often spoken of the mutual interests of developing countries and TNCs, it was not until recently that these shared interests were given substance in the activities of U.N. agencies. Even though the U.N. Code of Conduct for TNCs remains only a working document within a commission, to a large degree its goals have been achieved in practice, especially where it has tried to encourage transnational corporations to maximize their contribution to the development process. Today standards of corporate conduct in developing countries have been accepted that are broadly similar to the ones the OECD adopted ten years ago. The same is true where the code lays down guidelines for the treatment of TNCs by governments. The code aims to establish a stable, predictable, and transparent framework for foreign direct investment and the activities of TNCs. Special attention is given to determining what constitutes fair and equitable treatment and to ascertaining the right venue for the settlement of disputes [High-level Roundtable on the U.N. Code of Conduct on Transnational Corporations, 10/3–4/87].

These factors have led the U.N. Centre on Transnational Corporations to shift from a role of policy formation to one of coordination and support for member initiatives. The center also functions as a clearing house for information on bilateral agreements between nations and TNCs. This information has proven particularly useful to the center as it has worked over the last four years to develop **global accounting standards** for TNCs. The goal of this effort is full disclosure in all countries where TNCs operate by means of clear, standardized information on the structure, activities, and finances of the transnational corporation as a whole. Reporting requirements emphasize financial information, including corporate reports, investments in associates, and joint ventures; financial reporting by banks and other financial institutions; audits; and accounting for agents of branches and subsidiaries [E/C.10/AC.3/1987/2].

If the goal is simple, the issues underlying the development of a common standard of accounting are extraordinarily complex. Two considerations, however, may encourage TNCs to comply with a global standard of accounting. First, the TNCs need a fair valuation of the worth of their businesses abroad for the insurance and stockholder information required in many of their home countries. Second, over time a more consistent standard of accounting would greatly simplify the reporting and bookkeeping required of TNCs in host countries.

For the host countries, accounting standards promise to break down the barriers of distrust based on the governments' recognition that numerous loopholes, such as transfer-pricing, permit TNCs to avoid their jurisdiction. So far, the major accomplishment of the center's effort to standardize accounting procedures has been to bring together in a single forum the diversity of practices and viewpoints enforced in different host country environments.

Science and Technology Transfer

Like the U.N. Centre on Transnational Corporations, the **United Nations Conference on Science and Technology for Development** has gradually moved away from attempting to formulate policy for member states. Today it focuses more directly on technology transfer and on advising member countries not only on technologies but on the types of licenses and long-term agreements that can reasonably be negotiated, and their implications for both the licensor and licensee. The conference's original ideals and hopes for facilitating major technology transfer from advanced to developing countries through a code of conduct for TNCs or member nations remains far from realization. In the interim years, technology has moved faster than the commission has. Today newly industrializing countries are themselves creating demand for technology, while the developed countries are actively seeking to install advanced technology in developing countries to secure new markets, revenue streams, and access to lower-cost labor.

The **effects of technology transfer on the global environment** are likely to be a major concern for the U.N. in this field in 1987. The huge industrial accidents since 1985 have led to a greater understanding of the international dimensions of toxic waste problems, while the problem of acid rain across national boundaries has contributed to a heightened awareness of the global responsibility for the negative side effects of technology. Relatively less attention has been focused on the implications of increased exports of potentially toxic substances such as feedstocks to industries in developing countries. In a joint effort, the United Nations Committee on Transnational Corporations (UNCTC), the United Nations Environment Programme (UNEP), and the World Health Organization (WHO) are attempting to deal with some of these issues by creating a consolidated listing and review of "products harmful to the health and environment."

These multilateral efforts constrain technology transfer by limiting the potential damage to the technology-acquiring country. Technology exporters, however, are starting to impose their own constraints on the transfer of technology. Although the most forceful are justified on national security grounds, it is clear that some of these efforts to restrict licensing are based more on a desire to preserve economic advantage than on a need to enhance military superiority. The U.S. Department of Defense, for example, proposes to restrict international access to certain databases that contain nonclassified scientific research.

The issue of technology transfer is no longer confined to tangible products and merchandise: controversy has emerged in the area of **intellectual property**, where strict enforcement of patents, trademarks, and copyright protection is being insisted upon by the United States and other developed countries as a precondition for trade. The U.S. concern extends beyond the field of computers and software, to biotechnology, pharmaceuticals, and advanced materials. According to U.S. Department of Commerce figures, drug counterfeiting in 1986 alone resulted in a $240 million loss to the U.S. pharmaceutical industry. These discussions, however, especially those concerned with electronically stored information, are taking place neither within the World Information Property Organization (WIPO) nor within the International Telecommunications Union (ITU), but as a part of bilateral trade negotiations and within the **Uruguay Round of GATT.**

Another underlying division of interests between developed countries and developing nations concerning technology transfer has surfaced during the negotiations on **trade in services** at the new GATT round. The activities of TNCs in this arena and the regulatory issues are much more complex today than in the past. The technology of global communications has made regulations within individual nations much more difficult to apply. Underestimating the importance of such services for the international transfer of technology, as well as for the creation of economic wealth, has created perhaps the greatest imbalance in the approach of the U.N. today to transnational corporate activities.

As global computing and telecommunications technology facilitate the creation of new markets for the transfer of capital and financial services, the U.N. codes of conduct and regulations remain overwhelmingly focused on merchandise and the physical application of technology. These issues and the differences in perspective they imply are prominent in the divisions within GATT, with the sharpest confrontation occurring between the United States, as it represents the service exporters, and India and Brazil, as they seek to exclude services from the discussions. This new debate and the acute financial distress experienced by many developing nations in coping with their international debt burden constitute two of the greatest challenges the U.N. will face this year in dealing with transnational corporations, science, and technology transfer.

IV
Global Resource Management

1. Food and Agriculture

It has been a good year on the farm. Agricultural production was up in most of the world and food stocks increased as well. Even sub-Saharan Africa enjoyed bountiful harvests and began to bury the memory of the famine of 1984–85. For U.N. food agencies, however, hit by the system-wide financial crisis, it has been a lean year. Nevertheless, there are good prospects for multilateral action to reform agricultural policies that have led to huge food surpluses and depressed prices for agricultural commodities.

The **upturn in global food production** began in the growing seasons of 1984–85, and the trend has continued in 1986–87. According to the Food and Agriculture Organization of the United Nations (FAO), farmers harvested a record 1.85 billion tons of cereals (the most basic agricultural commodity) in 1985–86—over 40 million tons more than the year before—and FAO predicts a record 1.87 billion tons in 1986–87 [FAO, *Food Outlook*, 4/87].

Although this projected production figure for cereals represents an increase of only 1 percent worldwide, FAO estimates that in the **developing countries** output will rise about 2 percent, "mainly the result of increased production in several countries in Asia, notably China, India, Pakistan and Turkey" [*Food Outlook*, 2/87]. Obviously these gains have not been evenly distributed; and some developing countries have experienced worsening agricultural conditions.

(In a number of developed countries cereal production actually declined in 1986—by nearly 10 percent in the United States, owing to poor weather and to acreage-reduction policies contained in the Food Security Act of 1985, and by about 5 percent in the countries of the European Economic Community [*Ibid.*].)

The most dramatic increases in food production, though, have been registered in **Africa**. In March 1985, FAO's **Global Information and Early Warning System (GIEWS)** was reporting that twenty-one countries in **sub-Saharan Africa** had abnormal food shortages, but in March 1987 the GIEWS indicated that nine African countries were requesting international assistance to dispose of "exportable surpluses" [FAO Special Report, *Foodcrops and Shortages*, 2/87]. In 1984, Sudan was pleading for food aid to avert mass starvation, but today it too requests international assistance to export its surplus grain.

For the second year running, favorable crop conditions and excellent harvests have improved the food-supply situation in most of Africa. FAO reports that "the aggregate production of cereals in 1986 of the 45 developing countries of sub-Saharan Africa is provisionally estimated . . . at a record 55.7 million tons, some 1.8 million tons higher than the good 1985 harvest and 21 percent above the previous five years" [Food Outlook, 2/87].

In March 1987, however, FAO identified five African nations as having food shortfalls requiring "exceptional assistance." In three of these countries —Ethiopia, Mozambique, and Angola—civil strife has affected agricultural production and access to food. The other two—Botswana and Lesotho—have traditionally suffered from food shortages even in the best of years [Foodcrops and Shortages, 3/87].

Conditions could well have been disastrous throughout Africa. When **plagues of locusts and grasshoppers** swept through eastern Africa and the Sahel in mid-1986, many African and relief officials were predicting widespread crop damage and famine. FAO and several other international organizations, with the support of $50 million in donor contributions, coordinated an emergency control campaign that prevented devastating crop losses [U.S. State Department Bureau of Public Affairs, *Current Policy*, No. 925, 3/87]. FAO has warned that locusts and grasshoppers may again pose a serious threat to harvests in 1987 and that "donors and governments" must join in implementing control programs [Food Outlook, 2/87].

Despite the rapid recovery of sub-Saharan agriculture in the aftermath of the 1984–85 famine, Africa's agricultural future remains uncertain. In Africa's 1986 harvest, the amount of grain produced per person was 14 percent below that of 1969 [Lester R. Brown, "Sustaining World Agriculture," *State of the World 1987*, ed. Lester R. Brown et al. (New York, London: W.W. Norton & Co., 1987), p. 122]. Weak economic growth, environmental degradation, rapid population growth, and burdensome levels of debt are a continuing fact of life in Africa. Unless steps are taken to treat these underlying causes of the 1984–85 famine, bumper harvests are likely to be only temporary phenomena.

Owing to the good harvests, emergency operations have been suspended for most of Africa. The **United Nations Office for Emergency Operations in Africa**, the office credited with successfully coordinating international relief efforts during the famine, was closed in late 1986. This closing symbolizes the transition from emergency operations to long-term development programs for Africa—with the participation, at least in theory, of the entire international community.

The outline and rationale for this monumental development task is contained in **Africa's Priority Programme for Economic Recovery (APPER)**, which was drawn up by the Organization of African Unity (OAU) and became the focus of the General Assembly's **Special Session on the Critical Economic Situation in Africa**, held from May 27 to 31, 1986. The international community, unanimously endorsing APPER as the guide to medium- and long-term actions to address the serious development needs of sub-Saharan Africa, effectively agreed on a division of responsibilities with Africa for the recovery process. As both African and would-be donor governments acknowledged at the Special Session, this recovery will not be accomplished easily, nor will it be cheap. African nations themselves have pledged over $80 billion for the far-reaching five-year plan, and substantial foreign assistance will be needed.

The Special Session endorsed agricultural development as a priority for African development. In keeping with APPER's call for higher government expenditures in this area, OAU members have agreed to devote 20–25 percent of their public expenditures to agriculture—a considerable increase over the 10 percent or less that most governments had been allocating in years past. Of the estimated $127.9 billion it will cost to implement APPER, $57.4 billion, or 45 percent, will be invested in agricultural development. Still other programs of APPER, such as the development of agro-industries, measures to combat desertification, and policy reforms to stimulate agricultural production, affect this sector as well [Neal Spivack and Ann Florini, *Food on the Table* (New York: UNA-USA, 1987)].

The reform movement, involving increased investment in agriculture, price incentives for farmers, and reduced government control of the economy, seems to have taken hold in Africa. Twenty-two sub-Saharan countries have applied to the **World Bank's Special Facility for Sub-Saharan Africa**, created in 1984 to provide essential financial assistance for countries that adopt such structural adjustment policies. According to one expert, however, "there is little indication as yet . . . that the major donors, who have pushed for such reforms, are coming up with the additional resources which most of these programmes need if they are to succeed" [*African Recovery*, 2–4/87].

Several of the U.N. food agencies are now concentrating their energies on African agriculture. An FAO strategy for rebuilding the African agricultural sector, "African Agriculture: The Next 25 Years," was presented by FAO at the **Fourteenth Regional Conference for Africa**, held in Yamoussoukro, Ivory Coast, in September 1986. The report, describing present trends in sub-Saharan food production as "unsustainable," outlines a four-point action program to expand African agricultural production by 3 percent a year over the next quarter-century: (1) internal reforms to give priority to agriculture; (2) strategies for the conservation of natural resources; (3) an international economic environment conducive to growth; and (4) better incentives, inputs, institutions, and infrastructures for agriculture [ARC/86/REP].

The **Special Programme for Sub-Saharan African Countries Affected by Drought and Desertification** of the International Fund for Agricultural Development (IFAD) became operational in May 1986, when commitments to the program reached $40 million [DPI Press Release, IFAD/308, 11/7/86]. At present, more than $210 million of its target of $300 million has been pledged. Established by IFAD's Governing Council the previous January, the three-to-four-year program currently assists twenty-two countries in the sub-Saharan region with medium- to long-range projects to promote agricultural development.

Overall in 1986–87, however, **U.N. food agencies,** like other U.N. bodies, had to scramble for revenue because of reductions in funding by the United States, traditionally the largest donor. For fiscal year 1987 the United States has deferred payment of approximately a third of the funds appropriated for international organizations. **FAO,** the oldest of the U.N. food agencies, has been particularly hard hit, receiving less than $5 million of the $25 million appropriated for the specialized agency in FY87 [UNA-USA, *Washington Weekly Report,* 11/14/86]. The law states that the balance of monies for FAO is to be released on October 1, 1987, but current U.S. budgetary trends make it unlikely that the entire sum will be paid.

FAO's shortfall at the end of 1987 was expected to be about $90 million, or approximately 20 percent of its regular budget for the 1986–87 biennium. The agency has instituted a number of economies, reducing meetings and publications and putting a freeze on hiring for "non-essential" posts, but FAO Director-General Edouard Saouma has warned that FAO may have to borrow $30 million to meet its obligations in the next biennium [DPI Press Release, FAO/3408, 12/1/86]. No cuts were made, however, in the budget of the FAO's **Technical Cooperation Programme** (TCP), intended for short-term emergency projects. According to some members, funds for this program—whose projects do not require donor approval—have been misspent by Director-General Saouma on projects inconsistent with the original design of the program [*Food on the Table*].

The election of an FAO director-general is scheduled for November 1987. Edouard Saouma of Lebanon will face challenges from Gonzalo Bula Hoyos of Colombia, 1987 chairman of the Group of 77 developing countries, and from Moise Christophe Mensah of Benin, assistant president in charge of the Project Management Department at IFAD.

IFAD, following difficult but ultimately successful negotiations on the second replenishment of its funds, is looking ahead to negotiations in January 1988 on its third replenishment. Negotiations for the second replenishment had been going on for nearly three years when, in January 1986, IFAD's Organization for Economic Co-operation and Development (OECD) and Organization of the Petroleum Exporting Countries (OPEC) donors agreed on the figure of $500 million for the period 1986–88. This was, however, substantially less than IFAD's first replenishment of $1.1 billion for the period 1981–83 [*Issues Before the 41st General Assembly of the United Nations*, pp. 88–89].

After a preliminary study of IFAD's financial base by a panel of ten experts, the Fund's Governing Council appointed a high-level intergovernmental council to recommend ways of placing the agency's funding on a steadier footing. The council, expected to issue its report in January 1988, is considering such possibilities as setting a specific level of replenishment based on a set operating budget; including such nontraditional donors as South

Korea and Brazil in the replenishment negotiations; and empowering IFAD to borrow from capital markets.

IFAD, too, will soon be deciding on its future leadership. The three-year term of President Idriss Jazairy, an Algerian, was scheduled to expire in November 1987. Jazairy has already received a six-month extension of his term and seems likely to receive yet another extension because of general satisfaction with his leadership and the desire for continuity as negotiations begin on the third replenishment. At its meeting in January 1988, IFAD's Governing Council will likely approve a term of four years for future presidents of the fund.

Owing to large food surpluses in many donor countries, the **World Food Programme (WFP)**, the international agency chiefly responsible for food aid and food-for-work projects, has had no shortage of basic resources. Pledges in money and foodstuffs for the 1985–86 biennium reached a record $1.1 billion, or 83 percent of the pledging goal [*Food Outlook*, 2/87]. Contributions to the **International Emergency Food Reserve (IEFR)**, administered by WFP to meet emergency needs, surpassed the annual target of 500,000 tons [*Ibid.*]. James Ingram of Australia, executive director of WFP, was appointed to a second five-year term, which began in April 1987.

According to an FAO estimate, total food aid in cereals for July 1985–June 1986 amounted to 10.3 million tons, surpassing for a second year the target of 10 million tons set at the 1974 World Food Conference. FAO forecasts that food aid in cereals will reach 10.2 million tons in 1986–87 [*Food Outlook*, 4/87].

The **World Food Council (WFC)**, a political forum for the discussion of food policy, included self-analysis on the agenda of its twelfth annual meeting, held in June 1986. The meeting's participants recommended that WFC continue to serve as "a political catalyst, a forum for discussion of policy ideas and proposals" [*Report of the World Food Council on the work of its 12th session* (A/41/19)]. The 41st General Assembly in its annual resolution on food "invited" WFC to assist in the promotion of regional and subregional food strategies, to stimulate the progress of APPER, to assess the effects of economic adjustment on nutrition, and to study "the impact of the present agricultural trade situation" [A/Res/41/191].

That situation has caused many countries to reassess the effects of domestic agricultural policies on international trade and development. Since the early 1980s, prices for many major agricultural commodities have plummeted and now stand at levels unmatched since the Great Depression. Much of the responsibility for this situation rests with the European Economic Community (EEC), the United States, and Japan, whose **domestic agricultural programs** have distorted the relationship between supply and demand, leading to overproduction and a tremendous accumulation of carryover stocks. These programs—combined with the new-found agricultural self-sufficiency of many developed and developing countries at a time of slow economic growth and, thus, of slow growth in the demand for food—have created a glut that has caused the bottom to fall out of the agricultural commodities market.

The cost of storing its huge surpluses has nearly bankrupted the EEC; and according to FAO forecasts, by the end of the 1986–87 season the United States will be holding one-half of the world's cereal stocks [*Food Outlook*, 4/87]. The United States, the EEC, and a few other agricultural exporters have instituted export subsidies to raise farm incomes and dispose of surpluses through increased agricultural exports. Although these measures have not increased sales substantially, they have reduced world agricultural commodity prices further and have caused a number of trade disputes as exporters attempt to defend traditional export markets.

These trade disputes among developed countries have received wide press attention on both sides of the Atlantic, but far less attention has been paid to the effects of such farm programs on developing countries. Many have lost export earnings essential to development. The Dominican Republic is a case in point. In 1981 it exported almost 750,000 short tons of sugar to the United States, earning roughly $330 million; in 1987, with Dominican sugar exports to the United States limited to 160,000 tons, it will earn about $65 million— about a fifth as much [*Current Policy*, No. 927, 3/87].

More than anything else, it has been the heavy financial burden of domestic farm programs in many developed countries (in the U.S., for example, the farm support program of FY86 was equal to about 15 percent of the federal budget deficit that year) that has pushed agricultural exporters to the negotiating table. At the convening of the latest round of the **General Agreement on Tariffs and Trade** (**GATT**) in Uruguay in September 1986, the liberalization of agricultural trade was one of the items that held the spotlight. Undeterred by failures to reach agreement on agricultural issues in previous GATT rounds, a strong coalition of agricultural producers in both the developed and the developing worlds, with U.S. support, were successful in placing the question of agricultural subsidies on the agenda of the **Uruguay Round**. Under pressure from this coalition—known as the **Cairns Group**—and the United States, GATT has agreed to "fast-track negotiations" to identify the issues for negotiation this year and begin negotiations in the following year [*The Wall Street Journal*, 4/7/87]. It remains to be seen whether these multilateral trade negotiations, with the promise of future economic gains, will succeed in the face of opposition from domestic farm interests.

The 41st Session requested the Secretary-General to keep under review "problems which impede the liberalization of international agricultural trade" and report on these issues to the 42nd Session through the Economic and Social Council [A/Res/41/191].

2. Population

In 1987 the world's population reached **5 billion** after remaining below the billion mark for most of human existence. It has taken a mere thirteen years to reach the last 1 billion, and it will take only twelve more years to reach the next benchmark of 6 billion. Demographers predict that we can expect a world of 7 billion by 2010, 8 billion by 2022, and 10 billion by the end of the twenty-first century [UNFPA, Report of the Executive Director, *A World of Five Billion: State of the World Population*, 5/19/87].

All nations will not share equally in this growth, however. Population growth rates are three times higher in developing countries—already home to 75 percent of the world's people—than in developed ones, and about two-thirds of this growth will take place in the poorest developing countries.

More and more, **rapid population growth** is forcing analysts to reconsider the labels "developed" and "developing" that mark a nation's economic position in the world. For Lester Brown, for example, project director and an editor of the annual *State of the World* series, a more accurate and determinative classification divides nations into two different categories: those with little or no population growth and improving standards of living, and those with extreme rates of population growth and deteriorating—or soon to be deteriorating—standards of living.

Many of the nations traditionally designated as developed fall into the slow population growth category. These nations are characterized by low fertility rates and mortality rates and by population growth that is slow or even negative. In West Germany, for example, population growth is approaching zero, and Brown projects an inevitable negative growth rate, ultimately reducing West Germany's population to 15 percent below the current level. Another example is Japan, which has an annual growth rate of between 0.5 and 0.7 percent. Its rate of population growth will also decline, says Brown, eventually stabilizing at 128 million, 6 percent above the current level ["Analyzing the Demographic Trap," *State of the World 1987* (New York, London: W.W. Norton & Co., 1987), p. 23].

The majority of the nations designated as developing fall into the second group, among them Kenya, India, and Nigeria, with rates of growth that range from 2.0 to 4.2 percent. In most of these countries health conditions have improved, reducing infant mortality and increasing life expectancy but without a significant decline in fertility. The result has been historically high population growth rates. Kenya, for example, is expanding faster than any other country in the world, at 4.2 percent a year. At this rate, it will double its population every seventeen years [*Population*, 9/86], and the number of Kenyans will increase from 20 million in 1986 to 111 million in the twenty-first century. India, growing by 2.3 percent a year, will become the most populous nation at the beginning of the twenty-first century. Some demographers predict that its population will more than double, ultimately reaching 1.7 billion [Brown, *State of the World 1987*, p. 23].

It seems unlikely that the populations in many of these rapid-growth countries will actually reach the huge numbers predicted. According to another scenario, growth will be hindered by the gradual exhaustion of economic and environmental resources, leading to higher death rates and infant mortality in these countries. In either case, experts at the World Bank and the United

Nations Fund for Population Activities (UNFPA) agree that runaway population growth threatens to negate the improvements in living conditions that will come about as a result of future development. President Daniel T. arap Moi of Kenya noted in a 1985 radio address that "even if the Kenyan economy grew at 7 percent annually for 25 years, population growth would cancel most of the projected gains for the average person" [*The Humanist*, 7–8/86].

Already in some regions the carrying capacity—that is, the population that can be sustained by an ecological system—has been exceeded, and the consumption of the resource base itself has begun. Deforestation is the clearest example of population pressure on the environment. More mouths to feed has led farmers to clear forested land for planting. As a result, vast tracts of forest in Africa and South America have been lost. Demand for firewood has increased as well, in many cases exceeding the natural replenishment rate of the forest. Developing countries use an estimated ten to twenty times more trees than they plant [*A World of Five Billion*, p. 19]; and according to the World Bank, it will take a 20–30 percent reduction in firewood demand, accompanied by a fifteenfold increase in planting, to produce a sustainable yield by the year 2000 [*Population Growth and Policies in Sub-Saharan Africa* (Washington, D.C.: The World Bank, 1986), p. 28].

High population growth is a drag on social and economic development as well. Nations expanding at more than 2 percent a year will find it difficult to improve living standards, and even the cost of providing the same level of services per capita will be beyond the budgetary capacities of many governments. Were such services as education to be cut, this would seriously hinder the progress of birth-control programs.

For most **sub-Saharan nations**, attaining universal primary education over the next fifteen years may be impossible. The number of school-age children will more than double for most countries in the region, many of which already spend between 30 and 40 percent of their budgets on education. According to a World Bank study, "the cost of attaining universal primary education and rudimentary health services in fifteen years could reach as much as half the total expected governmental revenues in many African countries—nearly twice their current share" [*Population Growth and Policies in Sub-Saharan Africa*, p. 4].

Clearly, Africa has the most severe population crisis. The World Bank projects that the population of sub-Saharan Africa will rise from about 460 million in 1985 to about 730 million by 2000, and to 1.8 billion by 2050. The region's population is growing at the rate of 3 percent a year and is expected to continue expanding at that rate throughout the century. These rates could actually increase because of improvements in health in certain areas [*Ibid.*, p. 3].

In 1950 Africa had only half as many people as did Europe. By 2050, Africa's population will be nearly three times larger [*A World of Five Billion*, p.4]. Nigeria's population, estimated at 19 million in 1931, is now the world's eighth largest, at about 105 million. The population of its capital, Lagos, has expanded more than twentyfold over the past three-and-a-half decades and is now at 7 million [*The New York Times*, 3/27/87].

A major factor in this growth is the African preference for large families. The average Kenyan woman has eight children [*International Dateline*, 7/86]. In Ghana, where status is still largely determined by family size, the average has risen to seven children [*Popline*, World Population News Service, 9/86]. In Rwanda, which has the highest fertility rate in the world, the average is 8.5 children [*Popline*, 10/86]. Not unexpectedly, contraceptives are used by only a small percent of women—for example, fewer than 1 percent in Rwanda [*Ibid.*], 5 percent in Kenya, and 6 percent in the Sudan [*Population*, UNFPA Newsletter, 2/87].

Still, Africa has come a long way from the days when family planning was considered an imperialist scheme to control developing countries. At the time of the 1974 World Population Conference in Bucharest, only Kenya, Ghana, and Botswana favored policies to slow the rate of population growth. Now, family planning has the official sanction of over three-quarters of the countries in sub-Saharan Africa [World Bank, *Population Growth*, p. 1]. Although few of these countries offer widespread access to family planning services, some sub-Saharan nations have undertaken programs to expand family planning services dramatically.

Nigeria began its first national family planning program this year. The five-year program, to cost an estimated $100 million, aims at giving all Nigerians access to inexpensive contraceptives. The plan also seeks to improve child and maternal health, increasing the rate of child survival and ultimately reducing the need for high rates of fertility [*The New York Times*, 3/27/87].

The dangers of explosive population growth have the attention of policy-makers in **Asia** as well. The fifth United Nations Population Award was presented in June to Bangladesh President Hussain Muhammed Ershad for "strong personal leadership" in reducing his country's birthrate [*The New York Times*, 6/11/87]. In India, which in 1952 became the first country officially to promote a slower population growth, contraceptives have a prevalence rate of only 36 percent. The Indian government hopes to increase this rate to 60 percent by the year 2000, which is expected to lead to a leveling off of its population at 1.4 billion. Were the 60 percent prevalence rate to be reached twenty years later, India's population would level off at 1.9 billion [*Popline*, 12/86].

Population and development experts seem to share the belief that more resources need to be allocated to **family planning programs**. According to the World Bank, an increase in the rate of contraceptive use in sub-Saharan Africa from the current 3–4 percent to 25 percent would slow the rate of population growth by more than 1 percentage point. It would also raise program costs to $640 million in 2000—over six times current expenditures. Development assistance for population programs would have to increase at an equivalent rate [*Population Growth*, p. vi]. If applied worldwide, the Population Institute suggests in a recent report, swift measures to expand family planning programs could stabilize the world population at about 7.4 billion instead of the projected 10 billion. The institute recommends a nearly threefold increase in U.S. population assistance, raising the total to $750 million—the U.S. share of an estimated $1 billion needed to realize the lower world population figure [*The New York Times*, 4/20/87].

The **United States**, however, seems to be going in the opposite direction. Although the United States was for many years the leading international proponent of family planning as well as the largest donor to international population assistance programs—and even increased its aid to population programs during the first years of the Reagan administration—it has during more recent days played a much smaller part in the effort to reduce population growth. The United States cut its population assistance budget from $290 in 1985 to $250 million in 1986, retaining this figure in 1987. Gramm-Rudman-Hollings further reduced the 1987 appropriation to $234 million [*Popline*, 5/86]. It seems likely that this trend will continue; the Reagan administration has requested only $207 million for fiscal year 1988 [*The New York Times*, 4/20/87].

In fiscal year 1985 the U.S. Agency for International Development (AID) withheld $10 million out of $46 million that had been earmarked for the **United Nations Fund for Population Activities** (**UNFPA**), charging that the organization was involved in the management of China's population program, which allegedly involves coercive abortion and involuntary sterilization [*Issues Before the 41st General Assembly of the United Nations*, p. 91]. In fiscal year 1986, AID reprogrammed the entire $25 million in funding budgeted for UNFPA, distributing it among other family planning programs. The same $25 million was budgeted for FY87, but again it seems unlikely that these funds will be contributed to UNFPA.

In its 1985 decision to **withhold funds for UNFPA**, AID cited the language of the supplemental appropriations bill—known as Kemp-Inouye—barring U.S. assistance to any organization that "supports or participates in the management of a program of coercive abortion or involuntary sterilization." A suit challenging the withholding as exceeding the intent of the legislation was dismissed in September 1986. A bipartisan group of eight senators on the Appropriations Committee wrote to AID Administrator M. Peter McPherson to urge the restoration of funds for UNFPA and to voice the opinion "that UNFPA's 1 percent contribution to China's $1 billion population program cannot reasonably be said to amount to 'participation in management' consistent with the intent of the majority of Congress" [Letter to M. Peter McPherson, 10/17/86]. In reprogramming UNFPA's funds for FY86, the administration set a condition for future U.S. aid to UNFPA: China, in carrying out its family planning program, must act to prevent coercive abortion and involuntary sterilization *or* UNFPA must "radically change its assistance to the China program . . . such as by supplying only contraceptives" [*Issues Before the 41st General Assembly of the United Nations*, p. 92]. AID continues to maintain that "there have not been sufficient changes . . . to warrant a resumption of United States support for UNFPA" [AID press release, 8/28/86]. An amendment in the Senate version of the fiscal year 1988 foreign aid authorization bill rewrites the Kemp-Inouye language: Funds would be withheld from an organization only if that organization directly participates in coercive abortion or involuntary sterilization. Whether this new language is adopted awaits further steps in the budget process.

There are indications that China has significantly relaxed its one-child-per-couple policy, and many exceptions to the one-child rule have been allowed in rural areas. The result, however, has been an increase in the birthrate—from 17.18 per thousand in 1985 to 20.8 in 1986—and an increase in the average number of children per woman—from 2.2 in 1985 to 2.4 in 1986 [*The New York Times*, 4/21/87]—leading to speculation about the direction of China's policy in the future.

Despite the cutoff of U.S. aid, funding for UNFPA has remained strong. In 1987 voluntary contributions to the Fund are expected to reach a record $145 million, nearly $10 million more than when the United States last contributed to UNFPA in 1985 [Interviews with UNFPA officials, 4/87]. Increased donations from many European countries, including Finland, Denmark, West Germany, and the Netherlands, have made the difference. Public support also remains strong for UNFPA. In September 1986 the fund received the first Better World Society Medal "for worldwide leadership in addressing the crucial need for population stabilization and family planning" [*Population*, 10/86]. Despite such encouraging developments, funding for UNFPA falls short of the $165 million budgeted for 1987.

UNFPA suffered a setback with the death of its first executive director, Rafael M. Salas, in March 1987. Head of UNFPA throughout its seventeen-year existence, "Mr. Salas oversaw the growth of the agency from a minor body with a $2.5 million budget to one of the most influential United Nations agencies, spending over $150 million annually" [*The New York Times*, 3/5/87]. Salas's leadership helped bring population issues to the forefront of the international agenda.

Dr. Nafis Sadik, a physician from Pakistan and UNFPA's assistant executive director, was selected by Secretary-General Javier Pérez de Cuéllar to succeed Salas as director of the Fund—the first woman to head a U.N. agency. Previously in charge of all UNFPA operations, planning, and technical review, Dr. Sadik was chosen from a wide range of candidates nominated by a number of donor and developing countries [Population Crisis Committee, Legislative and Policy Update, 4/28/87].

Recently, Mr. Salas had been directing attention to the effects of **rapid population growth in urban areas.** In his report *State of the World Population 1986* he had warned that at an annual growth rate of 3.5 percent, urban populations would double in only twenty years. Furthermore, the number of "mega-cities," with at least 10 million inhabitants, will grow from three in

1950 to twenty-two by the year 2000. Eighteen of these cities will be in developing countries [*Issues Before the 41st General Assembly of the United Nations*, p. 95].

To address this problem, UNFPA convened in May 1986 the **International Conference on Population and the Urban Future** in Barcelona, Spain. At the conclusion of the conference, mayors and other officials of fifty-eight cities adopted a series of recommendations known as the Barcelona Declaration [*Popline*, 5/86]. The declaration called for the stimulation of rural economies to provide employment for people in the countryside and recommended the development of small- and medium-sized cities to divert growth from the larger cities. The declaration also "called for all national, state and city governments to integrate population and urban policies into overall socio-economic development planning, to give special attention to family planning programmes for potential rural-to-urban immigrants" [*Population*, 5/86].

At the meeting of the Governing Council of UNFPA in June 1986, emphasis was placed on giving priority to population policy in sub-Saharan Africa. The council also called for closer coordination between UNFPA and other U.N. agencies and for strengthening the evaluation process for UNFPA projects [*Population*, 7/86].

Population issues were on the agenda of the Economic and Social Council (ECOSOC) and were discussed at the 41st General Assembly. The Secretary-General submitted a report on action by the U.N. to implement the recommendations of the World Population Conference 1974, reviewing the monitoring of population trends and policies and the progress made in implementing the World Population Plan of Action. He also reported on the follow-up to the recommendations of the International Conference on Population 1984.

On July 11, 1987, UNFPA and other population organizations marked the "**Day of the Five Billion**"—an event, said the late UNFPA Director Salas, that "symbolizes both triumph and tribulation in the story of humanity."

3. Energy

The aftereffect of two shocks will dominate the debate on energy in the General Assembly this session.

The first shock was the precipitous drop in **worldwide petroleum prices**. A combination of rising supplies and falling energy consumption caused an oil glut. Spot prices plummeted from $40 a barrel in 1981 to below $9 a barrel in 1986. Although most consumers and debt-ridden Third World nations were relieved to see prices fall, energy analysts were concerned about the generally negative effect on investments in new energy production, including new and renewable sources [E/C.7/1987/9, p. 11].

The second shock was the **Chernobyl** nuclear plant explosion on April 26, 1986. In quantifiable terms, it killed 31, injured unknown thousands, and forced the indefinite evacuation of 135,000 Ukrainians from an eighteen-mile danger zone around the Soviet plant. In political terms, its fallout is still being felt.

As radioactive debris drifted across Europe, political and scientific responses differed country by country [*The New York Times*, "The Week in Review," 5/18/86]. Many banned milk products and leafy vegetables, but after a few weeks most countries lifted these warnings, with the notable exception of northern Scandinavia, where the sale of reindeer meat and freshwater fish is still forbidden one year after the accident [*The New York Times*, 4/27/87].

Once the dust began to settle, literally and figuratively, Soviet scientists surprised many in the West by giving a candid account of the accident to five hundred members of the international scientific community at an August 1986 **International Atomic Energy Agency** (IAEA) meeting [*The Economist*, 8/30/86].

Quickly incorporating the experiences of Chernobyl, two new international conventions were prepared for a **Special Session of the IAEA 30th General Conference**, held September 24–26, 1986, in Vienna—"a record time," according to Director-General Dr. Hans Blix. The conventions were adopted by consensus and opened immediately for signature [Transcript of *World Chronicle* broadcast, 11/12/86].

The **Convention on Early Notification of a Nuclear Accident** was signed by fifty-one states—including the five nuclear-weapon states—on the day it opened for signature at the Special Session. It was ratified on the spot when three countries (Czechoslovakia, Denmark, and Norway) agreed to be bound by it, and it entered into force on October 27, 1986, the earliest possible date. The **Convention on Assistance in the Case of a Nuclear Accident or Radiological Emergency**, signed at the same Special Session, was not ratified until January (by the Soviet Union and the Ukrainian and Byelorussian Soviet Socialist Republics). It entered into force on February 26, 1987. The **Convention on the Physical Protection of Nuclear Material**, which had languished since March 3, 1980, also benefited from the concern about nuclear safety; it was ratified and entered into force on February 8, 1987 [*IAEA Newsbriefs*, 10/1/86, 2/10/87].

Although the IAEA continues to defend nuclear power as the safest and most environmentally sound form of energy, in December 1986 its board of governors endorsed an expanded safety program, the details of which may be the subject of a report to the General Assembly at its 42nd Session [*International Atomic Energy Agency Bulletin*, Winter 1986].

At the beginning of 1987, eight months after the most serious reactor explosion in history, Chernobyl restarted two 1,000-megawatt units and once again began producing nuclear power. To protect plant workers from contamination, the destroyed reactor, Unit 4, had been smothered with five thousand tons of sand and entombed in a shell of concrete and steel.

A wide range of protective measures has been undertaken, said Dr. Yevgeny P. Velikhov, vice president of the Soviet Academy of Sciences, in an unusual appearance before a U.S. Senate committee. He testified that tens of thousands of workers sank a fifty-foot-deep concrete wall around the damaged reactor to block the movement of contaminated water, removed radioactive topsoil from an area of several square miles, decontaminated sixty thousand buildings in five hundred villages, and built twelve thousand new houses and two hundred community facilities.

Velikhov also announced Soviet plans to quintuple nuclear power production by the year 2000. At the end of 1986, Russia had fifty reactors producing more than 27,000 megawatts, or a tenth of the world's nuclear-generated energy [*The New York Times*, 1/21/87; *IAEA Newsbriefs*, 2/10/87].

By the beginning of 1987, IAEA Director-General Blix was forecasting a glowing future for nuclear energy. "I am convinced that for economic and environmental reasons there will be a renewed demand for nuclear power," he said. Although Chernobyl's health and environmental consequences may be severe, Dr. Blix continued, they will be far less than many people have been led to believe. He found it "reasonable to conclude" that health consequences outside the Soviet Union "will be so small that they will not be measurable or even identifiable" [IAEA Press Release PR 87/9].

The health and environmental consequences of Chernobyl are studied not by the IAEA but by a separate **U.N. Scientific Committee on the Effects of Atomic Radiation**, which the General Assembly established in 1955. It expects to provide an analysis of Chernobyl's long-term radiation effects for the 42nd Session [A/Res/41/62]. However, its preliminary report to the Assembly mentioned two problems: it did not yet have sufficient data for analysis, and it was "seriously concerned by the inadequacy of its present resources" [A/42/210]. Under the circumstances, the report noted, the committee secretariat's lone scientist "simply cannot be expected to coordinate the programme of work single-handed."

On the other hand, even with a committee of sixty-six, it had taken nearly a decade to prepare for the **United Nations Conference for the Promotion of International Cooperation in the Peaceful Uses of Nuclear Energy** [A/Res/32/50], referred to by its jaw-breaking acronym, UNCPICPUNE. Three months prior to the opening, the conference secretary-general, Ambassador Amrik S. Mehta of India, supplied as the reason for such lengthy preparations "the fact that no agreement could be reached . . . on some of the basic issues, like the content of the agenda, like the rules of procedure, the decision-making process in the conference . . . . And to some extent there was a certain confusion between the aims and objectives of this Conference" and previous ones of a purely technical nature [Transcript of *World Chronicle* broadcast, 12/10/86]. There were similar difficulties at the conference itself.

The General Assembly's invitation to all states to participate "at an appropriately high level" [A/Res/41/212] brought representatives of more than a hundred countries to Geneva for the three-week event, March 23 to April 10, 1987. Its technical sessions—offering scores of papers on the peaceful uses of nuclear tools for economic and social development in agriculture, industry, health, and medicine—generated an exchange that has been generally deemed positive.

Its political sessions had negative results. Any hope of agreement in such sessions had been undermined before the conference began, when it was decided that decisions would be taken by consensus: One negative vote would be sufficient to prevent a conference agreement. As a result, the delegates could not come to any formal agreement on principles that would enhance coopera-tion in the peaceful uses of nuclear energy, having encountered disagreement in such areas as nonproliferation, technical discrimination, disarmament, revers-ing the arms race, and diverting of financial and technical resources to aid the cause of cooperation in this area [U.N. Press Release EN/146,4/1/87]. Conference President Mohamed Shaker of Egypt was led to conclude that the UNCPICPUNE's main achievement was a "much greater understanding" of the various states' positions. The report to the 42nd General Assembly will urge the world's nations to overcome their differences [U.N. Press Release, EN/160,4/14/87].

"Did the Conference do any good?" a United Nations energy official was asked. "No," he responded, "I think it did bad." Noting that not one of the technical reports offered in Geneva had compared the economic feasibility of nuclear energy with other forms of energy for producing electricity, he saw consequences that "can be catastrophic." Had such a paper been present-ed, he maintained, the developing countries would find nuclear power not nearly as economic as oil and gas. Owing to the absence of such reporting at UNCPICPUNE, the conference "will be used by the nuclear industry, which is currently underemployed, as a rubber stamp for producing power stations for developing countries."

The adverse effects of nuclear power and weapons proliferation have been very much on the minds of those who have taken part in renewed public protests and political lobbying in the United States, Scandinavia, West Ger-many, and elsewhere in the developed world after the Chernobyl disaster. And as antinuclear forces have gained in strength, they have slowed the expansion of nuclear power and weapons deployment. "Since the accident," the World-watch Institute notes, "the pro-nuclear consensus has collapsed in country after country, and the future of nuclear power, already hanging by a thread in some nations, is now in greater jeopardy then ever" [Worldwatch Institute, Paper 75,

Reassessing Nuclear Power: The Fallout from Chernobyl, 3/87].
Austria's foreign minister, Peter Jankowitsch, addressed this new reality at the Special Session of the IAEA held on September 26, 1986:

> For us the lessons from Chernobyl are clear. The Faustian bargain of nuclear energy has been lost. It is high time to leave the path pursued in the use of nuclear energy in the past, to develop new alternative and clean sources of energy supply and, during the transition period, devote all efforts to ensure maximum safety. This is the price to pay to enable life to continue on this planet [*Ibid.*].

Coming from a top official of the country in which the IAEA has its headquarters, this statement indicates a seismic shift in attitude toward nuclear power.

The Italian Parliament halted work on four unfinished reactors. Finland, Denmark, Holland, Greece, Egypt, Turkey, and Brazil canceled or postponed plans to acquire reactors, and Sweden—already committed to abandoning nuclear power by 2010—moved up its schedule by fifteen years.

Only twenty-six, primarily industrial, countries—less than a sixth of the world's nations—have built nuclear power plants; and at the end of 1986 only 394 nuclear plants, producing 15 percent of the world's electricity, were in operation. Despite the Chernobyl accident, 1986 was also a year in which 21 nuclear reactors came on line: in Canada (2), Czechoslovakia (2), France (6), the Federal Republic of Germany (2), Hungary (1), Japan (1), the Republic of Korea (2), and the United States (5) [*IAEA Newsbriefs*, 2/10/87].

The United States, which led the world into the nuclear age, now appears to be leading it out. The last order for a nuclear plant in the United States that was not subsequently canceled bears the date 1974; orders for 108 reactors have been withdrawn. Yet U.S. capacity continues to rise as projects started in the early 1970s are finally completed. It is likely to peak in the early 1990s and then slowly decline as aging plants are decommissioned [Worldwatch Institute, *ibid.*]. At the end of 1986 the United States had ninety-eight reactors, twice as many as any other country, and produced a quarter of the world's nuclear-generated electricity—but only 16.6 percent of the nation's electricity supply [*The New York Times*, 4/26/87].

The several industrialized countries committed to nuclear power continued to push ahead: The United Kingdom authorized construction of the first of a new generation of reactors; West Germany brought its twenty-first reactor on line; and France—which leads the world by meeting 70 percent of its electricity needs with nuclear power—continued building new reactors at the rate of one every eighteen months.

Even before Chernobyl another reality—the market—had begun to contribute to the general slowdown. With a reduction in the projected demand for electricity came a decline in proposed reactors and the cancellation of several under construction [E/C.7/1987/9;*The New York Times*, 4/27/87].

This decline in energy consumption and demand and the fall in energy investment also slowed the development of **new and renewable energy sources**—including animal power, fuelwood, geothermal, solar, wind, wave, and hydropower—something that the United Nations, at an international conference in Nairobi in 1981, had recognized as especially important for developing countries. By 1986 the General Assembly was expressing "concern at the slow rate of implementation of the **Nairobi Programme of Action**" and its financing. It "invited" the **Committee on the Development and Utilization of New and Renewable Sources of Energy** "to review its working methods so as to ensure further improvement in the fulfillment of its mandate" [A/Res/41/170].

There is no overall coordination among U.N. bodies on energy issues. An example is the hybrid **Committee on National Resources**, with responsibility for a handful of natural resources: energy in some forms, minerals, and implementation of the 1977 Mar del Plata **United Nations Water Conference action plan.**

Kyle Scott, the U.S. delegate to the committee's tenth session in April 1987, remarked on the fragmentation within the U.N. on natural resource issues. Twenty-four U.N. bodies deal with energy, he noted, questioning whether this was the most rational use of the organization's limited resources [U.N. Press Release, NR/152, 4/10/87].

"The tragedy of the General Assembly," said a high-level U.N. energy official, "is that it looks at energy in bits and pieces. It should not deal with fragments; the agencies should. The General Assembly should look at the whole."

4. Environment

The General Assembly will have before it two blueprints for future action on the environmental aspects of development: "Our Common Future," a massive report by the independent World Commission on Environment and Development, and "Environmental Perspective to the Year 2000 and Beyond," the report of an intergovernmental committee.

Both will challenge governments—and the U.N. system—to reorient their planning and policies toward **sustainable development** by making environmental protection an inseparable component of economic growth.

The **World Commission on Environment and Development** was created by the General Assembly in 1983 [A/Res/38/161] at the behest of the **U.N. Environment Programme (UNEP)** [UNEP/GC.11/3].

Prime Minister of Norway Dr. Gro Harlem Brundtland chaired the group, leading twenty-one commissioners—politicians, economists, and scientists—

in a series of public hearings on every continent. The results were released with a publicity fanfare on April 27, 1987.

The Economist was impressed. "A press jamboree in London, a satellite link with America, a six-continent road-show: the UN's Brundtland Report on Environment and Development is getting about," it editorialized on May 2.

It was not by chance that the so-called **Brundtland Report** was getting widespread coverage—even six months before its presentation to the General Assembly. "First and foremost our message is directed towards people. . . . Unless we are able to translate our words into a language that can reach the minds and hearts of people young and old, we shall not be able to undertake the extensive social changes needed to correct the course of development," Mrs. Brundtland said in her foreword to the report [UNEP/GC.14/13]. She continued:

> Many critical survival issues are related to uneven development, poverty and population growth. They all place unprecedented pressures on the planet's lands, waters, forests, and other natural resources, not least in the developing countries. The downward spiral of poverty and environmental degradation is a waste of opportunities and of resources. What is needed now is a new era of economic growth—growth that is forceful and at the same time socially and environmentally sustainable.

This was the challenge to be taken up by governments with help from the United Nations Environment Programme.

UNEP's Governing Council of fifty-eight governments had started work on its own **Environmental Perspective to the Year 2000 and Beyond** in 1983, at the same time it initiated the World Commission on Environment and Development. The intergovernmental committee used the Brundtland Report to organize its thinking on strategies for environmentally sound development. Their succinct Environmental Perspective provides a basic environmental agenda for long-range national action and international cooperation [UNEP *North America News*, 2/87;UNEP/GC.14/4/Add.7]. The key to both plans is a stronger UNEP.

But one prescription of both reports was not welcomed by UNEP. The recommendation was that U.N. bodies assume full responsibility, operational and financial, for their own environmental programs, to free UNEP's human and fiscal resources for priority programs. UNEP Executive Director Mostafa K. Tolba was disturbed: "The proposed move would certainly not help in getting organs and organizations of the system to agree on a co-operative and complementary programme." It could "send the wrong signals [to the General Assembly] regarding the abilities of the Governing Council and the [UNEP] secretariat to carry out their functions," he told UNEP's Governing Council [UNEP/CG.14/4, p. 10]. Rather, Dr. Tolba suggested, the council might want to send a different message to the General Assembly, stressing UNEP's essential catalytic role within the U.N. system "and that the resources of the Environment Fund should be substantially enlarged, to facilitate . . . catalysing the sustainable development efforts of the United Nations system" [UNEP/GC.14/4/Add.7, p .3].

As it coordinated with the Brundtland Commission and the intergovernmental committee, UNEP evaluated itself and its work as the environmental coordinator and catalyst for action in the U.N. system. The result of this self-evaluation is an ambitious and thoughtful plan for orienting UNEP's future work [UNEP/GC.14/4/Add.4].

Its premise is that "solutions to serious environmental problems, whether global, regional or national, depend to a very large extent on the full integration of environmental considerations in the development process"—a conclusion in line with both the Brundtland Commission Report and the Environmental Perspective to the Year 2000 and Beyond. Accordingly, the UNEP plan sets goals for governments and the U.N. system, as well as specific targets for itself, to be accomplished between 1990 and 1995.

Executive Director Tolba believes UNEP should anticipate environmental problems and alert the world community to their potential dangers. He has already identified the most serious problems, setting goals for their solution by U.N. agencies, governments, and nongovernmental organizations. In Dr. Tolba's view, the priority problems are:

- Climate modification and atmospheric changes

- Fresh water shortage and degradation

- Desertification and soil degradation

- Deforestation and loss of biological diversity

- Marine pollution and the need for coastal management

- Environmental hazards of industry

- Degradation from uncontrolled urbanization

- Lack of access to low-waste and other environmental technologies

- The limited integration of environmental considerations into development policies, plans, programs, and projects

This plan for the future will be discussed in depth by UNEP's partners in the U.N. system prior to a General Assembly (43rd Session) review of the system-wide environmental program for 1990–95 [*UNEP North America News*, 4/87].

To lessen the risk of destructive development, UNEP's Governing Council decided on June 17 to adopt **Goals and Principles of Environmental Impact Assessment,** so that environmental and natural resource concerns are incorporated into national, regional, and international development plans. This forward-looking decision will go to the General Assembly for its endorsement [GC decision 14/25].

The United Nations Administrative Committee on Coordination had high praise for UNEP.

> Its 1984–1989 programme, as the only such system-wide effort, has proved to be of considerable value for the United Nations system—and not only UNEP—in planning and implementing environmental activities. It has fostered fresh forms of dialogue and cooperation. The lessons learned in the development of the programme may prove to be of value in other appropriate areas of multisectoral cooperation [UNEP/GC.14/8].

The lessons UNEP learned in working cooperatively with governments and within the U.N. itself led to an outstanding success in 1987, one in which UNEP helped governments anticipate a major environmental problem and start to resolve it.

Man-made chemicals were increasingly destroying the ozone layer that protects the earth from the sun's harmful rays. Scientists predicted that continued ozone depletion could cause a 40 percent increase in radiation effects, such as skin cancers [*UNEP North America News*, 12/86]. Because the problem belongs to no single country but to the whole earth, it required a global agreement and solution.

On April 30, 1987, UNEP announced that scientists and legal experts from thirty-two countries had taken a substantial step toward "a meaningful international agreement to protect the ozone layer." This **protocol to the 1985 Vienna Convention for the Protection of the Ozone Layer** was expected to be signed at a diplomatic conference in Montreal, September 14–16 [UNEP Press Release, 4/30/87], during the 42nd Session of the General Assembly.

The New York Times hailed the negotiators for "a degree of international foresight on the environment that had been no more than an elusive goal in recent decades. The negotiations also represented a dramatic success for a United Nations environmental agency that many experts had all but written off as ineffective." It was now widely perceived, the *Times* said in a May 5, 1987, article, that UNEP "played a key role in achieving the tentative agreement and that the U.N. body could be the much-needed forum for dealing with other pressing environmental problems in the future."

UNEP's increasingly important work on the international management of chemicals and other toxic substances has led to two sets of industrial guidelines that will go before the General Assembly at this session. The first, the **London Guidelines on the Exchange of Information on Chemicals in International Trade**, sets up a worldwide information exchange on chemicals, especially those banned and severely restricted. The **Cairo Guidelines and Principles for** the **Environmentally Sound Management of Hazardous Wastes** deals with these wastes from their generation to final disposal, and focuses particularly on movements across national boundaries [UNEP/GC.14/17; telephone interview with Jan Huismans, director of UNEP International Register of Potentially Toxic Chemicals, 5/15/87].

One transfrontier problem had become significantly worse. Ten years after ninety-four countries endorsed a massive United Nations campaign to stop the advance of deserts into agricultural land worldwide, not one single nation has been able to reverse the process, according to scientists and policy analysts at the American Association for the Advancement of Science (AAAS) annual meeting on February 18, 1987, in Chicago. On average, they said, 15 million acres of our planet's agricultural land turn into desert every year, primarily as a result of activities such as overgrazing and cutting of firewood [*The Boston Globe*, 2/18/87].

This issue has been a continuing concern of the General Assembly. The 1977 Nairobi **Plan of Action to Combat Desertification** called on governments to invest $4.5 billion every year, but in ten years just $6 billion has been spent, mostly on research and on infrastructure, such as roads, but very little on direct action to solve the problem [*Science*, AAAS, 2/27/87].

A special account to help UNEP mobilize financial resources for the plan [A/Res/32/172] has received a total of only $172,886. "In spite of repeated appeals by the executive director to the international community, pursuant to various General Assembly resolutions," UNEP reported in a decade-end review, this fund "is still short of the minimum needed to make it effective." At its June 8–19 meeting in Nairobi, the Governing Council tried once more to fill the arid coffers of UNEP's Special Account. It urged that UNEP's Executive Director Tolba discuss "a new and realistic approach" to soliciting contributions from governments and international financial institutions to halt the spread of deserts worldwide [GC decision 14/15S].

The UNEP Governing Council has experimented with a two-year meeting schedule and will recommend to the General Assembly that this biennial schedule be continued, to coincide with every-other-year review of UNEP by the General Assembly's Second (Economic and Financial) Committee. UNEP will, however, recommend one exception to this schedule—a special week-long session in 1988 and every six years thereafter—to consider the proposed U.N. systemwide environmental program and UNEP's role in the draft U.N. medium-term plan before they are submitted to the General Assembly for approval [UNEP/GC.14/4/Add.2].

5. Law of the Sea

During the last year only three nations ratified the 1982 United Nations **Convention on the Law of the Sea (LOS)**, the comprehensive treaty covering all ocean uses and developments. This brought the total to thirty-two—still far short of the sixty required for the convention's entry into force. Nonetheless, the convention holds an increasingly dominant position in law and practice in marine affairs. It is the work of the **Preparatory Commission**, now in its fourth year of preparing the institutions established by the convention, that is expected to have the greatest impact on the progress of actual ratification. At the close of the spring 1987 meeting of the commission, the delegation of Australia called the commission unrealistic for continuing to defer substantive discussion of such "hard-core" issues as financial decision making. The financial implications of the convention, the Australians noted in Jamaica, will greatly influence decisions about whether to ratify.

Another aspect of the commission's work that will influence national decisions about ratification is its mandate to draft regulations to implement technical aspects of the regulatory system for deep-seabed mining—the information to be submitted with requests for mining permits, procedures to be followed in applying, and the criteria and procedures that are to be used by the **International Seabed Authority** (ISA) and its organs in making decisions on such applications. Most of the nations contemplating deep-seabed mining in the future have indicated that they are waiting to see whether the commission's rule-making efforts actually create a practical and viable regime for mining before they will consider ratifying the convention. They have also placed on record their objections to some of the burdens imposed by the convention's mining regime, particularly as a result of changed market conditions for minerals.

At its summer 1987 meeting the commission will again face the problem of electing a successor to its chairman, Joseph S. Warioba, now prime minister of Tanzania. Warioba had agreed to stay on for more than a year after his appointment as prime minister in order to use his good offices to help conclude delicate negotiations on overlapping seabed mine-site claims of the pioneer investors in deep-seabed mining. These overlaps have delayed implementation of the interim regime set forth in Resolution II of the Law of the Sea Conference to protect the interests of the pioneers. At the spring meeting in Jamaica, the Eastern Europe regional group was unable to agree to the candidate proposed by the African group and endorsed by the Group of 77 developing nations.

To help implement the broader aspects of the LOS convention, U.N. headquarters announced on March 2 that most of the marine-related functions of the U.N. Secretariat would be consolidated in a new **Office of Ocean Affairs and the Law of the Sea**, to be headed by Under-Secretary-General Satya P. Nandan of Fiji. Nandan's office has served to date as the central repository for information on national maritime claims, has assisted member states in designing national ocean laws and policies to give effect to the convention's legal regime, and has monitored national marine laws and policies (publishing a periodic LOS *Bulletin* to record them) as well as broader developments and

trends at the regional and international levels. The new office is also expected to provide advice and assistance in matters pertaining to ocean development and management practices. By working cooperatively with such other U.N. specialized agencies as the Intergovernmental Oceanographic Commission (IOC), Food and Agriculture Organization (FAO), U.N. Environment Programme (UNEP), International Maritime Organization (IMO), and the International Hydrographic Organization (IHO), the new office will be a formidable resource for coastal states as they implement the convention regime. These organizations, particularly UNEP and the IMO, also have an important role in elaborating the international and regional agreements in such areas as marine environment protection and vessel safety and pollution control envisioned in the LOS convention. The annual report of the Secretary-General on the LOS provides an excellent and comprehensive summary of trends and developments in these areas, often drawing evidence from the activities of various international organizations as well as from other forums [A/41/742].

In addition to drafting implementing regulations for the **mining regime** and preparing for the establishment of the International Seabed Authority, its operating arm—the **Enterprise**—and the **International Tribunal on the Law of the Sea** (ITLOS), the Preparatory Commission has been working since 1983 to register the **pioneer investors** (PIs) in deep-seabed mining. Resolution II of the LOS Conference identified eight PIs: four nations (India, the Soviet Union, France, and Japan) and four multinational consortia. Each is to receive exclusive rights to develop mine-site areas where they have already expended significant funds so long as they comply with all other convention provisions. The four national mining groups have already applied to the commission for registration, but none of the consortia has done so. These consortia have been issued licenses to explore for seabed minerals under the domestic legislation of the United States, the United Kingdom, or the Federal Republic of Germany (FRG), all nonsignatories of the convention; and such unilateral actions have been deplored by the Preparatory Commission. In the commission, the interests of these multinational consortia are the concern of those signatory states that are home to companies that have been involved—Canada, Belgium, Italy, and the Netherlands. Companies based in the FRG and the United Kingdom, both of which are nonsignatory observers at the commission, are also members of the consortia, and so too are companies based in the United States, a nonobserver.

Of the four **national mining groups** that have applied to the commission for registration, three (the Soviet Union, France, and Japan) did so without first resolving problems of overlapping mine sites, a prerequisite under Resolution II. After three years of attempts to iron out such problems, using the good offices of the chairman of the commission, the Preparatory Commission reached an agreement on September 5, 1986, regarding the applications of the four states. This left only the problem of the unresolved overlaps between the

Soviet Union and some of the consortia. Consultations on the remaining overlaps have to be pursued outside the purview of the Preparatory Commission; but to take account of this situation, the commission in April 1987 reworked the timetable it had adopted on September 5, 1986, so that revised applications for registration by the four are now to be submitted on July 20, 1987, one week prior to the opening of the summer meeting of the commission. If the PIs fail to conclude an agreement in the course of intersessional consultations this summer—and, as a consequence, the applicants are unable to submit their revised applications for registration by the date established—the commission may meet to consider separately the registration of the Indian operation, a mine site located in the Indian Ocean.

Once registration is accomplished, there will have to be some agreement on the **obligations of the PIs to train personnel** and carry out other tasks to help launch the Enterprise, as required by Resolution II and the September 1986 understanding. At the spring 1987 meeting the PIs reiterated their commitment to undertaking these obligations but were still unwilling to submit substantive proposals until the remaining consultations were complete and registration under way. For some time the discussions have focused on the appropriate timing and duration of the training in light of current market conditions and the allocation of costs for such training.

Fundamental disagreement about the scope and manner of carrying out these obligations would delay further the effective implementation of the Resolution II regime and might also interfere with the ability of the commission to take on those hard-core issues that affect the ratification process. The hard-core issues were identified by commission Chairman Warioba in 1985 as those dealing with all aspects of decision making, the status of observers, the establishment of subsidiary bodies of the ISA, and financial and budgetary matters. At the time, Warioba deferred their consideration until some future date when it would be timely and appropriate to seek a consensus agreement on a "package" that could command widespread support. Since then various delegations have made proposals that, particularly on financial and budgetary matters, other states have claimed are not in accord with the convention's provisions.

The last year has witnessed the emergence of two significant trends in the commission. First, delegates from all the regional groups have engaged in debate on technical and substantive issues, seeking practical solutions to questions and problems. The developing nations have reaffirmed their position that it is not within the mandate of the commission to amend the convention, but they have indicated their willingness to be flexible in interpreting and clarifying the deep-seabed mining regime in response to criticisms leveled at it. They have also acknowledged that, should changing economic/market conditions render various portions of the convention's mining regime impractical or unworkable, they would be willing to consider adjusting, for example, details

of the formula limiting initial seabed production and the financial terms of contract, *as provided for in the convention.*

Second, the Eastern European group has effectively joined the Western industrialized nations with mining interests in advocating mining code provisions that permit "**a minimum level of profitability for contractors.**" These nations have urged the commission to remove ambiguities in the deep-seabed mining texts and to address the new economic/market circumstances affecting mining by developing in greater detail the general provisions on joint ventures and financial incentives, among others. Both groups have emphasized that commission regulations should not merely reiterate convention provisions but should specify in greater detail the criteria and procedures that will serve as a basis for decision making.

The work of the commission is divided among five working groups. Its informal plenary is responsible for the administrative, procedural, and budgetary rules of the ISA. **Special Commission 1 (SCN.1)** addresses the problems of land-based developing-nation producers likely to be affected by competition from deep-seabed mineral mining. **SCN.2,** preparing for the Enterprise, is concentrating on the question of training, recommendations on the initial needs of the Enterprise, and studies of the different options the Enterprise could adopt for its first mining operation. **SCN.3** drafts the implementing regulations for mining—the mining code—and is currently concentrating on such aspects as the financial terms of contracts. **SCN.4** is preparing for the establishment of the International Tribunal on the Law of the Sea, drafting rules of procedure, considering a draft headquarters agreement, and dealing with privileges and immunities related to the ITLOS function.

SCN.4 is also faced with the politically charged question of what to do in the event that the FRG, identified in the convention as the **seat of the Tribunal,** has not ratified the convention by the time it enters into force. At the April 1987 meeting West Germany acknowledged that states envisaged as sites for the institutions of the convention must be parties to it upon its entry into force, noting the government's hope that "the matters concerning deep-sea mining can be cleared up in such a way as to enable the FRG, as well as other states with an interest in deep-sea mining, to become Parties before the UNCLOS enters into force" [LOS/PCN/SCN.4/L.8].

After a period of unexpected delays, the current possibility of registering pioneer investors and the more flexible attitude taken in commission debates offer hope for a not-too-distant agreement on the means to address the issues and problems that have stood in the way of widespread support for the LOS convention—issues involving the regulatory system for mining and the desire of states to have a relatively firm grasp on the scale and timing of their financial obligations before they ratify the convention and it enters into force. Many of these issues can be addressed adequately in the implementing regulations, but others may require that convention provisions effectively be amended even before the attempt is made to formulate implementing regulations that can gain wide support. It will be far easier to reach agreement on any such changes before the convention enters into force, since only states that are parties to the Law of the Sea Convention may take advantage of the formal amendment procedures.

6. Antarctica

For two years now consensus has eluded the General Assembly on its resolutions dealing with Antarctica, and the Assembly debate on Antarctica in 1986—its fourth— indicated that there is little room for maneuver in achieving a consensus between the nations that are party to the **Antarctic Treaty** and to the related international agreements that form the **Antarctic Treaty System** (**ATS**) and the nations that are taking issue with certain aspects of the ATS role as governing agent in Antarctic matters.

The three resolutions offered in 1986 (41/88 A, B, C) were similar to those adopted in 1985. One addressed in general terms the availability of information on Antarctic affairs from the **Antarctic Treaty Consultative Parties** (**ATCPs**)—those with decision-making powers under the Antarctic Treaty. One, specifically related to the Antarctic minerals regime negotiations, addressed the Assembly's 1985 call upon the ATCPs to make information on these negotiations available to the United Nations; and one called for the exclusion of South Africa from the **Antarctic Treaty Consultative Meetings** (**ATCMs**) and for informing the Secretary-General of actions taken in this regard. The 1986 resolutions differed from the 1985 resolutions in including a call for a moratorium on the minerals regime negotiations "until such time as all members of the international community can participate fully in such negotiations" and a call for a report by the Secretary-General on actions taken with respect to South African participation in the ATCMs.

The Secretary-General's report for the 1986 debate dealt with three specific questions [See *Issues Before the 41st General Assembly of the United Nations*, pp. 108–9; A/41/722]; his 1987 report will update information about all aspects of Antarctica as well as inform the Assembly of actions taken on South African participation in ATCMs. It is expected that the ATCPs as a group will refuse to respond to the requests for information contained in the General Assembly's resolutions, as they did in 1985, citing the breakdown of consensus in the General Assembly.

The call for a moratorium on the minerals regime negotiations reflects growing frustration with what has been characterized as the ATCPs' "stonewalling" when it comes to providing information on the status and substance of these negotiations, which are expected to conclude in the first half of 1988. The debate in the 41st General Assembly had left open the possibility that there would be less criticism of the Antarctic Treaty itself if the emerging minerals regime were to allow for universal participation. But the refusal of the ATCPs to respond to the Assembly's request for information on these talks in time for the 41st Session [A/41/688 and Add.1] contributed to the resumption of such criticism. Several speakers took direct issue with two fundamental elements of the Antarctic Treaty System: the distinction between ATCPs and **Non-Consultative Parties** (**NCPs**) in ATS decision making, and the validity of territorial claims in Antarctica. In early Assembly debates the sponsors of the agenda item on Antarctica withheld judgment on the role of the NCPs, which received their first invitation to attend the ATCMs in 1983 and the minerals negotiations in 1985, expressing interest in the development of ways in which the NCPs, as observers, might exert their influence upon the ATS. It was believed at the time that developing the role of the NCPs, together with improving the flow of information about Antarctic affairs and expanding working relationships between the ATS and international organizations with relevant scientific and technical expertise, could effectively respond to outside criticism of the ATS.

The debate of 1986 indicated that those outside the system are no longer interested in the developing NCP role as long as decision making is reserved for those nations able to pay the price of undertaking substantial scientific research in Antarctica. It indicated as well that outsiders will no longer ignore the fact that claims to territorial sovereignty in Antarctica obstruct application of the "**common heritage of mankind**" **principle** to that continent. In 1986 several countries challenged the validity of these claims and called attention to their incompatibility with the "common heritage" concept. It is such challenges that leave little room for compromise with the parties to the Antarctic Treaty, who continue to support the ATS and the tenets of Article IV of the Treaty, which preserves both claimant and nonclaimant positions.

The debate of 1986 highlighted anew the participation in the ATCMs of South Africa's "racist *apartheid* régime." On this issue as well it will be difficult for the ATCPs as a group to act, since decision making at the meetings takes place by consensus. In the General Assembly, however, an increasing number of treaty parties are voting in favor of the Assembly resolutions on South Africa, even while refusing to participate in the voting on the other two resolutions. In 1985 the People's Republic of China, India, Peru, and Romania were in this number. They were joined in 1986 by Argentina, Brazil, Bulgaria, Cuba, Czechoslovakia, the German Democratic Republic, Hungary, Poland, and the Soviet Union.

There were relatively few comments in the 41st Session on the Secretary-General's study of Antarctic matters, since it was issued just one day before the debate commenced. Preliminary questions were raised about the section on the significance of the 1982 **Law of the Sea Convention in the Southern Ocean**, owing to its failure to address offshore claims in general or the role of the

International Seabed Authority, whose mandate covers seabed areas *beyond* national jurisdiction. Participants in the debate noted with approval the active coordination between the ATS and a number of international organizations, although one speaker indicated a preference for direct interaction between these organizations and the ATS over the more usual indirect interaction that is taking place through the **Scientific Committee on Antarctic Research (SCAR)**—a committee of the International Council of Scientific Unions, established during the 1957–58 International Geophysical Year to coordinate continuing research activity and scientific cooperation in the Antarctic following the year.

At the 1983 ATCM it was decided to consider inviting international organizations to send **observers** to future ATCMs for discussion of relevant agenda items, but the ATCPs did not act on the matter for the 1985 ATCM. In May 1987, SCAR and the **Commission of the Convention on the Conservation of Antarctic Marine Living Resources (CCAMLR)** were invited to designate observers to report to the October 1987 ATCM, and experts from the World Meteorological Organization and the International Union for the Conservation of Nature and Natural Resources (IUCN) were invited to contribute to discussions on relevant meteorological and environmental matters.

With respect to the availability of information issue, all parties to the debate acknowledge that, with the exception of the minerals regime negotiations, a wide variety of materials on Antarctic issues and activities is now available to the United Nations. The 41st Session's resolution on this matter suggests that the U.N. could function as the central repository of all such information. On the agenda of the XIV Antarctic Treaty Consultative Meeting in Brazil in 1987 is the **declassification of documents** from ATCMs IV to VII and continuing improvement in making available to the U.N. system current information on ATS developments. Also to be considered is the establishment of an Antarctic Treaty secretariat, which could facilitate the dissemination of Antarctic information, among other functions.

Another agenda item of the XIV ATCM deals with the gradual move toward **long-term, integrated management and conservation of Antarctica**, drawing heavily on the advice of SCAR. In May 1986 a joint working group, composed of representatives from the nongovernmental SCAR and the IUCN, developed an outline of such a plan, its details to be completed by the end of 1988. The XIV ATCM will be considering some elements of this plan as SCAR reports on the progress made toward designating additional protected areas, elaborating protected-area concepts, improving the code of conduct governing waste disposal practices in Antarctica and the accessibility and comparability of scientific data on the region, and applying environmental impact assessment procedures to scientific and logistics facilities in Antarctica, as outlined by SCAR in its report to the XIII ATCM and endorsed by various SCAR meetings.

In the course of the year three more states have acceded to the Antarctic Treaty (South Korea in November 1986; North Korea and Greece in January 1987), and South Korea is developing plans for establishing a research station in 1987–88. Italy is seeking ATCP status before the XIV ATCM in October 1987. South Korea, India, and Brazil are the newest members of the CCAMLR Commission, having joined in 1985–86. In 1987, Spain and Uruguay are expected to seek commission status. Guidelines for the type of information to be submitted by states seeking commission status were developed under the CCAMLR in 1985. Similar guidelines for information about "substantial scientific research" to be supplied by nations seeking ATCP status will be considered at the XIV ATCM.

The **Antarctic minerals regime negotiations** continued at meetings in Hobart, Australia (April 1986), Tokyo (November 1986), and Montevideo (May 1987). As in the previous year, there were discussions of legal matters, such as compliance and enforcement, liability, dispute settlement, amendment, and withdrawal, and on guidelines and procedures for operators planning to submit applications to explore and develop minerals. The key questions remain: (1) What are to be the composition and decision-making procedures of the institutions of a minerals regime and their relation to each other? (2) Who will participate in the institutions of the regime and in approved activities pursuant to it, and who will reap the potential benefits from such activities? What is now required is the political will to obtain final agreement on these matters and to complete the drafting process. A proposal to convene a final meeting to adopt the regime in 1988 may provide the necessary impetus to agreement.

The fifth meeting of the commission and the Scientific Committee established by the CCAMLR took place in September 1986, and the sixth is scheduled for October–November 1987. Adoption of effective conservation measures for **fin fisheries** continues to be slowed by disagreement over whether the available data justify them. In 1986, for the first time, the parties explicitly refused to permit a consensus on continued fishing of some species, registering frustration with the failure to agree on conservation measures. The fishing states have doubled **krill** harvests between 1984–85 and 1985–86; and amidst indications that krill fishing will continue to increase, the parties to CCAMLR are now turning their attention to krill conservation. Educational and monitoring measures to control **marine debris** were adopted at the 1985 and 1986 CCAMLR meetings. Implementation of the system of observation and inspection called for in the convention to ensure compliance will be reconsidered in 1987. Its adoption grows more important with increased harvesting and the adoption of additional conservation measures. The persistence of difficulties in implementing and enforcing the far-sighted conservation standard set forth in the CCAMLR calls into question the ability of the ATS to act as an effective monitor and manager of Antarctic conservation more generally.

The General Assembly debates on Antarctica have served not only to ferret out a considerable amount of information on the ATS and make it widely available but also to prompt the ATCPs to open up their system in other ways—for example, by inviting NCPs and international organizations as observers at their meetings. Two years of a breakdown of consensus have created the need for a forum in which those within and outside the ATS can take steps to move the debate off dead center. Many have suggested the possibility of a **review of the Antarctic Treaty** after 1991, but any amendments resulting from such a review would also require the consensus of ATCPs to go into effect. It seems unlikely that such a review conference could produce results more acceptable to the international community than those that can be identified now as the General Assembly continues to debate Antarctica.

V
Human Rights and Social Issues

1. Human Rights

In his report on the work of the United Nations to the 41st Assembly (A/41/1), Secretary-General Javier Pérez de Cuéllar noted that the United Nations has been successful and comprehensive in defining rights and freedoms in authoritative form and is now facing the more complex task of promoting respect for them in practice. The central and most important international standards that define these rights are the Universal Declaration of Human Rights and the International Human Rights Covenants that translate the principles enshrined in the declaration into legally binding form. These are the foundation of a universal system for the promotion and protection of human rights worldwide.

In his message on Human Rights Day, December 10, 1986, the Secretary-General set forth broad goals aimed at translating the rights provided for in the Universal Declaration and the International Covenants into social reality. The observance of these latter instruments, he said, the conformity in practice with their provisions, is one of the foremost aims of the United Nations. "We are, however, still far from our goal," he continued.

> Oppression in various forms, the practice of torture, the persecution of individuals or groups on grounds of belief or political persuasion, detention without trial, summary executions . . . none of these has yet become an unfamiliar phenomenon in global society as a whole. In many parts of the world, human beings are still deprived of their basic means of survival; assaults are still made upon their physical or mental integrity. Racial discrimination is still entrenched in an important corner of the globe [DPI press release SG/SM/3944, 12/9/86].

The **International Human Rights Covenants** were adopted in 1966, and last year the United Nations commemorated the twentieth anniversary of their adoption. Each state party to the International Covenant on Economic, Social and Cultural Rights is pledged to take steps, to the maximum of its available resources, to achieve the rights recognized in the covenant. States party to the **International Covenant on Civil and Political Rights** undertake to respect and to ensure to all individuals within their territories the rights recognized in this covenant. The General Assembly has emphasized that the rights recognized in the covenants are indivisible and interdependent and that equal attention and urgent consideration should be given to the implementation, promotion, and protection of civil and political as well as economic, social, and cultural rights.

The 41st General Assembly called upon all states that had not yet done so to mark this anniversary by ratifying or acceding to the covenants. At present, eighty-nine states are party to the **International Covenant on Economic, Social and Cultural Rights**, eighty-five to the **Covenant on Civil and Political Rights**.

Only thirty-eight states have accepted the **Optional Protocol to the Covenant on Civil and Political Rights**, which allows individuals to complain to the Human Rights Committee if their rights under the covenant have been violated and domestic remedies have been exhausted. The Human Rights Committee monitors the compliance by states parties with the rights set down in the Covenant on Civil and Political Rights. Thus far, governments have shown reluctance to allow citizens under their jurisdiction such international recourse.

The year 1988 will mark the fortieth anniversary of the adoption of the **Universal Declaration of Human Rights**. The 41st Session of the General Assembly, in preparation for this anniversary, recommended a number of measures at both the national and international level for its commemoration [A/Res/41/150]. It asked states that had not yet ratified or acceded to international instruments in the field of human rights to give special consideration to becoming party to them. It also recommended the establishment or strengthening of national or local institutions for the promotion and protection of human rights, the encouragement of teaching programs on human rights at various educational levels, and the dissemination of the Universal Declaration of Human Rights in national languages, including the languages of minorities. The participation and organization of activities by nongovernmental organizations to commemorate the anniversary was also recommended.

The 41st Session of the General Assembly took place at a time of financial and political crisis for the United Nations. It is still not clear how the crisis will affect the United Nations human rights program in 1987. In a report on funding prospects and economy measures for 1987, issued in December 1986, the U.N. Secretary-General said that "the United Nations will begin 1987 with only $10 million cash in hand, substantially less than the cost of one week's operations." Although many member states took steps to pay their contributions early in 1987, it is still far from clear how the U.N. and its specialized agencies will survive financially in 1987.

In these circumstances of crisis, it is difficult to predict what measures will be taken to ensure the continuation of ongoing programs. Since the U.N. human rights programs account for less than 1 percent of the annual budget, nongovernmental organizations working in the field of human rights have suggested that cuts would not affect the program at all. In fact, however, the human rights program was badly affected in 1986. Meetings of important human rights bodies, such as the Human Rights Committee, the Committee on the Elimination of Racial Discrimination, and the Sub-Commission on Prevention of Discrimination and Protection of Minorities and its various working groups, were cancelled. Important areas of the work of the U.N. Centre for Human Rights in Geneva also suffered as a consequence of the prohibition on the employment of temporary staff and consultants. It is feared that the 42nd Assembly's consideration of human rights could be adversely affected as well.

In May 1987, however, when the Committee on Programme and Coordination considered the program budget proposed by the Secretary-General for the next biennum, it recommended to the 42nd General Assembly that the human rights program not be affected by the overall 15 percent cut in regular staff posts that the 41st Assembly had asked the Secretary-General to implement.

Human rights questions are considered primarily by the General Assembly's Third Committee on Social, Humanitarian and Cultural matters, although the work of other committees also addresses, directly or indirectly, issues relevant to human rights. The Third Committee deals with a broad and complex range of questions that do not lend themselves to easy summary. What follows is a review of the committee's agenda in the field of human rights. This is based largely on its consideration of item 12 of its agenda, which deals with the report of the Economic and Social Council, to which the Commission on Human Rights reports.

Among the issues addressed by the committee are measures to combat racism and racial discrimination, especially in South Africa and Namibia; the adverse effects on human rights of assistance to South Africa; and questions relating to self-determination—the assertion, for example, that the use of mercenaries violates human rights and impedes the exercise of self-determination. In 1983, at its 38th Session, the General Assembly proclaimed the Second Decade to Combat Racism and Racial Discrimination and approved a program of action for the Second Decade. The 42nd Session will review activities to date and discuss a program of activities for the second half of the decade. Lack of financial resources to fund the decade's activities has been a continuing problem.

The committee will also consider the effect of scientific and technological developments on human rights, the question of the human rights of migrant workers, regional arrangements for the promotion and protection of human rights, and the establishment and strengthening of national institutions for the promotion and protection of human rights, all of which have been longstanding items on its agenda.

The annual report of the U.N. High Commissioner for Refugees will be before the committee; and, in this context, the committee will also consider assistance to refugees, especially in Djibouti, Chad, the Sudan, and Ethiopia and to student refugees in Southern Africa. It will review as well the problem of mass exoduses of refugees and displaced persons. It will review the U.N.'s program and activities in the field of crime prevention and criminal justice and human rights in the administration of justice. There are now four U.N. regional crime-prevention institutes; the most recent addition, currently being established, is the regional institute in Africa.

The 41st Session of the General Assembly's **Declaration on the Right to Development** proclaimed the right to development among the inalienable human rights. The 42nd General Assembly will consider measures following the adoption of this declaration, which was accepted by a vote of 146 for, 1 against (the United States), and 8 abstentions.

The Third Committee will comment on the reports from the four major treaty bodies in the field of human rights: the **Committee on the Elimination of Racial Discrimination**, the **Committee on the Elimination of Discrimination against Women**, the **Committee on Economic, Social and Cultural Rights**, and the **Human Rights Committee**. The committee will detail their consideration of states parties' reports during the year. The reporting obligations of states parties under the different human rights treaties will also be taken up. Concerned that many reports are overdue at these various bodies, the General Assembly of late has been urging states parties to make every effort to fulfill their obligations under these treaties as soon as possible; at the same time, the Secretariat and the chairmen of the groups have been working on ways to make the reporting task less burdensome, including the organizing of training seminars for this purpose. The need to strengthen the servicing provided to these treaty bodies by the Secretariat has been frequently voiced.

An initiative taken at the 41st Assembly on further standard setting in the human rights field will be pursued at the 42nd. This resolution called upon member states and U.N. bodies to accord priority to the implementation of existing standards and urged broad ratification of or accession to existing treaties. Any further standards should be consistent with the existing body of human rights law [A/Res/41/120]. Many argue that further standard setting is at present a luxury and can be an excuse for avoiding the more complex task of protecting and promoting respect for existing standards in practice.

The committee will also review the status of the **International Convention on the Suppression and Punishment of the Crime of Apartheid**, and of the **Convention on the Prevention and Punishment of the Crime of Genocide**.

The **question of the elimination of all forms of religious intolerance** will also be on the agenda. In a resolution coordinated by Ireland, the 41st General Assembly reaffirmed that freedom of thought, religion, and belief is a right guaranteed to all without discrimination [A/Res/41/112]. It welcomed the work being undertaken by the Commission on Human Rights to prepare a compendium of the national legislation and regulations of states on the question of freedom of religion or belief. It took note of the commission's appointment of a special rapporteur to examine incidents and governmental actions inconsistent with the provisions of the Declaration on the **Elimination of All Forms of Intolerance or Discrimination based on Religion or Belief**. The rapporteur was appointed in 1985 and submitted his first report to the commission at its 43rd Session, in February 1987. The Assembly also asked the commission to consider further measures to implement the declaration and to report back at its 42nd Session.

Among the most difficult challenges before the committee is to formulate a response to government practices that the international community has condemned and that are not permitted under any circumstances—not even in times of war. These include: torture and other cruel, inhuman, or degrading treatment or punishment; summary or arbitrary executions; and enforced or involuntary disappearances. The Commission on Human Rights has appointed a working group and two special rapporteurs to consider and to respond to these practices on a global basis and to make recommendations for their eradication. Although this is a significant development, it nonetheless remains clear that a more focused response from the international community is required when a government persists in gross violations of the human rights of individuals under its jurisdiction.

The committee will consider the human rights situations in Afghanistan, Chile, El Salvador, Guatemala, and Iran, where such practices have been reported. At the 41st General Assembly many observers noted that the discussions of human rights situations in the committee were marked by more ideological and political conflict than in the past.

The General Assembly will have before it a report from the Secretary-General on the status of the **United Nations Convention against Torture and Other Cruel, Inhuman or Degrading Treatment or Punishment**, which was adopted in 1984. The convention entered into force on June 26, 1987, one month after the requisite twenty states had ratified/acceded to it: Afghanistan, Argentina, Belize, Bulgaria, Byelorussia, Cameroon, Denmark, Egypt, France, Hungary, Mexico, Norway, the Philippines, Senegal, Sweden, Switzerland, Uganda, the Ukrainian SSR, the Soviet Union, and Uruguay. Canada shortly became the twenty-first. A further forty-three states have signed the convention. The resolution adopted by the 41st Assembly expressed satisfaction at the number of states that have ratified or signed the convention, while requesting all those that have not yet done so to become parties as a matter of priority. The General Assembly also expressed its serious concern at the number of reported cases of torture and other cruel, inhuman, or degrading treatment or punishment taking place in various parts of the world [A/Res/41/134].

On adoption of the convention by the General Assembly on December 10, 1984, Secretary-General Javier Pérez de Cuéllar noted: "The world community has thus outlawed once and for all the abominable practice of torture."

The convention obliges states parties to prevent torture in their jurisdictions and to make torture a punishable offense. To oversee implementation of the convention, a Committee against Torture is now to be set up. The committee is to consist of ten experts of recognized competence in the human rights field elected by states parties to serve in their personal capacity. States parties will be required to report to the committee every four years on measures they have taken to give effect to the convention. Further, the committee has the power to examine *ex officio* reliable information alleging the systematic practice of torture in a state party, provided that the state party did not reject this provision upon ratification of the covenant.

If states make declarations under the appropriate articles that they recognize the competence of the committee to do so, the committee may consider complaints (under Article 21) from one state party that another state party is not fulfilling its obligations under the convention, or (under Article 22) from individuals who claim to be victims of a violation of the convention's provisions. Five declarations recognizing the competence of the committee in this regard were necessary before these provisions entered into effect. When such declarations were made by Argentina, Denmark, France, Norway, Sweden, and Switzerland, these provisions entered into force with the convention.

In 1981, having noted with deep concern the acts of torture carried out in various countries, the General Assembly established a **Voluntary Fund for Victims of Torture** to provide assistance to such victims and members of their families. Contributions received by the fund will be detailed in a report to the 42nd Session. The report before the last assembly gave the information about contributions that appears in table 5–1.

The fund's Board of Trustees pointed out the desirability of receiving contributions from governments on a regular basis, and from as wide a spread of governments as possible, in order to be able to give continuing support to certain projects and programs. It also mentioned various publicity activities undertaken to make the fund more widely known. The board's account of the programs supported by the fund showed how the focus of its grants has shifted, from training projects to therapy and rehabilitation projects.

Under a separate agenda item, a working group of the Sixth Committee of the General Assembly will have before it once again the **Draft Body of Principles for the Protection of All Persons under Any Form of Detention or Imprisonment**. In 1975, when the General Assembly adopted the Declaration on the Protection of All Persons from Torture and Other Cruel, Inhuman or Degrading Treatment or Punishment, it called on the Commission on Human Rights to formulate a set of principles intended to afford greater protection against arbitrary detention and to reduce the risk of torture and ill-treatment of detainees. While many of the draft principles are derived from existing international instruments, several are new. The draft principles have been on the U.N.'s agenda for ten years now. Provisional agreement has been reached on the texts of all the principles, and on the definition of the words *arrest,*

Table 5–1
Contributions to the Voluntary Fund for Victims of Torture, by Country
(In U.S. Dollars)

Country	Contribution
Austria	5,000.00
Cameroon	1,344.90
Canada	7,103.00
Denmark	120,402.14
Finland	104,304.95
Federal Republic of Germany	79,032.64
Greece	5,000.00
Ireland	10,872.00
Japan	50,000.00
Liechtenstein	2,958.58
Netherlands	44,799.38
New Zealand	13,400.00
Spain	13,176.09

detained person, imprisoned person, detention, and *imprisonment*. A number of square brackets remain in the text, denoting wording on which agreement has not yet been possible, but some observers note that agreement should be easier to reach now that the definitions have been arrived at. The Secretary-General was asked to circulate to member states the report of the working group from the 41st Session. At the 42nd Session, the working group will need to consider the text as a whole, look for uniform usage of terminology, and eliminate overlaps. Some governments will also seek to ensure that the principles do not fall short of existing international standards, a concern also shared by nongovernmental organizations.

At its 41st Session, in a resolution introduced by Denmark and adopted without a vote, the General Assembly strongly condemned the prevalence of **summary or arbitrary executions**, including extralegal executions, in various parts of the world, and welcomed the renewal of the mandate of the special rapporteur, first appointed by the Commission on Human Rights in 1985 [A/Res/41/144]. The resolution contained an important new paragraph endorsing a recommendation made by the special rapporteur in his 1986 report to the Commission on Human Rights. He proposed that international standards be developed to ensure that proper investigations are conducted by appropriate authorities into all cases of suspicious death, including provisions for adequate autopsy. The recommendation invited the special rapporteur to receive information from appropriate U.N. bodies and other international organizations and to examine the elements to be included in such standards.

In resolution 41/145, introduced by France, the 41st Assembly expressed its concern about the practice of **enforced or involuntary disappearances**. It welcomed the decision of the Commission on Human Rights to experiment with extending the mandate of the Working Group on Enforced or Involuntary Disappearances from one year to two, while maintaining the principle of annual reporting by the group. The working group is pursuing cases of "disappearances" in a number of countries. The working group was established in 1980 to provide an international response to the massive disappearances occurring in Argentina at the time.

In its report to the Commission on Human Rights in 1987, the working group reported on the more than twenty cases of disappearances—still mostly unresolved—it had transmitted to the following eighteen governments: Brazil, Colombia, Cyprus, El Salvador, Guatemala, Guinea, Honduras, Indonesia, Iran, Iraq, Lebanon, Mexico, Nicaragua, Peru, the Philippines, Sri Lanka, and Uruguay. In its concluding observations, the working group stated:

> Making people disappear seems to be a convenient tactic for any Government suppressing insurgence or espousing a policy for stifling dissent, for it takes the victim out of the protective precinct of the law. Disappearances may manifest themselves in many ways. In some instances, arrests are brazenly carried out in broad daylight by uniformed men in the presence of witnesses. In others, the victim suddenly vanishes leaving no clue as to the identity of those responsible. The enforced disappearance of defense lawyers and human rights advocates at the hands of government agents also appears to be on the increase. The same fate is being suffered by relatives of missing persons, particularly those occupying leading positions in organizations for victims of repression. Many others, if not made to disappear, have been menaced or murdered, their offices ransacked and their meetings dispersed. Those who, with exemplary courage, persevere despite such onslaughts, putting their lives in danger while seeking justice for themselves and others, deserve the respect and protection of the international community [Report of the Working Group on Enforced or Involuntary Disappearances, to the Commission on Human Rights, 43rd Session: E/CN.4/1987/15, p. 44].

The group stated that although cooperation with the governments concerned had substantially improved in the course of time, some had consistently failed to respond to the group's communications. It did not specify which.

Country-Specific Issues

The 41st Assembly considered reports from the Commission on Human Rights' rapporteurs or representatives on the human rights situations in Afghanistan, Chile, El Salvador, and Iran. Although there was no report on Guatemala—the Commission having decided in March 1986 to end the mandate of the special rapporteur for Guatemala following the establishment of a popularly elected civilian government the previous January—the 41st Session of the General Assembly nonetheless retained Guatemala on its agenda.

Citing the need for cost-cutting in a time of financial crisis, the U.N. Secretariat decided to circulate the reports on Afghanistan, Chile, and El Salvador in truncated form, rather than in their entirety as documents of the General Assembly. (Owing to its brevity, the report on Iran was not affected.) Not only were the intregral parts of the reports excluded—those providing detailed information on the human rights situation in each of these three countries—but the partial reports were sent to the permanent missions in the original language of submission. This posed particular problems for non-Spanish-speaking missions, since the reports on Chile and El Salvador were in Spanish only. Discussion of human rights in Afghanistan was less affected, since the language of submission was English. The Third Committee demurred, however, requesting the circulation of the reports in their entirety and in all the official languages of the U.N. These became available in January 1987.

Dissatisfaction with the quality of the reports by the Commission on Human Rights' special rapporteurs or representatives has been widespread. One problem has been the lack of experience of many of the rapporteurs when it comes to the exacting task of assessing and reporting on the human rights situations. There has also been confusion about their role—specifically, whether they are to act as mediators between the U.N. and the government or whether they should investigate and establish the facts of the human rights situation. Rapporteurs have understood their mandate and role in different ways. The quality and accuracy of reporting has often suffered when they have given undue emphasis to their mediating role.

Although the emergence in the past several years of the rapporteur system to respond to gross violations of human rights is considered an important development by (among others) nongovernmental organizations working in the human rights field, the system is the most controversial of the U.N. human rights programs. Often, political interests are given greater attention than the actual human rights violations under investigation. For example, the Soviet Union is not happy about the report on Afghanistan, and the attitude of the United States and certain Latin American governments has, some believe, damaged the quality of reporting on Chile, El Salvador, and Guatemala. As a result, the reports have been criticized as biased in favor of the governments in question.

Consideration by the 41st Session of the human rights situations in the five countries was accompanied by considerable government lobbying in capitals as well as at U.N. headquarters. Many were concerned that the situation in Guatemala would not be discussed at all, the mandate of the special representative on El Salvador would be ended, and that there would be insufficient support for a resolution on the situation in Iran. The two situations considered to be "safe," relatively speaking, were Chile and Afghanistan. A similar situation is expected to prevail at the 42nd General Assembly.

A report on the situation of human rights in **Afghanistan** will come before the 42nd Assembly. The report and resolution on Afghanistan were the least controversial of those under consideration by the last Assembly, since the vast majority of U.N. member states oppose Soviet intervention in Afghanistan. Resolution 41/158, introduced and coordinated by Belgium, was adopted by a vote of 89 for, 24 against, with 36 abstentions [A/Res/41/158]. It expressed "grave concern" about the consequences for the civilian population of continuing warfare and called on the parties to the conflict to apply fully the principles and rules of international humanitarian law and to admit humanitarian organizations, in particular the International Committee of the Red Cross (ICRC). It expressed profound distress at the widespread violations of the right to life, liberty, and security of person, including the commonplace practice of torture and summary executions of the opponents of the regime; it was also deeply concerned about the number of persons detained for seeking to exercise their fundamental human rights and freedoms and about detentions under conditions contrary to internationally recognized standards. It urged the authorities in Afghanistan to cooperate with the Commission on Human Rights and its special rapporteur, who had been denied access to Afghanistan. The ICRC has since been allowed to resume its activities; the special rapporteur has recently been invited to visit and is expected to do so in July or August 1987. His report to the 42nd General Assembly will therefore be of particular interest.

There will also be a report on the situation of human rights in **Chile** before the 42nd Session. The report of the special rapporteur [A/41/719] was criticized by some delegations and nongovernmental organizations during the Assembly's 41st Session as misrepresenting and understating the gravity of the human rights situation in Chile. In its resolution the General Assembly did not commend the report but, instead, noted it "with interest" [A/Res/41/161]. Mexico led and coordinated the resolution, which was adopted by 94 in favor, 5 against (Chile, Indonesia, Lebanon, Paraguay, and the United States), with 52 abstentions. The United States, in explaining its "no" vote, stated that it considered the resolution on Chile neither balanced nor constructive and that it failed to reinforce the constructive recommendations made by the special rapporteur.

The Assembly resolution on Chile expressed deep concern at the persistence of serious violations of human rights and called on the government of Chile to restore and respect human rights in conformity with the Universal Declaration of Human Rights and in compliance with the obligations it has assumed under various international instruments. In particular, it called on the government to put an end to states of siege and of emergency; to put an end to torture, intimidation, persecution, abductions, arbitrary arrests, and detention in secret locations; to investigate all reports of death, torture, abductions, and other human rights violations; to investigate and clarify the fate of disappeared persons; to reorganize the police and security forces; to ensure the independence of the judiciary; and to respect the activities of organizations and persons related to the protection and promotion of human rights.

The 42nd Assembly will have before it a provisional report from the special rapporteur on **El Salvador**. While his report to the 41st General Assembly [A/41/710] was "commended" in the resolution, it was also subject to criticism by delegations and some nongovernmental organizations for overreliance on materials prepared by the government of El Salvador and on U.S. sources, for failing to give an accurate picture of continuing violations of human rights, and for ignoring information submitted by nongovernmental organizations.

The text of the Assembly's resolution, coordinated by Peru, underwent considerable revision to accommodate the views of the Contadora Group and the United States. This enabled Costa Rica to withdraw an alternative text it had tabled, which was positive about the human rights situation in El Salvador and would have invited the next Commission on Human Rights to consider the possibility of terminating the mandate of the special rapporteur. The revised text was adopted by a vote of 110 for, none against, with 40 abstentions [A/Res/41/157].

The resolution recognized the importance of the special representative's indication in his report that the question of human rights figured prominently in the policy of the government, which was achieving increasingly significant and commendable results. At the same time, it expressed deep concern that "serious and numerous violations of human rights continued to take place in El Salvador." It also deplored the inability of the judicial system to investigate, prosecute, and punish violations of human rights. The resolution deals largely with the humanization of the conflict and requests the government and the insurgent forces to observe the Geneva Conventions of 1949 and the Additional Protocols of 1977. It also recommends the resumption of dialogue between the government and the opposing forces in order to reach a comprehensive political settlement.

The assembly will consider an interim report from the Commission on Human Rights' Special Representative on **Iran**. His report to the 41st General Assembly [A/41/787] contained no information about the actual situation of human rights in Iran, describing instead his efforts to contact the government of Iran since his appointment in July 1986. The report for this reason was much criticized and provided little guidance for the contents of the resolution on the situation. The resolution, led by Canada, expressed in strong terms its deep concern over specific and detailed allegations of violations of human rights, in particular over those related to the right to life, liberty, and security of person; to freedom from torture, arbitrary arrest, and detention; and to the right to a fair trial and to freedom of thought, conscience, and religion [A/Res/41/159]. It was adopted by 61 votes for, 32 against, with 42 abstentions. The special representative's report to the 43rd Commission on Human Rights

[E/CN.4/1987/23] was more comprehensive and did address the human rights situation in Iran. The resolution was almost defeated through a procedural move by Pakistan. The discussion on Iran at the 42nd General Assembly is expected to continue to evoke sharp responses.

There will be no report on the human rights situation in **Guatemala** before the 42nd Assembly, owing to the decision of the Commission on Human Rights to terminate the mandate of the special rapporteur, but Guatemala will be on the Assembly's agenda once again. Troubled by word of continuing violations of human rights in Guatemala, the 41st Session decided to examine the Guatemalan situation at its next session [A/Res/41/156]. The resolution was adopted by 122 votes for, none against, with 18 abstentions. Guatemala voted in favor.

The Commission on Human Rights at its 1987 session asked the Secretary-General to appoint an expert to assist the new government, through direct contacts, in taking the necessary action for the further restoration of human rights, and requested the expert to report on his contacts and to formulate recommendations for further actions to restore human rights. The commission decided to continue to observe the situation of human rights in Guatemala but has not yet announced an appointment.

At the 41st General Assembly, the United States offered a resolution on the human rights situation in Cuba. Cuba retaliated by offering resolutions on the human rights situation in Puerto Rico and in the United States proper. All texts were withdrawn by mutual agreement on a motion by India. There were similar events at the Commission on Human Rights in February and March 1987. The U.S. Mission has indicated that its initiative will be pursued at the 42nd General Assembly or in other forums.

The Third Committee will also address—as it has for years—the important and pressing question of **public information activities and education in the field of human rights** in the realization that people must know their rights in order to exercise them. Although (with Australia taking the lead) increasingly detailed resolutions have been adopted, urging governments and the United Nations to adopt a more active role in public information and education in this field, little actual progress has been made. The 41st General Assembly requested all member states to accord priority to the dissemination of the Universal Declaration of Human Rights, the International Covenants on Human Rights, and other international conventions in their respective national and local languages. It emphasized the need to make available U.N. materials on human rights in simplified, attractive, and accessible form, in national and local languages, and to make effective use of the mass media and new audio-visual technologies to reach a wider audience, giving priority to children, other young people, and the disadvantaged, especially those in isolated areas. It called upon all relevant parts of the U.N. system, including the specialized agencies and the regional commissions, to assist further in the dissemination of U.N. materials on human rights.

Recommending to all member states that their educational curricula include materials relevant to a comprehensive understanding of human rights issues, it invited them to consider nominating national focal points to which the U.N. could supply copies of relevant materials. The Assembly requested the Secretary-General, within existing resources, to complete work on a draft teaching booklet on human rights and to build up collections of reference works and U.N. materials at each United Nations information center. The Commission on Human Rights reiterated these requests. It also asked the Secretary-General to arrange a public presentation on Human Rights Day, December 10, 1987, of a selection of audio-visual and other materials in the field of human rights prepared by the U.N. Department of Public Information. The presentation is to enable member states to review these materials and to draw public attention to the U.N.'s activities in the field of human rights. In view of the financial crisis and the slow progress that has been made over the years, it remains to be seen whether these relatively simple requests will be implemented.

The question of **East Timor** is the province of the Assembly's Fourth Committee, which deals with decolonization matters. The main question under discussion is that of the self-determination of the East Timorese, to which the human rights situation in East Timor is relevant. Under resolution 37/30, which the General Assembly adopted in 1982, the U.N. Secretary-General was requested "to initiate consultations with all parties directly concerned, with a view to exploring avenues for achieving a comprehensive settlement of the problem" and to report thereon to the General Assembly. Each year since then the Assembly has deferred its consideration of the question until the following year, and it is probable that it will do likewise at the 42nd Session.

In a note of September 12, 1986, the Secretary-General informed the General Assembly that substantive talks undertaken by Indonesia and Portugal under his auspices, with a view to achieving a comprehensive and internationally acceptable settlement of the question, were continuing and that he was not in a position to submit a report to the Assembly but would do so as soon as possible. The General Committee of the Assembly decided to defer a decision on whether or not to include the question of East Timor on the agenda for the 41st Session—leaving open the possibility of discussion of the question if the Secretary-General did submit the report. None was forthcoming. The situation in East Timor did get some mention, however, during the General Assembly's discussion of **New Caledonia**. The Assembly approved the inscription of New Caledonia on the list of non-self-governing territories and will return to this question at its 42nd Session.

The situations in **South Africa** and **Namibia** will be considered in plenary sessions. Assembly resolutions address a wide range of issues here, including civil and political rights. The Assembly has repeatedly demanded the immediate and unconditional release of political prisoners and detainees in South Africa, naming Nelson Mandela and Zephania Mothopeng, in particular. It has strongly condemned the South African authorities for killings, torture, arbitrary mass arrest, and the detention of mass organizations as well as individuals for opposing the apartheid system and the state of emergency. It has also condemned the continued and increasing use of capital punishment in defiance of international protests and appeals. Condemning South Africa for its massive repression of the people of Namibia, the Assembly continues to demand that South Africa immediately release all Namibian political prisoners, account for all "disappeared" Namibians, and release any who are still alive. It has also condemned the introduction of compulsory military service for Namibians.

The question of human rights in the **territories occupied by Israel** will be considered by the Assembly's Special Political Committee, on the basis of the report of the Special Committee to Investigate Israeli Practices Affecting the Human Rights of the Population of the Occupied Territories (a body established by the General Assembly in 1969 and composed of representatives from three member states—Somalia, Sri Lanka, and Yugoslavia). The 41st Assembly condemned the eviction, deportation, expulsion, displacement, and transfer of Arab inhabitants of the Occupied Territories and denial of their right to return. It also condemned collective punishment, mass arrests, administrative detention, and ill-treatment of the Arab population and the ill-treatment and torture of persons under detention.

Since 1981 the Secretary-General has submitted reports for the consideration of the Assembly's Fifth Committee concerning **breaches of the privileges and immunities of United Nations staff members,** many of whom have been arbitrarily imprisoned, abducted, or have died in detention or "disappeared." This is a matter of deep concern to the Secretary-General and the staff. The U.N. Staff Union is concerned over the lack of progress in obtaining clarification or resolution of such cases by the governments concerned, and a group within the union is active on behalf of their colleagues. The staff holds vigils on Human Rights Day each year to draw attention to the plight of their colleagues.

The Secretary-General's report to the 41st General Assembly [A/C.5/41/12] stated that a total of ninety-five cases of arrest and detention or "disappearance" of staff members had been reported from September 1985 to June 1986, the period covered by the report. In the majority of cases, the release of the detainees was achieved or the reasons for their arrests were held to be unrelated to their U.N. duties.

Among the cases still to be resolved, as of the last report, is that of Tesfamariam Zeggai, a staff member of the Economic Commission for Africa (ECA), who has been detained in Ethiopia since March 1982. He is reported to have gone almost blind while in detention. In Afghanistan, eight staff members from UNICEF, UNESCO, UNDP, and FAO were detained; one has died. The cases of two staff members from the Economic Commission for Latin America and the Caribbean (ECLAC) who were killed in Chile in 1973 and 1976, respectively, have not been investigated. Twelve staff members have been detained or have "disappeared" in Syria. Several have been detained by the Israeli authorities in Lebanon, Gaza, and the West Bank. Others have been abducted by "unknown elements" in Lebanon. Cases in Argentina, Guatemala, Jordan, Bahrain, and Equatorial Guinea have still to be resolved. In all these cases, no satisfactory explanation has been given by the governments concerned.

The 41st Assembly [A/Res/41/205] deplored the growing number of cases where the functioning, safety, and well-being of U.N. staff had been affected. It called upon member states currently holding U.N. personnel under arrest or detention to resolve each case with all due speed, and urged the Secretary-General to give priority to the reporting and prompt follow-up of cases of arrest and detention relating to the security and proper functioning of U.N. staff officials. The 42nd Session will have before it a new report by the Secretary-General covering the period September 1986–June 1987.

In the process of reform and renewal currently taking place in the United Nations, supervisory responsibility for human rights activities in the U.N. Secretariat has been transferred to the Director-General of the U.N. Office in Geneva from the office of the Under-Secretary-General for General Assembly and Political Affairs at U.N. headquarters in New York. This change has renewed concern about the need for a well-staffed liaison office for the Human Rights Centre in New York in order to ensure that proper priority is accorded to human rights at U.N. headquarters and to give adequate service to delegations, Secretariat staff, and NGOs throughout the year as well as during the General Assembly. The decision also involved the abolition of a senior assistant secretary-general post previously held by the director of the Centre for Human Rights—something that has been described as a positive step but nonetheless gives rise to concern that abolition of this post could undermine rather than strengthen the United Nations' human rights program.

2. Refugees

"Unless the humanitarian objectives pursued by UNHCR and the political interests guiding Governments move closer in the direction of convergence, at least temporarily, nothing solid or lasting can be achieved for the vast majority of the world's refugees," noted the United Nations High Commissioner for Refugees (UNHCR), Jean-Pierre Hocké [CA/7423, 11/12/86]. Mr. Hocké's words highlight the seemingly intractable problems of refugees around the world.

Although the United Nations system, working with governments and voluntary agencies, has established an honorable record in meeting the humanitarian needs of refugees, there are today more than 11 million refugees in need of a lasting solution to their situation. Yet the three universally recognized durable solutions—**voluntary repatriation, local integration into the country of first asylum, and resettlement to a third country**—remain elusive for the majority of refugees.

The outcome most favored by governments and international organizations, as well as by most refugees, is voluntary repatriation. Although there have been modest successes in 1986 with officially sponsored as well as spontaneous repatriation in Somalia, Sudan, and Honduras, most of the countries with the largest, long-term care and maintenance refugee populations—Pakistan (2.8 million), Iran (2.3 million), Sudan (914,000), and Thailand (405,300)—have not seen significant decreases in the number of refugees [U.S. Committee for Refugees, *World Refugee Survey, 1986* (New York, Washington, D.C.: American Council for Nationalities Service, 1986)].

The second most desirable solution is integration into the country of first asylum. Some countries have advocated humanitarian policies that offer refugees a chance to resume a normal life in the host country. Generous settlement or at least asylum policies found in countries such as Tanzania, Sudan, and Pakistan have permitted refugees to become as economically self-sufficient as possible or to obtain vocational skills to help them in the future. These policies serve the dual purpose of helping refugees lead more normal lives and of lessening the financial burden of assistance. However, many of these countries are facing severe economic problems and development challenges. While sharing what they can, they need the contributions of other U.N. member states to lighten the economic, ecological, social, and political burdens placed on countries of first asylum in the developing world.

Third country resettlement, while continuing to be the most "visible" example of a durable solution, is also regarded as the least desirable and has led to tension between countries of first asylum and receiving states over refugee admission levels. Similarly, the high number of asylum seekers in 1986 going to the industrialized countries of Europe and North America led a number of countries to revise current or adopt stricter immigration policies and procedures. This trend of tightening immigration policies shows no sign of diminishing during 1987. As the Secretary-General noted in his report on the Work of the Organization [A/41/1, Sup.1], "Even if the refugee problem abates somewhat, . . . the United Nations may be called upon to deal with new problems connected with mass migration for economic and related reasons." In this atmosphere of restricted immigration, third country resettlement remains an option for only a small percentage of the world's refugees.

The 42nd Session of the United Nations General Assembly will be examining a number of special issues and concerns regarding refugees as well as receiving institutional reports from the two United Nations organizations established to handle refugee affairs.

The **United Nations High Commissioner for Refugees (UNHCR)** was created in 1949 by General Assembly resolution 319/A/IV to provide for the physical and legal protection of refugees, to facilitate in coordinating efforts to assist refugees, and to engage in repatriation and resettlement programs. Jean-Pierre Hocké of Switzerland assumed the office of the United Nations High Commissioner for Refugees on January 1, 1986.

The UNHCR was originally established for a period of three years. After the initial period, the office has been extended for successive periods of five years by the General Assembly. The question of extension comes up again at the 42nd Session [A/Res/37/196], and it is expected that the General Assembly will decide in favor of UNHCR continuing its humanitarian work.

During the past year, UNHCR has undergone major changes: the structure of its headquarters has been reviewed, its chain of command has been modified, and its working methods and procedures are being revised. One major institutional change, the primacy of the regional bureaus, is a reflection of UNHCR's efforts to become more field-oriented.

Currently, the UNHCR assists some 11.7 million refugees in more than eighty-five countries and is charged with carrying out an assistance program costing $360 million. The ability to meet these financial needs is a most pressing issue from an institutional perspective. At the 41st Session the General Assembly recognized the work of the UNHCR and urged states to contribute generously to its programs [A/Res/41/124].

The second major U.N. agency working with refugees is the **United Nations Relief and Works Agency (UNRWA)**. UNRWA is concerned specifically with assisting Palestinian refugees in the Middle East. Since its creation in 1949, UNRWA has shifted its assistance from administering emergency relief aid to providing services primarily in the fields of education and health care. UNRWA has a noticeably weaker mandate than UNHCR. For example, it is not charged with providing legal protection to the 2.1 million refugees it serves.

Although the 41st Session of the General Assembly extended the mandate of UNRWA until June 30, 1990 [A/Res/41/69], its financial situation still remains precarious. Funds must be approved on a yearly basis by the General Assembly. A working group was set up to assist in ensuring the agency's financial security. For the first time, the budget for 1987 was put together on the basis of a medium-term plan and was estimated at only 5 percent higher than the 1986 budget.

The 42nd Session will hear the reports of Giorgio Giacomelli, the UNRWA commissioner-general; the working group on the financing of UNRWA [A/Res/41/69B]; and the United Nations Conciliation Commission for Palestine [A/Res/41/69A]. The Secretary-General will report on progress made in a number of matters regarding scholarships, education, protection, ration distribution, and the situation of Palestinian refugees living in the Gaza Strip and on the West Bank [A/Res/41/69D to K].

The 41st General Assembly adopted several resolutions about which it requested progress reports at the 42nd Session. The first concerns the Second International Conference on Assistance to Refugees in Africa—ICARA II [A/Res/41/122]. It emphasized the complementarity of refugee aid and development assistance in order to achieve durable solutions for the refugees in Africa. It further requested the UNHCR to keep the situation of refugees in Africa under constant review. The Secretary-General was asked to monitor the follow-up to ICARA II and report back to the General Assembly at the 42nd Session. Many African countries have expressed disappointment with the low level of funding for the ICARA II proposals.

A second resolution [41/123] focused on the measures of assistance provided to South African and Namibian refugee women and children. It called upon governments, intergovernmental organizations, and nongovernmental organizations to intensify solidarity and support for refugee women and children outside South Africa and Namibia. This resolution also requested U.N. bodies to work toward maximizing publicity on the situation of the refugee women and children in these areas. Measures of assistance provided to South African and Namibian refugee women and children will be considered at the 42nd Session. The High Commissioner was asked to report on the current status of assistance programs for student refugees in Southern Africa [A/Res/41/136].

In recent years the General Assembly has requested reports on refugee problems in specific countries. In response to those made by the 41st General Assembly, the High Commissioner will provide information on assistance to refugees in Djibouti, Somalia, and Sudan; emergency assistance to voluntary returnees and displaced persons in Chad; and assistance to displaced persons in Ethiopia [A/Res/41/137, 138, 139, 140, 141].

Both physical and legal protection of refugees are long-standing issues of key concern to the United Nations. One of the most important aspects of the legal protection provided to refugees is the **freedom from refoulement,** or forced repatriation. The 42nd Session will consider the draft resolution, "International Procedures for the Protection of Refugees," which was deferred from the 41st Session to permit consultations on the issue.

During 1986 **armed attacks on refugee camps** and attempts to militarize camps continued. Such attacks were condemned at the 39th Session of the General Assembly [A/Res/39/140]. Nevertheless, the South African military attacked refugee sites in Botswana, Zambia, and Zimbabwe; the Afghan Air Force dropped bombs on refugee villages in Pakistan; and conflicts in the Middle East, Central America, and Southeast Asia have made it difficult for refugees to feel safe even when they have found asylum in another country.

In some cases the barrages are relentless. Since November 1986 refugee camps administered by UNRWA in the Beirut and Tyre areas have been beseiged by fighting between the PLO and Amal militia. Despite calls from the Security Council for an immediate cease-fire, which would allow the safe passage of UNRWA relief convoys into the camps, the situation remains precarious. The condition of the civilians within the camps continues to deteriorate owing to the lack of food and medical and sanitation supplies. A few UNRWA convoys managed to enter some of the camps, but two convoys were attacked, resulting in injuries and death to UNRWA staff. Several governments have sent letters to the Secretary-General expressing concern over this situation, and these will be circulated as documents of the 42nd General Assembly under items 38 and 80 on the preliminary agenda. On March 19, 1987, the Security Council issued a statement expressing concern that the necessary humanitarian assistance had not been reaching the Palestinian refugee camps and described the situation as "critical" [WS/1327, 3/20/87].

The continuing attacks on refugee camps throughout the world demonstrate the need to analyze refugee situations with regard to the root causes of the problem. The Secretary-General himself has shown a special interest in the question of **human rights and mass exoduses.** The United Nations has been conscious of the fact that human rights violations are among the factors leading to mass exoduses of people [E/CN.4/1503]. At the 41st Session of the General Assembly a group of governmental experts presented a final report, "International Cooperation to Avert New Flows of Refugees" [A/41/324, annex]. The General Assembly also welcomed the steps taken by the Secretary-General to establish an early warning system, as mentioned in his report on the work of the organization [A/41/1]. The General Assembly will review the question of human rights and mass exoduses at its 42nd Session.

3. The Information Issue

Issues relating to communications and the dissemination of information have played an important role in the discussions of certain United Nations bodies since the introduction by the Soviet Union of the "Draft Declaration on the Role of the Mass Media" before a general conference of the United Nations Educational, Scientific, and Cultural Organization (UNESCO) in 1974 [UNESCO 18C/35]. The centerpiece of these discussions has been the controversial call by Third World nations for a **New World Information and Communication Order (NWICO).**

The decade-old debate on NWICO emerged from the developing world's perception that there is a marked imbalance in the international flow of news. These nations claim that the developed world—which owns 90 percent of global communications facilities and the four dominant news agencies (United Press International, Associated Press, Agence France-Presse, and Reuters)—

effectively dominates the content of the world press. Third World representatives—with some justification—contend that the news reported by the West reflects only Western priorities: insufficient coverage is given to their own needs and achievements, while all too often their problems and failings are overemphasized or dealt with in an unsympathetic way.

Debate over the definition and implementation of NWICO has been extensive and bitter. Western governments have balked at the concept of an "order" regulating the media and have contended that UNESCO discussions have worked to promote acceptance of greater government control of the press, including the licensing of journalists.

Despite the strong Western opposition, however, interest in the concept of NWICO spread quickly from UNESCO to the General Assembly. "Questions relating to information" has been on the General Assembly's agenda since its 33rd Session, and by the late 1970s resolutions had begun to acknowledge the "potential of the fields of communication . . . to further enhance the economic and social progress of developing countries" and the "essential role of information in the implementation of international decisions concerning economic and social development" [A/Res/33/115C]. In 1978 the General Assembly responded to UNESCO's call for a NWICO by affirming "the need to establish a new, more just, and more effective world information and communication order, intended to strengthen international peace and understanding and based on the free circulation and wider and better-balanced dissemination of information" [A/Res/33/115B].

The debate on the NWICO reflects the conflicting philosophical views of Western, Soviet, and developing countries as to the proper role and function of the state, the individual, and the media in society. Western nations— including the United States—are strongly committed to the free flow of information. The media in these countries operate free of government interference, a condition that allows them to serve as an independent watchdog of the state's activities.

The media model espoused by most of the developing world is based upon far different assumptions as to the proper role of the press. The media in these countries are expected to play a positive role in development by demonstrating support for basic government policies and, in most cases, for the regime itself. In these countries, news is regarded not as information but as a means of guiding social processes. According to Freedom House, "guided" journalism, which may among other things include the licensing of journalists, is practiced in 25 percent of the countries of the world, all of which (with the exception of Poland) are developing countries.

Most of the Soviet-bloc countries, and some others, follow a similar, if more rigorous model. Forty-one percent of the countries of the world operate under this model, which views the media as a servant of the state and an active force for the achievement of state goals. Not only is dissension from government policies not tolerated, but the press must serve as a constant propagandist and progovernment agitator. To quote Malaysian Prime Minister Datuk Seri Mahatir Mohamad in a speech to ASEAN journalists, the role of the press under the "communist" model is to "act as an instrument of revelation, not information" [*Far Eastern Economic Review*, 10/10/85].

Prompted by the withdrawal of the United States (1985) and the United Kingdom (1986), UNESCO has begun to take a far less contentious stand on information issues than previously, concentrating instead on practical ways to build communications infrastructures in the Third World. Third World nations kept their criticism of Western news media out of UNESCO meetings in 1985, for example, and the second United Nations/UNESCO-sponsored roundtable on the New World Information and Communication Order, held in Copenhagen in April 1987, was comparatively free of acrimony.

As a result of UNESCO's disengagement from the NWICO debate, discussion of the political aspects of information has now moved almost entirely into the **United Nations Committee on Information (COI)**, which reports to the General Assembly on information issues. At the same time, the omnibus information resolutions submitted by the committee to the General Assembly have increasingly concentrated on ideological issues, rather than on the policies and activities of the United Nations in the field of public information. In the committee's most recent set of resolutions, for example, 25 percent directly related to NWICO.

The committee is supposed to arrive at its recommendations by consensus, but decreasing Western support for its positions have made this impossible since 1982. The West has had some success in modifying the language of recent information resolutions, however. In the June 1986 meeting of the COI, Western delegates successfully pressed for the adoption of a new formulation—included in UNESCO resolutions since 1982—describing the NWICO as "an evolving and continuing process." The United States voted against the resolution anyway, contending that by emphasizing the dissemination of information on certain political issues—apartheid, Namibia, and the question of Palestine, for example—the resolution imposed limitations on press freedom [A/Res/41/68].

The **United Nations Department of Public Information (DPI)** has come under close scrutiny lately as a result of two recent, widely publicized reports—by the Heritage Foundation and the United States General Accounting Office (GAO)—that have charged that a great many of DPI's information products contain elements of anti-Western propaganda. While DPI responded that the two reports contained numerous errors of fact and logic and that, in the case of the GAO report, the methodology badly skewed the results of the research, the papers' conclusions had harmful repercussions in Washington. The GAO report, in particular, prompted an amendment by Congressman Patrick Swindall (R–Ga.), which reduced the U.S. contribution to the U.N. regular budget by $7.57 million—that portion of the contribution ordinarily designated for DPI. In offering the amendment, Congressman Swindall maintained that the U.N. media arm "has been engaging for some time in the dissemination of information which has a clear bias against the U.S." [UNA-USA, *Washington Weekly Report*, 7/25/86].

The decision by ABC's entertainment division to air the controversial twelve-hour, $32 million miniseries "Amerika" led to protests by the United Nations. The miniseries depicted the organization as a Soviet pawn and the U.N. peacekeeping forces as Gestapo-like troops who enforce a brutal Soviet regime. A spokesman for DPI harshly criticized "Amerika," noting that "The U.N. flag, its logo, and above all the reputation of its peacekeepers are gravely damaged by this kind of nonsense" [*The InterDependent*, 12/86-1/87]. Initially threatening a lawsuit against ABC for the unauthorized use of its logo, the United Nations finally chose to use the opportunity to launch a publicity campaign emphasizing the very positive contributions of its peacekeeping troops. In December 1986 the United Nations Association of the United States (UNA-USA) issued a public statement criticizing the program's treatment of the U.N. over the signatures of former U.S. permanent representatives to the U.N. and U.S. secretaries of state.

Responding to proposals by the Group of High-Level Intergovernmental Experts (the Group of 18) and UNA-USA's blue-ribbon panel on U.N. reform, the Secretary-General established the **Office for Research and the Collection of Information** in March 1987 [ST/SGB/225]. The office is responsible for the collection and dissemination within the Secretariat of political news and information, and is designed to provide the Secretary-General with early warning of situations that threaten to erupt into violent conflict or to create a humanitarian emergency. The office will use the United Nations Information Centres (UNICs)—DPI's "branch offices"—the wire services, and the U.S. media as the principal sources for its data.

The formation of the new unit has been justified as a budget-cutting move because it will consolidate several scattered functions and use fewer staff. For example, the U.N.'s existing Political Information News Service (PINS), formerly administered by a department directed by a Soviet national and, as such, a long-time target of U.S. criticism, has been made part of the new office under an assistant secretary-general, James Jonah of Sierra Leone, who reports directly to the Secretary-General.

Although inspired by U.S. proposals and endorsed by the office of the U.S. Ambassador to the U.N., Vernon Walters, the new information-gathering service has been attacked by U.S. officials, who charge that "manipulation and illegal penetration" of the U.N. Secretariat staff by Soviet government officials led to its formation [*The Washington Times*, 3/3/87]. In addition, several U.S. senators have attempted to block the new unit, charging that it would benefit Soviet spy operations. Responding to this charge, one high-ranking American said, "The whole thing is off the wall. . . . There is no intelligence-gathering function here.

The new office will read newspapers and analyze the stuff that bears on the U.N. This is something that we want to happen" [*The Washington Post*, 4/16/87]. Nevertheless, it is likely that controversy over the Office for Research and the Collection of Information will continue well into the 42nd Session.

Among the Group of 18's recommendations for the improvement of U.N. administrative and financial functioning—adopted by the General Assembly on December 19, 1986 [A/Res/41/213]—are three that will most certainly affect the operations of the Department of Public Information. Recommendation 37(1) calls for a

> thorough review of the function and working methods as well as the policies of the Department of Public Information (DPI) conducted with a view to bringing its role and policies up to date in order to improve the capacity and ability of the Department to provide information on UN activities as approved by the inter-governmental bodies. To this end, the working methods of the Department should be rationalized in order that the funds allocated to the Department should, to a larger extent than hitherto, be used for program activities [A/41/49].

The **review of the activities of DPI** began on March 1, 1987, and consists of three phases: the first, completed in June 1987, examined the department's major fields of activity and its management system, including access to technologies and funding policies. The second stage, to be completed before the 42nd Session of the General Assembly, will examine the distribution of human, technological, and financial resources, and ways and means of achieving more effective policies and programs. The final stage of the reform will consist of the implementation of a new departmental structure and should be in place by the end of 1987 [A/42/234].

Several departments and offices in the Secretariat—for example, the Centre Against Apartheid and the Office of the Commissioner for Namibia— have their own information capabilities and perform certain information dissemination activities on their own. The dispersion of the U.N. public information activities among other Secretariat units makes coordination of these activities difficult and virtually assures some duplication of outputs. In recommendation 37(2), the Group of 18 sought to consolidate these activities in the Department of Public Information.

Finally, recommendation 37(3) called for a long overdue review of the functions and activities of the U.N.'s sixty-eight information centers, which have been established on the ad hoc basis at the request of member states, with the result that there is a high concentration of centers in some areas and relatively few in others. In addition, despite the fact that throughout the U.N.'s history secretaries-general and the General Assembly have repeatedly stressed the need to strengthen the functioning of the UNICs, the centers are generally acknowledged to be ineffective.

The reorganization of the department will be presided over by a new under-secretary-general for public information—Thérèse Paquet-Sévigny—who replaced Under-Secretary-General Yasushi Akashi on March 1, 1987. The new under-secretary-general is Canadian and has extensive experience in the fields of journalism and public relations.

4. Other Social Issues

In response to an earlier proposal by Sri Lanka's Prime Minister R. Premadasa, a former minister of housing, the General Assembly in December 1982 adopted resolution 37/122 designating 1987 as the **International Year for the Shelter of the Homeless (IYSH)**. This resolution also named the Commission on Human Settlements as the U.N. intergovernmental body responsible for organizing the year's activities and the United Nations Centre for Human Settlements (HABITAT) as the secretariat and coordinator of the IYSH-related activities of cooperating organizations and agencies.

The problems of the homeless—although by no means a recent phenomenon—deteriorated rapidly in the late 1970s, largely as a result of population increases and a worldwide recession. It is estimated that up to a billion people—a fifth of the world's population—are inadequately housed, and 100 million have no form of shelter at all. Every day more than fifty thousand people—mostly children—die of malnutrition and other diseases linked to a lack of adequate housing [*Building for the Homeless*, United Nations Department of Public Information, 1987]. Arcot Ramachandran, the executive director of HABITAT, has defined the homeless as "the pavement dwellers, those who sleep in doorways, subways, and recesses of buildings, those made homeless by natural and man-made disasters, and the hundreds of millions who do not have access to safe water and sanitation, who do not have security of tenure, and who because of their poverty are confined in slums and shanty towns" [*Secretariat News*, 1/31/87].

The problems of the homeless are by no means restricted to the developing world. Within industrialized nations, large numbers of homeless have resulted from the deterioration of the inner cities; the increase in the numbers of individuals made unemployable by drug and alcohol addiction; and, in the United States, the policy of some states (notably New York) of "deinstitutionalization," which has released thousands of disturbed people onto the streets. Nevertheless, the problem is much worse in developing countries, where up to 50 percent—in some cities 80 percent—of a country's urban inhabitants live in slums and squatter settlements. As a result, the population of these settlements is increasing at twice the rate of the cities themselves—a yearly growth of 3.5 percent or 49 million [*Building for the Homeless*, United Nations Department of Public Information,

1987]. In rural areas conditions are often not much better, marked by malnutrition and by inadequate sanitation and water supply.

The foundation for U.N. action on behalf of the homeless lies in the **Vancouver Declaration on Human Settlements**, a product of a 1976 United Nations Conference on Human Settlements. The Declaration contains sixty-four recommendations for national action to improve the quality of life for all peoples through the development of human settlements. In 1977 the General Assembly established an intergovernmental Commission on Human Settlements, and it created the United Nations Centre for Human Settlements in Nairobi, Kenya. The center, built upon existing U.N. units dealing with settlement issues, was charged with assisting the commission with the coordination of U.N. settlement activities.

The International Year for the Shelter of the Homeless has two main objectives: to improve the shelter and neighborhoods of some of the poor and disadvantaged by the end of 1987, especially in the developing world; and to demonstrate, by the year 2000, ways and means of continuing to improve the shelter and neighborhoods of the poor and disadvantaged [A/Res/37/221]. The IYSH also seeks to encourage international political commitment to the improvement of shelter for the homeless and to emphasize the importance of shared knowledge and experience among countries as a means to develop practical alternatives for improving the neighborhoods of the poor.

The General Assembly followed resolution 37/221 with the "Plan of Action" for the IYSH, adopted in 1983 [A/Res/38/168]. The plan encouraged countries to be innovative in their attempts to improve the situation of the homeless and suggested that they undertake "shelter demonstration projects" in order to test new approaches to their own basic housing problems. In addition, the international community was urged to review and evaluate the effectiveness of present policy regarding the homeless and to develop improved legislative, organizational, and financial measures to improve the shelter and neighborhoods of the poor.

The $4.3 million budget submitted to the General Assembly by the Secretary-General for IYSH activities was mostly to cover the costs of projects and project support services and was to be met entirely through voluntary contributions. Contributions have ranged from Sri Lanka's pledge of $1 million to Equatorial Guinea's pledge of $624, although the fund is still short of its goal.

As early as 1982, national governments and nongovernmental organizations began to design projects to help the homeless. To date, some four hundred projects have been submitted to HABITAT as offerings for IYSH. The projects fall into eight action areas: shelter, services, construction, employment, legislation and regulation, management and finance, research and education, and training and information. Some projects also involve issue areas, such as the role of women in shelter programs and barriers to women's access to land and credit.

Although the Plan of Action did not call for a major global conference in connection with the year, the tenth session of the commission—held in Nairobi, April 6-16—reviewed and evaluated the activities of the IYSH to date. The session was attended by five hundred delegates representing 104 countries, who set a new agenda to guide national human settlements policies up to the year 2000. The new agenda takes human settlements as the framework of development and points out the need for an "enabling strategy" to mobilize a country's human, material, and financial resources to meet development goals. Delegates to the session informed the commission of short- and long-term measures that had been taken by their countries to alleviate the problems of the homeless, and they identified a number of critical issues in the shelter field. The commission provided guidance for the preparation of the human settlements aspects of the U.N.'s new medium-term plan for the period 1990-95.

In a policy statement before the U.N.'s Economic and Social Council (ECOSOC) in 1985, the Secretary-General proposed that a world conference at the ministerial level be held in 1987 to consider all aspects of **drug abuse and illicit drug trafficking**. The General Assembly acted on the Secretary-General's proposal, and in resolution 40/122 it determined to convene an International Conference on Drug Abuse and Illicit Trafficking (ICDAIT) in Vienna in June 1987. The mandate of the conference was to generate universal action to combat the drug problem in all of its forms at the national, regional, and international levels and to adopt a comprehensive multidisciplinary outline of future activities that focuses on concrete and substantive issues relating to drug use and illicit trafficking.

The U.N. has been involved in drug abuse issues since its earliest days. Under U.N. auspices, several protocols and conventions have been adopted to deal with drug problems. The 1961 Single Convention on Narcotic Drugs, as amended by the 1972 Protocol, consolidated many early instruments dating as far back as the League of Nations; and the 1971 Convention on Psychotropic Substances extended and modernized the drug control system. Most of these early conventions concentrated on limiting and regulating the movement of drugs. ICDAIT, however, moves beyond this to a more positive approach that focuses not only on control of the supply of drugs but also on the prevention of drug abuse in all its forms through international cooperation, drug law enforcement, education and prevention, and treatment of drug-addicted persons.

The United Nations' new focus on the drug abuse problem was prompted by the widespread increase in drug use and a growing recognition of the far-reaching and dangerous economic, social, and health consequences of drug abuse. In an address to ECOSOC, William B. Buffum, at that time Under-Secretary-General for General Assembly and Political Affairs, pointed out that "the problem of drug abuse and trafficking is so severe that the total amount of drugs seized by law enforcement agencies is now being quoted in billions rather than millions [of dollars] . . . and requires strenuous efforts by all of us" [*The InterDependent*, 9-10/86]. At the same time, countries have developed an awareness that the drug menace transcends national and regional boundaries. For example, the Soviet Union, which has in the past attributed drug use to unemployment and poverty bred by capitalist systems, last spring admitted having its own serious drug problem. According to Alexander Vlasov, the minister of Internal Affairs, "The struggle with drug addiction and the criminal activities that go with it has moved up to become one of the top priority tasks of the internal forces" [*The Washington Post*, 1/19/87].

The United States has long struggled with its own well-documented drug problems. According to the U.S. National Institute on Drug Abuse, there are 500,000 heroin addicts and 5.8 million cocaine addicts in the United States. National programs to combat drug abuse, such as those currently being undertaken by the United States and the Soviet Union, are important complements to the U.N. efforts, and most countries have been very supportive of the organization's activities in this area. In fact, despite major cutbacks in U.S. contributions to most U.N. organizations, the U.S. pledge to the United Nations Fund for Drug Abuse Control (UNFDAC), the U.N.'s financer of drug control projects, has actually increased over the past few years and now represents 27 percent of UNFDAC's total monies.

In April 1987 the United Nations Association of the United States of America, in cooperation with several other nongovernmental organizations, convened a conference in Washington on the subject of drug abuse and illicit trafficking in preparation for the international conference. The UNA conference drew together nationally recognized experts on drug abuse problems, governmental leaders, and representatives of nongovernmental organizations. The focus of the conference was on strategies for community action, and participants were encouraged to build support within their communities for activities to reduce the demand for illicit drugs, as well as to urge support for government policies to curb the manufacture of and international traffic in illicit drugs.

The **International Conference on Drug Abuse and Illicit Trafficking** was held in Vienna June 17-26, 1987. The conference drew high-level government ministers, representatives of U.N. agencies and affiliates, and representatives of more than a hundred nongovernmental organizations. The principal document considered by the ICDAIT was the Comprehensive Multidisciplinary Outline (CMO) of future activities, focusing on practical and concrete actions that can be taken at the national, regional, and international level to combat the twin problems of drug abuse and trafficking, and taking advantage of the full potential of the U.N. system in carrying out these activities. Drug-related issues examined at the conference included several major subject areas: eradication of raw material sources for illicit drugs through crop substitution and rural development; restriction of the use of narcotics to medical and scientific purposes; reinforcement of national legislation and international treaties and instruments relating to enforcement and penalties for traffickers and cooperation in dealing with drug abusers; promotion of education and community participation to heighten awareness of the effects of drug abuse. Another important item on the ICDAIT agenda was a progress report on a new draft convention that is intended to close several loopholes in the 1961 Single Convention and the 1971 Convention on Psychotropic Substances by including provisions for tracing, freezing, and forfeiting the proceeds from drug trafficking.

One of the major achievements of the **U.N. Decade for Women** has been the adoption of the Convention on the Elimination of All Forms of Discrimination against Women. The convention, which amounts to a bill of rights for women, was adopted by the General Assembly in 1979 [A/Res/34/180 annex]. As of July 1987 the convention had been signed by 94 countries and ratified or acceded to by 93 countries. Signing the convention obligates governments not to contravene the principles set forth in the specific articles; ratification obligates them to pursue, by all appropriate means, a policy for the elimination of discrimination against women.

The Committee on the Elimination of Discrimination against Women (CEDAW) held its sixth session in Vienna in April 1987. The committee consists of twenty-three experts elected by states party to the convention to consider the progress made in the implementation of the convention and to monitor compliance with its principles. (The United States has signed the convention but has yet to ratify it and therefore cannot nominate an American to serve on CEDAW.) Under the terms of the convention, states parties are obliged to submit reports every four years on measures they have taken to implement the convention. The committee's sixth session examined the status of women in eight countries: Bangladesh, Colombia, France, Greece, Poland, the Republic of Korea, Spain, and Sri Lanka. In addition, it urged states parties to adopt education and public information programs to help eliminate stereotyped concepts of women and encouraged states that have expressed reservations to the convention to reconsider them with a view to withdrawing them. To improve its efficiency, the committee requested ECOSOC—through which it reports to the General Assembly—to approve, on an exceptional basis, eight additional meetings of the committee next year, due to the large number of reports it must consider [E/1987/L20].

The 1987 session of the Commission on the Status of Women was held in New York in January 1987. The commission, which was formed in the early years of the United Nations to promote equality for women, examined the Secretary-General's draft for a proposed systemwide medium-term plan for women and development. The Administrative Committee on Coordination, incorporating the commission's comments, then presented the proposed systemwide medium-term plan to ECOSOC. The proposed plan addresses ways in which the U.N. system can implement the **"forward looking strategies for the advancement of women for the year 2000,"**adopted at Nairobi in 1985. Significantly, for the first time, program activities for the advancement of women are not described as separate activities requiring separate funding and organizational structures but are dealt with as core activities to be integrated into the United Nations' substantive work. An important goal of the plan is to integrate women into the management and decision-making process at the United Nations. In the words of the Secretary-General, "The U.N. cannot present itself to the world as a principal advocate of women's advancement nor claim to be a source of inspiration in this area, if women are not involved in these activities, at high levels of responsibility" [Press Release, SG/SM/3975/Rev.1].

In 1985 the Secretary-General presented to the General Assembly an action program for the improvement of the status of women, which contained detailed work plans in the areas of recruitment, career development, training, conditions of service, and administration of justice. The General Assembly approved this program [A/Res/40/258] and set the target of 30 percent for the representation of women in posts subject to geographical distribution. In resolution 41/111, adopted last year, the General Assembly amended the previous resolution slightly and called upon the Secretary-General and the heads of specialized agencies to establish new targets every five years for the percentage of women in professional and decision-making positions.

A recruitment freeze, instituted in 1986 in response to the organization's financial crisis, has had some effect on hiring practices; but women have nonetheless made significant strides of late—notably the advancement in 1987 of three women (the first ever) to posts at the under-secretary-general level. These are: Dr. Nafis Sadik, Executive Director of the U.N. Fund for Population Activities; Margaret Joan Anstee, Director-General of the U.N. Office in Vienna; and Thérèse Paquet-Sévigny, head of the U.N. Department of Public Information. Prior to the freeze, efforts to increase the number of women in professional posts had been fairly successful: the percentage of professional women in U.N. service jumped from 16.9 percent in 1976 to 24.7 percent in 1986 [A/41/627]. The Secretary-General is expected to present a detailed report on this progress to the General Assembly at its 42nd Session.

In general, the General Assembly will be looking at the progress of the forward-looking strategies through a report by the Secretary-General and through considering the recommendation of ECOSOC that the Committee on the Status of Women meet annually—rather than biannually, as has been suggested for other U.N. committees—until the year 2000 in order to promote the implementation of the strategies. The 42nd General Assembly will also be concerned with the follow-up to several other programs of action, including the Vienna Programme of Action on Aging, and programs on crime, the disabled, and youth.

VI
Legal Issues

Several bodies of the United Nations deal with questions of international law. The International Law Commission seeks to produce conventions that codify international law on important and pressing topics. The International Court of Justice makes determinations on international law in the particular cases before it. Other U.N. bodies draft conventions on the topics within their jurisdiction. However, it is the Sixth Committee that has been specifically entrusted with legal issues. In an age when consensus in any area of international relations is difficult to achieve, the Sixth Committee's task has become especially onerous. Its members squabble over what items should be added to the committee's agenda and then are often unable to achieve progress on the topics chosen. However, real progress on less controversial topics is still within the committee's reach.

1. The International Law Commission

The International Law Commission (ILC) continues to codify the law of nations. Because of strained resources, however, and the commission's failure to reelect one of its special rapporteurs, at its thirty-ninth session in the spring of 1987 the ILC was only able to discuss legal issues relating to two of the topics it has undertaken: the Law of Nonnavigational Uses of International Watercourses, and State Liability for the Injurious Consequences Arising Out of Acts Not Prohibited by International Law.

Faltering work on the **Law of Nonnavigational Uses of International Watercourses** continued. The commission's work on this difficult topic began in 1974 with the establishment of a subcommittee, which sent out a questionnaire to states on the topic. The commission has since then made little progress, in part because of the high turnover of rapporteurs. At the thirty-eighth session, the commission received the second report of the special rapporteur, who recommended various points for the consideration of nine draft articles that the previous rapporteur had prepared and referred to the Drafting Committee in 1983. There was general support in the Sixth Committee for the rapporteur's suggestion that the ILC continue to approach the convention as a framework agreement to provide guidelines for regional cooperation regarding particular international watercourses [A/CN.4/L.410].

The special rapporteur on the topic of **International Liability for Injurious Consequences Arising Out of Acts Not Prohibited by International Law** introduced six preliminary articles to the commission at its thirty-ninth session. The articles were discussed but were not referred to the Drafting Committee.

At the thirty-eighth session, the ILC provisionally adopted and submitted for the review of the Sixth Committee draft articles on the Convention on the **Status of the Diplomatic Courier and the Diplomatic Bag Not Accompanied by the Diplomatic Courier** [A/41/10]. There is still substantial controversy over the articles on the extent of inviolability of the unaccompanied diplomatic and consular bags [A/CN.4/L.410]. Not treated in other conventions, those articles are the essential ones to the draft convention.

Fourteen more draft articles were adopted on the **Jurisdictional Immunities of States and Their Property**. Currently, the draft articles allow exceptions to state immunity for injury to person or property where both the act and injury occurred in the forum, under some conditions for contracts of employment with the state where the contract was to be performed in the forum state, and for certain other commercial contracts unless the parties agree otherwise. Government-to-government arrangements are excluded from the provision on commercial contracts [A/41/10]. Controversy still rages over whether the enumeration in the articles of cases in which there is no immunity will be exclusive [A/CN.4/L.410].

Slow progress was marked in the development of draft articles on **State Responsibility**. The commission has now provisionally adopted on first reading all of parts 1 and 2 of the draft convention, which deal with international responsibility and its extent. Attention is now focused on the last part, which would provide for mandatory dispute settlement through the International Court of Justice or possible referral to compulsory conciliation if a state has not made a reservation to the contrary upon ratifying the convention.

The Sixth Committee continued to consider the ILC's **Draft Code of Offenses against the Rights of Mankind** as a separate agenda item in the 41st General Assembly [See *Issues Before the 41st General Assembly of the United Nations*, p. 142; A/Res/41/75]. The draft code is an ILC project dating back to 1947, when the General Assembly directed the ILC to formulate the principles developed in the Charter and Judgment of the Nuremberg Tribunal. The commission finished its first draft code in 1954, but the Assembly was unable to accept the draft because of difficulties with the closely related Definition of Aggression. In 1974, the Assembly adopted a Definition of Aggression, and in 1981 it authorized the commission to begin work on the code again in light of that definition [See A/41/10, par. 66–70]. At its thirty-eighth session, the commission reviewed the general discussion on the nature of the topic in the special rapporteur's fourth report [A/CN.4/38, and corr. 1–3]. The commission deferred consideration of the revised draft articles in the fourth report. The commission's Drafting Committee was likewise unable to pass upon the rapporteur's earlier drafts of some preliminary articles, as had been intended [*Issues Before the 41st General Assembly of the United Nations*, p. 142; A/41/10, par. 76]. The commission is also still awaiting guidance from the General Assembly on whether the code should provide for international criminal jurisdiction [*See* A/38/10, par. 69(c)(1); A/41/10, par. 185].

The current draft code would include separate provisions on crimes against humanity and war crimes [A/41/10, p. 104, n. 84]. The rapporteur has considered adding apartheid and serious damage to the environment to those crimes against humanity enumerated in the 1954 draft. The draft code also contains articles on crimes against peace that incorporate a definition of aggression. However, the code itself currently applies only to "persons." Nonaligned states wish to expand the code's application to cover conduct by states, but Western and Soviet-bloc states reject the concept of criminal liability of states [*Issues Before the 41st General Assembly of the United Nations*, p. 142]. As some delegations have noted, if the code were applied to states in its current form, it would cause significant legal difficulties [A/C.6/41SR.29].

2. The International Court of Justice

After winning the judgment of the International Court of Justice (World Court) in its case against the United States, **Nicaragua** on July 28, 1986, filed two more actions with the registrar—against its neighbors. It brought suit against **Costa Rica** based on that country's failure to curb border and transborder armed actions by contras originating from that state. A similar claim filed against **Honduras** also denounced the participation of the Honduran military in aiding the contras in armed conflict against the Sandinistas [A/41/4].

On December 22, 1986, the Court delivered its decision in the case of the frontier dispute between **Burkina Faso** (formerly Upper Volta) and the **Republic of Mali**. The judgment considered and applied several rules of international territorial sovereignty law, including intangibility of frontiers inherited from colonization, the principle of *uti possidetis juris* (which gives pre-eminence to legal title over effective possession as a basis of sovereignty), the principles of delimitation, and the right of peoples to self-determination. Both states have accepted and are abiding by the Court's decision.

On May 27, 1987, the Court delivered its advisory opinion on an application for Review of Judgement No. 333 of the U.N. Administrative Tribunal. The Committee on Applications for Review of Administrative

Tribunal Judgements is authorized to ask the Court for advisory opinions on administrative issues by virtue of Article 96 of the U.N. Charter. The case in question, *Yakimetz v. the Secretary-General of the United Nations*, concerns a refusal by the Secretary-General to renew the appointment of, or grant a new appointment to, Vladimir Victorovich Yakimetz, a Secretariat staff member from the Soviet Union who had defected to the United States in 1983. By a vote of 11–3, the Court decided that the Administrative Tribunal did not err on any question of law relating to the U.N. Charter—in effect confirming the action of the Secretary-General.

The Court selected the five judges to compose a chamber to hear the complaint of the **United States against Italy** for the latter's requisition of an Italian subsidiary wholly owned by two U.S. corporations. The U.S. withdrew from the compulsory jurisdiction of the Court last year, but brought the case with Italy's consent under Article 36(1) of the Statute of the Court. The deadline for the filing of the U.S. memorial was May 15, 1987. The Italian countermemorial is due November 16 [U.N. press release, ICJ/454].

The Court also agreed to hear the case, brought jointly by the **Republic of El Salvador** and the **Republic of Honduras**, concerning a land, insular, and maritime frontier dispute between those two states.

Election for a vacancy on the court was scheduled for September 14 following the March 10 death of Guy Ladreit de Lacharrière of France, vice president of the Court. Article 14 of the statute designates the Security Council to set the date of an election to fill a vacancy on the court. To be elected, a candidate must receive a majority in simultaneous voting in the Security Council and the General Assembly. The new elected official will fill the rest of Lacharrière's term, which expires in 1991. Judge Lacharrière had been on the Court since 1982 and had represented France in various U.N. conferences on international law [U.N. press release, SC/4912].

The 42nd General Assembly will also be electing five new members to the Court in November 1987, replacing Brazil, the Soviet Union, Italy, the United States, and Algeria, whose nine-year terms expire on February 5, 1988. The Court is composed of fifteen members, who are elected by an absolute majority of both the Security Council and the General Assembly. Every three years five new judges are elected, and the five who have completed their term step down.

3. Outer Space

As expected, the 41st General Assembly adopted the Committee on the Peaceful Use of Outer Space's (COPUOS) **Draft Principles on Remote Sensing**

by Satellites [A/Res/41/65]. The principles allow for the collection and dissemination of information on a country without its prior consent, contrary to the wishes of many developing countries and the Soviet Union. The principles do provide that remote-sensing activities are to be carried out for the benefit and interests of all countries, giving special consideration to the needs of developing countries.

The Legal Subcommittee of COPUOS continued work on the two items currently on its agenda and deferred consideration of choosing a third. Under the first of its agenda items, on regulating the **use of nuclear power sources in outer space,** the subcommittee considered a revised Canadian working paper [A/AC.105/C.2/L.154/Rev. 1] consisting of five principles. In the last session, the group had approved two of those principles, on notification of reentry and assistance to states. In its latest session, discussion centered on the duties of states to assess the safety of nuclear power sources launched into space and to notify other states of the existence of the power source, guidelines and criteria for safe use of the nuclear power source, and state responsibility for damage caused by space objects with nuclear power sources.

A revised Canadian draft produced at the end of the subcommittee's session increased the number of principles but incorporated few substantive changes [A/AC.105/C.2/L.154/Rev. 2]. The subcommittee has thus far been unable to resolve whether and when a state must inform other states of the presence of a nuclear power source aboard one of its spacecraft. Questions also persist as to the convention's safety standards. Some delegates oppose a provision that would incorporate the standards of COPUOS's Technical Subcommittee and would require their update every ten years [A/AC.105/C.2/L.158/Add.3].

Another working group considered the issues of regulating the **geostationary orbit** and the definition of the **boundary of outer space** [A/AC.105/C.2/L.158/Add.4]. The geostationary orbit is a band about 22,000 miles above the earth's equator in which satellites stay in the same position relative to a fixed point on earth. For this reason, the band is particularly of value for communications satellites. Currently, the International Telecommunications Union assigns slots in the orbit on a first-come, first-served basis. However, developing nations fear that by the time they have developed the technology to put up communications satellites of their own, no more room will be left in the orbit. In addition, equatorial countries lay special claim to the orbit based on their position underneath it. The position of the equatorial countries is reflected in a working paper presented by Ecuador, Colombia, Indonesia, and Kenya. They argue that other countries must ask their consent before placing satellites in the orbit superjacent to their territory.

The developed countries argue that the 1967 Outer Space Treaty applies to the geostationary orbit, so that it is not subject to claims of sovereignty. They argue for an "equal use" principle, which translates in practice into the retention of the Telecommunications Union's first-come, first-served approach. Their position is reflected in the working paper of East Germany [A/AC.105/C.2/L.153].

The current rule is found in Article 33 of the International Telecommunications Union Convention, which provides that "in using frequency bands for radio services members shall bear in mind that radio frequencies and the geostationary satellite orbit are limited natural resources and they must be used efficiently and economically . . . taking into account the special needs of developing countries and the geographical situation of particular countries." In October of 1985 the union, through the secretary-general of the World Administrative Radio Conference, communicated to the Secretariat its determination that it was incompetent to judge the claims of the developing countries [A/AC.105/370].

In the latest session, the chairman identified similarities between the two working papers and arranged for the preparation of a draft that would incorporate those similarities. It is unclear how that draft will find an effective compromise between the principle of first-come, first-served and the demands of the equatorial and developing countries.

The working group also continued to consider the proposal of the Soviet Union that the boundary of outer space be defined as beginning at 110 kilometers above sea level. (Under the Soviet view, the geostationary orbit is therefore definitely a part of outer space and subject to the 1967 treaty.) In addition, the Soviet Union seeks assurances of a right of "innocent passage" to outer space. The Western states have argued that a definition is unnecessary.

4. Economic Relations

At the 41st Assembly the United Nations Commission on International Trade Law (UNCITRAL) again received the acclaim of developed and developing nations —this time for a novel proposal in connection with the almost finished **Convention on International Bills of Exchange and International Promissory Notes**. It suggested that the convention be adopted through the General Assembly rather than through a diplomatic conference [A/41/17, A/C.6/41/SR.3]. No previous convention had been adopted in such a manner. The proposal was generally supported in the Sixth Committee because the subject matter of the treaty is not so controversial as to require an expensive and time-consuming diplomatic conference [A/C.6/41/SR.4].

UNCITRAL also reported to the 41st Assembly that its draft legal guide on **electronic funds transfers** was well received by governments and international organizations, and that the commission had authorized the Secretariat to publish it in all official U.N. languages. The commission plans to take up the formulation of model legal rules in a working group in late 1987 [A/C.6/41/SR.3].

A working group of the commission also continued drawing up uniform legal rules on international contract practices regarding the **liability of operators of transport terminals** [A/CN.9/275].

As the commission expected, one of its earlier efforts, the **United Nations Convention on Contracts for the International Sale of Goods,** entered into force in December 1986, when Italy, China, and the United States deposited their instruments of ratification with the U.N. The convention attempts to ease trade dispute settlement and encourage foreign trade by standardizing international law in the area of buyer and seller rights and obligations [*Department of State Bulletin, 3/87, p. 55*].

UNCITRAL also accepted the Secretary-General's proposal that it undertake several joint projects with the working group on the **New International Economic Order (NIEO).** This year, the working group submitted for the commission's review a report on its progress on the draft legal guide on drawing up international contracts for the construction of industrial works. The commission planned to review the working group's draft in its twentieth session. In addition, it planned to take up an analysis of procurement with the working group as their first joint effort [A/C.6/41/SR.3].

As for the principles on the NIEO, dispute continued within the Sixth Committee as to which body should undertake drafting them, or whether they should be drafted at all [A/C.6/41/SR.47]. The General Assembly again adopted a resolution calling for the Sixth Committee to find procedures for development of the NIEO [A/Res/41/73].

5. Peace and Security

With the Soviet concession that it would not call for a world treaty on the non-use of force, the Special Committee on Enhancing the Effectiveness of the Principle of Non-use of Force in International Relations made swift progress in preparing a **draft declaration** on the topic [A/42/41]. The chairman of the committee, Tullio Treves of Italy, prepared the draft on the basis of two working papers, one submitted by Belgium, France, West Germany, Italy, Japan, Spain, and the United Kingdom; the other by Benin, Cyprus, Ecuador, Egypt, and Nepal. The draft will be considered in the next session.

The Sixth Committee's approval could end a decade of debate on the issue. The draft declaration reaffirms the Charter, the Definition of Aggression, and the Manila Declaration on the Peaceful Settlement of Disputes, and declares that it neither enlarges nor diminishes the scope of provisions of the Charter concerning cases in which the use of force is lawful. The declaration incorporates the wishes of the nonaligned countries with denunciations of the use of mercenaries, propaganda, economic coercion, intervention, and wars of aggression. It makes a concession to the Soviets with a nod toward disarmament in the preamble and a paragraph in the body declaring that states "should take effective measures in order to . . . prevent an arms race in outer space and to reverse it on earth." The United States is satisfied with the draft declaration as a termination of the item on the Special Committee's agenda.

The Subcommittee on **Good Neighborliness** continued to experience difficulty in defining the principle. Some delegations expressed doubt as to whether a separate principle of good neighborliness existed [A/C.6/41/SR.50]. Others squabbled over whether the principle should be defined to cover border state relations or whether the concept was broader [A/C.6/41/L.14]. A resolution passed by the Sixth Committee altered the existing definition of the principle to cover the relations of states not in geographic proximity [A/C.6/41/L.17].

6.   Effectiveness of the Organization

The Special Committee on the Charter of the United Nations and on the Strengthening of the Role of the Organization continues to dissatisfy all those who expect it to live up to its name. The committee is unable to make the sweeping changes necessary to strengthen the role of the organization without losing the support of members who do not want the organization to be more powerful. Thus, nonaligned states complain that the Special Committee provides support for detractors of the U.N. who claim that the organization is ineffective [A/C.6/41/SR.17]. Other members note that at least part of the committee's ineffectiveness is attributable to the duplication of its efforts in other U.N. forums [A/C.6/SR.18].

Of the committee's three projects, its work on the **rationalization of procedures** is the most innocuous and the most duplicated. The committee continues to consider the revised working paper of the United Kingdom and France, and members continue to criticize that paper for dealing only with the General Assembly [A/C.6/41/SR.16]. Rationalization is being discussed outside the Sixth Committee by the Asian-African Legal Consultative Committee (AALCC) Working Group of the Whole and by the Working Group of High-Level Intergovernmental Experts to Review the Efficiency of the Administrative and Financial Functioning of the United Nations [A/C.6/41/SR.16]. A move to consider the AALCC's findings was rejected as a waste of time [A/42/33, par. 23].

The committee also continues to labor over two projects related to the **peaceful settlement of disputes.** Work continued on a draft handbook on the topic, although the Secretariat delayed convening the Consultative Group until all the handbook's sections had been completed [A/42/43, par. 11]. Consideration by the Special Committee of the creation of a commission for the peaceful settlement of disputes remained tied to a revised working paper of Romania.

The Romanian working paper has been so weakened to appease its critics that it is now subject to attack as being devoid of substance.

The Special Committee also continued to consider the two working papers on the **maintenance of international peace and security**. The older of the draft declarations, submitted and revised by West Germany, Italy, Japan, New Zealand, Spain, and Belgium, provides that the Security Council or the General Assembly should resort to the International Court of Justice for advisory opinions to help in resolving situations threatening international peace and security, that the Security Council should widen its fact-finding efforts, and that more information on threatening situations should be provided to the Council and the Assembly. It is subject to criticism by delegations in the Eastern bloc, who argue that too much power is granted to the General Assembly under the scheme [A/C.6/41/SR.18]. The draft declaration of Czechoslovakia, Poland, and East Germany places emphasis on the existing scheme of the Charter and the duties of the Security Council. It also contains controversial provisions on disarmament and the non-use of force.

The committee came close to adopting the Western paper in the last session, but the Soviet bloc refused to support that draft declaration in lieu of its own. There is little likelihood of merging the two papers, so discussion in the next session is likely to focus on whether adoption of one draft precludes subsequent adoption of another.

7. Violence by Individuals and Groups

The Sixth Committee will approach its biennial discussion of **terrorism** in an atmosphere of considerable discord in the next session. In 1985 the General Assembly adopted resolution 40/61 unequivocally condemning "all acts, methods and practices of terrorism wherever and by whomever committed," as criminal [A/Res/40/61]. But a December 1986 letter from the Syrian foreign minister, Farouk Al-Sharaa, to the Secretary-General calls for a United Nations conference to find an internationally acceptable distinction between terrorism and racism [A/42/58]. The Syrian proposal asserts that the failure to distinguish national liberation movements from terrorism "allows scope for the forces of imperialism and racism . . . to resort to the pretext of combating terrorism in order to commit aggression against independent states."

There is some support in the Sixth Committee for reviving the Ad Hoc Committee on International Terrorism. The committee has been at a standstill since 1979 because Western members seek a general condemnation of terrorism, whereas Eastern-bloc, Arab, and nonaligned nations favor recognition for national liberation movements, as the latest Syrian proposal contemplates [*Issues Before the 41st General Assembly of the United Nations*, p. 145]. The United States will seek "implementation" of resolution 40/61 and calls for increased bilateral and multilateral cooperation to combat terrorism.

The U.S. government, however, decided against seeking ratification of part of a major revision of the 1949 Geneva Conventions on treatment of combatants and war victims. President Reagan said he would not submit Protocol 1 because it would legitimize insurgent movements and terrorist groups by giving them legal status and protection as combatants and prisoners of war. Protocol 2, which deals with internal conflicts, is awaiting consideration by the U.S. Senate.

The work of the Ad Hoc Commmittee on the Drafting of an International **Convention against the Recruitment, Use, Financing and Training of Mercenaries** was deferred from 1986 to this year [A/C.6/41/SR.25]. As previously, discussion within the last session of the Sixth Committee focused on the applicable definition of a mercenary and whether states shall be held liable for the acts of mercenaries. The position of the Soviet and nonaligned countries is that the definition of a mercenary should be broader than that encompassed in Article 47, paragraph 2 of the Additional Protocol to the 1949 Geneva Conventions. The definition in the current draft convention is limited to those individuals who are not nationals or residents of a state party to the conflict and who are "promised . . . on behalf of a party to the conflict, material compensation substantially in excess of that paid to combatants . . . in the armed forces of that party." The Soviet and nonaligned states would like both qualifications eliminated [A/C.6/41/SR.25].

There is apparent agreement that states must refrain from training mercenaries and from allowing nongovernmental organizations (NGOs) to engage in such training within their territory [A/42/42]. The U.S. has taken a cautious position on the development of the convention because of its potential application to the contra movement in Nicaragua.

Every year the Sixth Committee reviews a report of the Secretary-General on measures to enhance the **protection, security, and safety of diplomatic and consular missions and representatives.** Last year eight states made reports in connection with the protection, security, and safety of their diplomatic and counsular missions and representatives to the Secretary-General. However, the Secretary-General was concerned that a number of incidents had gone unreported [A/C.6/41/SR.22]. In the future, it was suggested, the Secretariat should send a form to each state requiring a response even if the state had not experienced any incidents. There was also some support for requiring reports to be more detailed [A/C.6/41/SR.22].

8. International Organizations and Host Country Relations

On the recommendation of the Legal Counsel [A/C.6/41/SR.45] and the Sixth Committee [A/C.6/41/SR.55], the Secretary-General signed the **Vienna Convention** on the Law of Treaties between States and International Organizations. The Sixth Committee resolution recommending signature followed debate in which Eastern-bloc states argued against signature because the treaty provided for compulsory jurisdiction of the International Court of Justice [A/C.6/41/SR.46]. Other controversial provisions were those allowing for the invalidation of treaties contrary to peremptory norms of *jus cogens* (inalienable rules) [A/C.6/41/SR.45], and several articles paralleling those in the Vienna Convention on the Law of Treaties between States, which provide that treaties cannot create obligations for parties without their consent [A/C.6/41/SR.46].

The Sixth Committee again passed a resolution calling on states to accede to the Vienna Convention on the Representation of States in Their Relations with International Organizations and to grant the privileges and immunities provided for therein, along with observer status, to **national liberation movements** recognized by the Organization for African Unity or the League of Arab States [A/C.6/41/SR.47]. Western states opposed the resolution, noting that the 1975 convention was not yet in force as of the end of 1985 because it had failed to receive sufficient support, and that at any rate the convention did not refer at all to the status of national liberation movements.

Discussion within the Committee on Relations with the Host Country focused on the U.S. demand that the three Soviet missions make **phased reductions in their permanent staff**. The United States required that the total permanent staff be reduced from 275 to 170 by April of 1988. The first of the four reduction deadlines was October of 1986. The Legal Counsel expressed its opinion to the committee that sending states had a duty to assure that the size of their missions did not exceed what was "reasonable and normal," but that the Vienna Convention on the Representation of States in their Relations with International Organizations and the U.N. Headquarters Agreement required that disputes between the sending country and the host state be resolved through consultation [A/41/26]. The Soviet missions protested the U.S. moves before the committee [A/41/26] and to the Secretary-General [A/41/207; A/41/208; 1/41/209] but have thus far complied with the staff reduction deadlines.

9. Other Legal Developments

The International Atomic Energy Association (IAEA) rapidly responded to the April 1986 Chernobyl disaster by completing by September of that year two **draft conventions on state responses to nuclear accidents**. The Convention on Early Notification of a Nuclear Accident provides for notification of significant past or anticipated transboundary releases resulting from accidents of nuclear reactors, nuclear waste management facilities, and "the use of radio-isotopes for power generation in space objects." The convention may therefore overlap with the COPUOS draft convention on nuclear power sources in space [see earlier section on outer space]. The convention specifies the sort of information that must be made available and requires that states parties must have designated contact authorities continuously available to other states or the IAEA. Information provided under the convention shall be made generally available except where it has been given in confidence by a state party.

The Convention on Assistance in the Case of a Nuclear Accident or Radiological Emergency would provide general rules for states asking and providing assistance after an accident. It would allow for a state to ask assistance of other states whether the accident had originated within its territory or elsewhere. The convention includes provisions for maintaining the confidentiality of both the sending and the receiving states.

Each convention will enter into force after three states have ratified it. Both contain mandatory dispute settlement procedures to which an acceding state can make a reservation [IAEA Final Documents, Resolutions, and Conventions, 9/24–26/86].

The Sixth Committee came close to finalizing a **Draft Body of Principles for the Protection of All Persons under any Form of Detention or Imprisonment** and hopes to finish its drafting in the next session. The General Assembly adopted a **Declaration on Social and Legal Principles Relating to the Protection and Welfare of Children** [A/Res/41/85] providing guidelines for legislation by states. The United States was among those pushing for the stringent standards incorporated in the declaration. The declaration covers only those institutions recognized and regulated by the domestic law of a state for foster placement and adoption of children.

VII
Administration and Budget

1. U.N. Budget and Finance

There were 142 items on the agenda of last year's General Assembly, but, as one Asian diplomat noted, there was "only one issue: money" [*The New York Times*, 9/16/86]. Financial questions have concerned the United Nations for many years; in 1986, however—amid talk of "payless paydays" and major cutbacks in programming—the organization's longtime financial instability reached crisis proportions.

The U.N.'s current **financial emergency** began in late 1985, when U.N. officials learned that the United States—assessed at 25 percent of the regular budget ($210 million out of $841 million)—intended to withhold a large portion of its contribution for U.S. fiscal year 1987 (U.N. calendar year 1986). By that time, the cumulative withholdings and late payments of other members had already depleted the organization's slim cash reserves.

Secretary-General Javier Pérez de Cuéllar moved swiftly to **cut U.N. spending** in early 1986, imposing economies in travel, documentation, meetings, hiring, and outside consultancies. These economies yielded savings of about $70 million in 1986 and are expected to save an additional $85 million in 1987. Some member states responded to the crisis as well: In April 1986 the Soviet Union made a special voluntary contribution of $10 million to the regular budget, and both Argentina and Brazil—struggling with their own financial crises—managed to pay their arrearages. In the fall, the Chinese government paid $4.3 million that it had withheld from bonds issued in the 1960s to pay for peacekeeping forces in the Congo, while asserting that it did not wish to retract its original objections to the debt issue.

Despite these efforts, the U.S. Congress continued to slash away at its contribution to the U.N. regular budget, and the future of the U.N. began to look even more bleak as the year progressed. Initially, the Reagan administration appeared to be behind the cuts. Testifying before the House Committee on Foreign Affairs in March 1986, Assistant Secretary of State for International Organization Affairs Alan Keyes said, "We see this situation as providing the leverage needed to press forcefully for program and budget forms . . . . We should not engage in a fruitless search to escape from cutbacks that cannot be avoided. The U.S. wants to use this situation as an opportunity to achieve the fundamental reforms required to renew the efficiency of the United Nations agencies" [*The InterDependent*, 9–10/86].

In the fall, however, fearing the loss of some of its leverage at the world body as well as of U.S. jobs (distribution of U.N. posts is linked to contribution levels), the Reagan administration mounted a campaign to restore some of the congressional cuts. These efforts were unsuccessful, and the 1986 U.S. contribution to the United Nations regular budget totaled $100 million, less than half of its assessment of $210 million.

Congress justified most of its U.N. withholdings as a means of pressuring the world body to improve its efficiency and to reform what the United States regarded as flawed administrative and budgetary processes. The largest of these cuts—$42 million—came about as a result of the **Kassebaum Amendment,** which placed a ceiling of 20 percent on the United States contribution to the U.N. regular budget unless the organization took steps to adopt weighted voting on budgetary matters to give a greater say to the largest contributors. Still other cuts were made to protest the United Nations' allegedly anti-Western attitudes, among them the Sundquist Amendment, which was aimed at U.N. personnel who are required by their governments to pay part of their salaries to their national missions; and the Swindall Amendment, which targeted allegedly biased U.N. publications and broadcasts. The Sundquist and Swindall amendments reduced payments by $17.5 million.

A further blow took the form of a motion, approved by the Senate Appropriations Committee, to defer until October 1987 $130 million in payments to all international organizations, including the North Atlantic Treaty Organization (NATO) and the Organization for Economic Cooperation and Development (OECD). Contributions to the U.N. regular budget were not affected by the deferral; however, $87.1 million of the amount consisted of funds previously earmarked for U.N. specialized agencies.

Administrative and budgetary reform has been a vexing problem at the U.N. for decades, but the financial crisis that threatened to close the organization's doors in late 1986 made progress on reform a matter of urgency. In December 1985, responding to an initiative by the Japan delegation, the General Assembly passed resolution 40/237 establishing an eighteen-member Group of High-Level Intergovernmental Experts to conduct a "thorough review of the administrative and financial matters of the United Nations with a view to identifying measures for further improving the efficiency of its administrative and financial functioning." The group was asked to focus on medium and long-term goals for establishing organizational efficiency and effectiveness, paying particular attention to the issues of priority-setting, management, the content and level of progam budgets, and the establishment of an orderly process for reaching consensus—or at least broad agreement—on major budgetary questions.

The difficulty in reaching agreement on budgetary questions has in large part been caused by persisting differences between two major groups at the U.N.: on the one side the major donors who want greater influence, especially on budgetary matters; and on the other side the smaller, mostly Third World members who want to preserve the one-nation one-vote principle. The panel saw the need to acknowledge such differences from the first, agreeing that the U.N. would benefit from "budget procedures which would associate Member States more actively with the preparation of the medium-term plan and the programme budget and which would better facilitate broad agreement among Member States on budgetary matters, while preserving the principle of sovereign equality of States enshrined in the Charter" [A/41/49].

In mid-August, after a series of closed session meetings, the group released a forty-page report containing a large number of specific recommendations aimed at improving the overall efficiency of the organization. Among these were proposals for structural adjustments, cutbacks in staff and spending, and a call to the United States and other contributors to pay promptly their assessed share of the U.N. budget. That the Group of 18, with so many competing priorities and individual agendas, was able to agree on so many specific proposals for reform was widely regarded as encouraging. Nonetheless, the group was unable to agree on a single set of budgetary procedures and, in fact, submitted three alternative solutions.

On December 19, 1986, the United Nations General Assembly adopted by consensus resolution 41/213, containing the elements of a plan for reforming a wide range of administrative and budgetary practices of the U.N. The reform resolution draws heavily on the recommendations of the Group of 18, which are to be fleshed out by the Secretary-General, approved by the General Assembly, and put into effect over the next three years. A crucial and hard-won element of the reform concerns a **modified budget process**, similar to the one recommended by a majority of the Group of 18. That this was a recommendation of an international U.N. Management and Decision-Making panel of current and former government leaders called together by the United Nations Association of the United States of America [*Leadership in the U.N.: The Role of the Secretary-General and the Member States*, 12/7/87] influenced the General Assembly's surprise acceptance of the new procedure in the final hours of the session [*The InterDependent*, 2–3/87].

The most significant change in the new budgetary procedure concerns the expanded role it gives to the twenty-one-member **Committee for Programme and Coordination** (CPC)—a body that traditionally operates by consensus and has involved the major powers. Under the new procedures, the Secretary-General will work closely with the CPC on the preparation of his introduction to the medium-term plan. (The medium-term plan sets out projected program developments at six-year intervals and is accompanied by an introductory section that sets the overall direction for the organization's activities over this period.)

In addition, the biennial budgeting process will henceforth begin with CPC's setting a ceiling for the budget. The committee will also agree on a contingency fund—expressed as a proportion of total budget—for add-ons to support programs approved by the General Assembly after the budget has been finalized. Major donor countries have been highly critical of what they view as an excessive use of add-ons. Traditionally, budget ceiling and spending priorities have been set by majority vote of the General Assembly. The move to define these limits by consensus in the CPC means major donors would have a greater voice in U.N. budgetary decisions than in the past.

The revamped budget process adopted by the General Assembly consists of two sequential parts. In off-budget years it calls for the Secretary-General to submit a budget outline to the CPC and the **Advisory Committee on Administrative and Budgetary Questions (ACABQ)** containing his estimate of resources required for the biennium; priorities; the rate of growth—positive or negative—associated with the activities proposed; and a contingency fund for meeting any emergency expenses unforeseen at the time the budget is adopted. The CPC, acting as a kind of gatekeeper for the General Assembly, then reviews the outline, makes whatever changes it considers necessary, and submits this to the General Assembly, through the Fifth Committee, for its approval. The Assembly's decision provides the Secretary-General with guidance and a mandate to develop a full budget proposal. In budget years the Secretary-General returns to the CPC with the budget he has developed on the basis of the committee and the General Assembly's reactions to the outline described above. This fully developed budget is also submitted to the ACABQ. Both bodies submit their recommendations to the General Assembly through the Fifth Committee, and it is on this basis that the Assembly takes final action.

By mid-1987 many observers saw that to bring about broader agreement on the level and content of the organization's budget, several ingredients had to be present. First, to avoid divisions that could prevent the CPC from reaching consensus and thus make it unable to play a gatekeeper role, members would have to avoid too broad an application of the consensus rule by focusing primarily upon the overall level and growth of the budget and the allocation of priorities among major programs. Second, since the opportunity of major donors to influence the budget is directly proportionate to their ability to reach agreement with the other members, they will have to engage in the kind of give and take that will make the committee a success. Third, to avoid the breakdown in consensus that triggered the budget crisis, developing-country members will have to resist the temptation to rely on their numerical advantage in the General Assembly to achieve results they failed to get by consensus in the CPC. Finally, the Secretary-General and his senior staff will have to take a direct role in shaping and proposing programs—and in providing the kind of overall programmatic leadership that the unwieldiness of the U.N.'s intergovernmental bodies has always required but that few Secretaries-General have been willing to take on.

The reform resolution was greeted with praise on all sides. In a statement issued by the White House on December 22, 1986, President Reagan described the General Assembly's actions as "an historic step to adopt sweeping reforms of [the U.N.'s] organizations and methods of operation." Although not formally acknowledged at the time, there was a tacit understanding among participants in the negotiations that resulted in resolution 41/213 that any serious efforts by the U.N. toward reform would encourage the United States to end its withholdings from the U.N. budget. Passage of the resolution has therefore increased the possibility of a return to nearly full payment by the United States of its assessed contributions. (The United States will undoubtedly continue to hold back funding—as it has for many years—from U.N. programs that it finds objectionable, such as those supporting the Palestine Liberation Organization.)

Shortly after the General Assembly passed its resolution, President Reagan reportedly telephoned Secretary-General Javier Pérez de Cuéllar to offer his congratulations and to promise that he would personally seek restoration of the cuts in 1987. In the following months Secretary of State George Shultz, Assistant Secretary of State for International Organization Affairs Alan Keyes, and U.S. Permanent Representative to the U.N. General Vernon Walters each testified to the administration's satisfaction with the U.N.'s progress toward reform and about its desire to see Congress restore the full assessment. Only one nagging omission undermined the administration's position: its failure to include full funding for the U.N. in its budget request to Congress. Administration officials claim that the December 19 agreement had come too late for the State Department to amend its budget request but that a supplemental request for U.N. funding would be submitted in the near future.

In May 1987 the Senate Foreign Relations Committee approved language modifying the Kassebaum Amendment, recommending nearly full payment of U.S. contributions to the U.N. and its specialized agencies in fiscal year 1987. The modifications—proposed by the original amendment's author, Senator Nancy Kassebaum (R-Kans.)—provides for a three-part disbursement of U.S. contributions that would be contingent upon the progress of reform at the U.N. Under the new practice, the President would have authority to contribute the first 40 percent of the U.S. appropriation for 1987 after October 1, 1987, which is the beginning of U.S. fiscal year 1988. If the President reports to Congress that the consensus-based budgetary procedures outlined by the General Assembly are being implemented, a second 40 percent would be contributed after the Assembly's adjournment around December 15. The final 20 percent would become payable thirty days after the President had made his report to Congress. During that period Congress would have the option of passing a joint resolution prohibiting the final payment. Such a resolution would require the President's signature to become law. The entire process would expire in September of 1989.

Some within Congress and the administration have expressed unease about restoring the cuts before they are able to see whether the new budget mechanism is working. Consequently, the first meeting of the CPC since the passage of resolution 41/213, held between April 29 and May 29, attracted an unusual degree of American attention. As one top administration official noted prior to the meeting: "If, in fact, they have to come to a vote on even one item, or if they cannot begin work on establishing a ceiling for the budget, then we will have to throw out the whole thing and start all over again." With twice as many countries observing this year's meeting as had last year, and the Secretary-General himself in attendance for the first time, delegates to the CPC could not fail to be aware of the significance of their actions for the future of the U.N.

Officials at the U.N. breathed a sigh of relief when the U.S. Mission announced in the early weeks of June that it considered the meeting to have been "a major accomplishment." Although the CPC had deferred the difficult decision on a budget ceiling for the organization until a special resumed session scheduled for September, it had been able to adopt by consensus budgetary recommendations in areas ranging from public information to the evaluation of electronic data-processing.

Nevertheless, congressional aides have made it clear that the fate of U.N. funding depends not so much on the progress of U.N. reform as on U.S. fiscal considerations. "If we had no budget constraints, the U.S. might pay its arrears as well as the assessment," commented John Shank, Minority Clerk of the Senate Subcommittee on Appropriations. "But in recent years, U.S. policy has followed the budget and not the other way around. If the administration is unwilling to cut other programs or to raise revenues, then we will get nowhere fast." Not only was it unlikely that the U.N. would receive full funding this year, Shank predicted, but there would probably be little change until after the 1988 election year.

2. Personnel and Administration

Although United Nations personnel issues were to some extent overshadowed in 1986 by the more pressing matter of the financial crisis, the special attention paid to them by the eighteen-member **Group of High-Level Intergovernmental Experts** and the obvious effect of austerity measures on salary levels, pensions, and recruitment ensures that these issues will be in the spotlight during the 42nd Session of the General Assembly.

The most striking recommendations of the Group of 18—endorsed in December 1986 by the General Assembly [A/Res/41/231]—concern the **Secretariat,** which the report labels "complex, fragmented, and top heavy." The report calls for a greatly simplified Secretariat structure and for the establishment of clearer lines of authority and accountability. To overcome duplication and waste, it also calls for far greater coordination of the work of U.N. departments, offices, and units and for the consolidation, whenever feasible, of U.N. offices located in the same city or country.

With regard to staff, the group called for a 15 percent reduction in posts funded by the regular budget and a 25 percent reduction in the number of **under-secretary-general and assistant secretary-general posts** over the next three years —reductions that could result in the elimination of 1,700 jobs. In fact, Secretary-General Javier Pérez de Cuéllar had taken steps along these lines some weeks previously. As part of a cost-cutting reorganization, the U.N.'s top official told fourteen high-level staff members that their contracts would not be renewed at the end of the year. Some of the positions were to be eliminated completely. Under the United Nations system, the twenty-seven under-secretaries-general (USG) and twenty-eight assistant secretaries-general (ASG) are appointed by the Secretary-General for terms ranging from one to three years. There is no guarantee that their contracts will be renewed at the end of their terms. U.S. officials, who have pushed hard for such cuts, praised the step highly. According to one U.S. Mission official, "It's the first big chop following the American push for reform, and there will be more" [*The New York Times*, 11/4/86].

Other proposals of the Group of 18 attempt to objectify **recruitment procedures** through the use of competitive exams at the P-1 though P-3 levels and drafting tests at the P-4 and P-5 levels in an effort to improve the quality of a staff that has been characterized as "inadequate." The report urged that the Secretary-General be guided in the implementation of these reforms by such concerns as equitable geographical distribution, the avoidance of negative effects on programs, and the continuing need to recruit new staff, particularly at the junior officer levels. The panel echoed the criticism of the United States and other member states that the pay and benefits of U.N. employees are greatly out of line with those received by most national civil servants and recommended specific cuts in some entitlements. It also recommended reductions in travel, in the use of outside consultants, and in the number of conferences and meetings held each year.

In adopting the recommendations of the Group of 18, the General Assembly imposed certain conditions. The percentages by which the Secretariat staff are to be reduced should be regarded as "targets" rather than as numbers set in stone. Given the continued uncertainty of the U.S. level of support for 1987, the Secretary-General has continued the **hiring freeze** imposed in 1986. It is expected that a large number of the **staff cuts** targeted by the reform resolution will come about through attrition. In addition, a newly initiated vacancy-management system will review vacant posts to determine which should be filled in the light of program priorities, workload, and classified job descriptions. A rotation and mobility system is being designed to facilitate the redeployment of staff in different duty stations and functions.

The General Assembly resolution repeated the Group of 18's request that personnel reforms be implemented with flexibility "in order to avoid *inter alia* negative impact on programs and on the structure and composition of the Secretariat."

The fundamental rationale for the level of U.N. salaries is rooted in the **Noblemaire principle**, which dates from the League of Nations. According to this principle, in order to recruit highly competent international civil servants, an international organization must be willing to pay at least as much as the highest-paying national civil service, which since the earliest days has been the U.S. Civil Service. **U.N. salaries** at the professional levels are compared to the salaries of U.S. civil servants holding comparable jobs. (Salaries for the general service staff, recruited locally, are determined by the "best prevailing local rates"—that is, the most favorable conditions of employment in the locality of the office concerned.)

Comparisons are based on the findings of a 1978 job equivalency study prepared by the International Civil Service Commission (ICSC), a fifteen-member panel responsible for regulation and coordination of the U.N. common system of salaries, allowances, and other conditions of service. A new study is currently being conducted by the ICSC and is expected to be released soon. The ICSC has requested its own secretariat to study methods of comparing ASG/USG posts to those in the U.S. Civil Service—not generally included in past equivalency studies—and to present the results of these findings at its next session in 1987. Member state criticism has been directed primarily at the pay and benefits of international civil servants at these levels.

A comparison between U.S. and U.N. net pay in New York that takes the form of a ratio, with U.S. salaries given the numerical value of 100, reveals the extent to which U.N. pay is higher than that received by U.S. counterparts. In the case of U.N. professionals, a postadjustment is added to (or in some cases subtracted from) base U.N. salary to equalize purchasing power in all duty stations. There is also a salary advantage, known as the "margin," to compensate for certain features unique to the International Civil Service, such as expatriation, less security of tenure, and less-favorable opportunities for career development.

Reacting to government pressures, the General Assembly in 1985 approved a range of 110 to 120, with a desirable midpoint of 115 for the margin between net remuneration of officials in the professional and higher categories of the United Nations in New York and officials in comparable positions in the U.S. Civil Service [A/Res/40/244]. In its report to the 41st Session of the General Assembly, the ICSC, by majority, recommended that remuneration comparisons in the future be carried out on the basis of net remuneration of the two civil services in New York (rather than by comparing U.N. New York salaries with U.S. Washington salaries, as previously) and that the differential factor in the margin calculation that had been used to account for differences in cost-of-living between New York and Washington, D.C., be dropped. In making this recommendation, the ICSC noted that their implementation would result in significant changes in the margin calculation methodology, the level of the margin, and the margin range itself. At the request of the General Assembly, the commission is to reexamine this issue and submit recommendations at the 42nd Session.

In recent years, the General Assembly has been calculating and reporting a margin based on total compensation comparisons covering only nonexpatriate benefits available to each service. The possibility of extending these comparisons to include expatriate benefits is being considered by the commission. The 41st General Assembly requested the International Civil Service Commission to examine the "total entitlements (salaries and other conditions of service) of both services with a view to determining the feasibility and usefulness of a comparison and to report thereon to the General Assembly at its 42nd session" [A/Res/41/207]. The ICSC will also have before it a recommendation of the Group of 18 to reduce the amount of total U.N. entitlements, which, according to the report, have reached a level that "gives reason for serious concern" [A/41/49]. In particular, the ICSC recommends the elimination of the education grant for postsecondary studies and the establishment of a four-week annual leave system for all staff members (annual leave is currently set at six weeks).

In resolution 41/207, the General Assembly approved the introduction of a revised scale of staff assessment for staff in the **general service and related categories**. The staff assessment, an internal U.N. "tax," is paid into a tax equalization fund that is used to reimburse those staff members who are required to pay taxes to their governments (nationals of Canada, Laos, the United States, and Mexico fall into this category) and to compensate governments that do not tax their nationals in U.N. service—under the tax-related provisions of the United Nations Convention on Privileges and Immunities. The new scale is lower than the previous one and will therefore yield a somewhat lower scale of gross salary to staff in these categories. Since the gross salary serves as the pensionable remuneration for these staff, the Assembly also approved transitional measures whereby the existing gross salary would be maintained until overtaken as a result of future adjustments to the salary scales.

Like the U.N.'s salary system, the **U.N. pension plan** has been criticized as being overly generous. Significant differences in the definition of and method used to determine pensionable remuneration between the U.N. and the U.S. systems have resulted in U.N. pensions that are significantly higher than those of the comparator. In recent years the United Nations has changed its method of determining pensionable remuneration, resulting in reductions in scale. The newest scale, adopted by the 41st General Assembly and effective April 1987 [A/Res/41/208], uses as its starting point the net remuneration in New York, which is determined on the basis of comparisons with U.S. Civil Service net remuneration. Because the new scale is lower than the one in effect since January 1985, the new system should bring about a significant reduction in costs—approximately $10 to $11 million per annum for all organizations and all sources of funds [Report of the International Civil Service Commission, A/41/30]. The next comprehensive review of pensionable remuneration for the professional and higher categories is to be carried out in 1990. In the meantime, the April 1987 scale will be adjusted whenever net remuneration of officials in the professional and higher categories in New York is adjusted.

A margin range of between 10 and 20 percent above U.S. pensionable remuneration—much like the calculation that determines U.N. salary levels— was proposed by the commission in its 1986 report to the General Assembly. Among the reasons cited by the ICSC for the margin was shorter careers, more limited opportunity to rise to the highest levels in the U.N., and a mandatory retirement age of sixty years (there is no mandatory retirement age for U.S. civil servants). The 41st General Assembly did not adopt a margin range for pensionable remuneration, believing it to be unnecessary, since there is a margin range for net remuneration, which itself serves as the starting point for calculating pensionable remuneration. The General Assembly also failed to give its endorsement to the ICSC recommendation that the same level of pensionable remumeration be applied to both assistant secretaries-general and under-secretaries-general. The Assembly did accept, however, the Pension Board's recommendation that—subject to transitional measures—a ceiling be imposed on the size of the lump-sum payment that employees can opt to receive in lieu of up to a third of their pensions.

Four years ago, in response to an actuarial imbalance in the joint staff pension fund, which caused outflows to exceed income, the General Assembly authorized the first of several increases in the size of contributions to the fund by staff and participating organizations. Consideration of the second stage of the increased contribution rate, postponed since the 40th Session, will come before the 42nd Session as well.

Recommendation 46 of the Group of 18 calls on the Secretary-General to take additional measures to ensure greater **representation of women** in the professional category and above. In fact, the improvement of the status of women in the Secretariat has been one of the cornerstones of U.N. personnel policy in recent years. The Secretary-General appointed a Co-ordinator for the Improvement of the Status of Women in the Secretariat in 1985 and presented a detailed plan to the 40th General Assembly for improving the recruitment, career development, training, and conditions of service of women staff members [A/C.5/40/30]. The General Assembly approved the program in December 1985 and set a target of 30 percent for the representation of women in posts subject to geographical distribution [A/Res/40/258]. The austerity measures imposed as a result of the financial crisis have had a largely negative impact on this program. As long as the recruitment freeze is maintained, for example, it will be difficult to increase the percentage of women in the professional category. There are notable exceptions, however. In early 1987 the Secretary-General appointed two women to the highest levels of the Secretariat, each to bear the title of under-secretary-general.

Article 101 of the U.N. Charter sets out as the paramount considerations for the selection of U.N. employees "efficiency, competence and integrity" but adds that "due regard" should be given to establishing the widest **geographical representation**. For the past several years, General Assembly resolutions on personnel issues have emphasized "equitable geographical distribution" in the recruitment of staff and have required the Secretary-General to deliver an annual status report on his efforts in this area. As a result of the suspension of recruitment, there was little progress in this area in 1986, and in fact there has been a slight deterioration in the figures since last year. Twelve member nations currently have no nationals on the U.N. work force at all, while twenty-four countries are underrepresented and twenty-nine countries are overrepresented [A/C.5/41/6].

In 1980 the General Assembly affirmed that "no post should be considered the exclusive province of any member state or group of member states" and requested the Secretary-General to ensure that this resolution is applied faithfully in accordance with the principle of equitable geographical distribution. Nevertheless, the tradition persists in the U.N. of considering certain posts, offices, or divisions the domain of particular member states—a situation that makes concepts of efficiency in work force management and fairness in career development difficult to apply. In response to a recommendation of the Group of 18, the Secretary-General has stated his intention to maintain adequate representation for all member states, in accordance with General Assembly resolution 35/210, while at the same time ensuring that no post is regarded as the exclusive preserve of any member state.

According to the United Nations Staff Union, some forty-five U.N. employees are currently imprisoned, illegally detained, or believed dead—an abridgement of the right of the U.N. staff "to demand respect for [its] independence and international character." The greatest number of these incidents has taken place in Afghanistan and Syria, but there have been others in areas as politically diverse as the Gaza Strip, Guatemala, and Burma. It was recently alleged that the Polish government—in contravention of a U.N. rule that a staff member may not resign while away from headquarters—is preventing Wlodzimierz Cibor, a Polish staffer in the U.N. Council for Namibia, from returning to New York after his recall to Warsaw. The United Nations continues to pursue with the government of Romania the case of Liviu

Bota, a U.N. staffer in Geneva who has been barred from returning from Bucharest since Christmas 1985.

Appendix

THE UNITED NATIONS AT A GLANCE

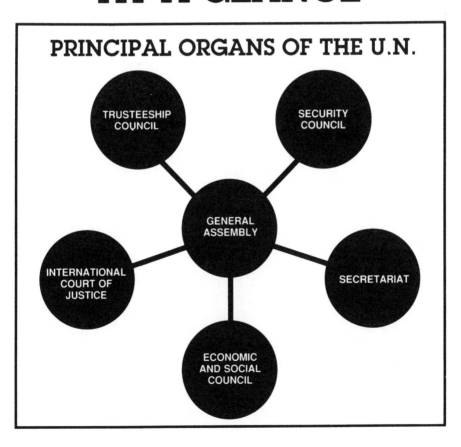

PRINCIPAL ORGANS OF THE U.N.

TRUSTEESHIP COUNCIL

SECURITY COUNCIL

GENERAL ASSEMBLY

INTERNATIONAL COURT OF JUSTICE

SECRETARIAT

ECONOMIC AND SOCIAL COUNCIL

I. GENERAL ASSEMBLY

All U.N. members are part of the General Assembly, and each has one vote. The General Assembly controls the U.N.'s finances, makes nonbinding recommendations on a variety of issues, and oversees and elects some members of other U.N. organs. The Assembly meets in plenary session from the third Tuesday in September through mid-December. As the length of the agenda has grown in recent years, there has been a tendency to resume the plenary shortly after January 1 for a few weeks in order to address all items. The Assembly can also meet in special session, as it has done for two special sessions on disarmament. Most business is delegated to the Assembly's seven main committees, which prepare recommendations for the approval of the Assembly.

President of the 41st General Assembly: Humayun Rasheed Chaudhury (Bangladesh).

Main Committees

First Committee (Political and Security)
Special Political Committee (Other political issues, including most disarmament issues)
Second Committee (Economic and Financial)
Third Committee (Social, Humanitarian, and Cultural)
Fourth Committee (Decolonization)
Fifth Committee (Administration and Budget)
Sixth Committee (Legal)

Chairpersons

Siegfried Zachmann (East Germany)

Kwam Kouassi (Togo)
Abdallah Saleh Al–Ashtal (South Yemen)
Alphons C.M. Hamer (Netherlands)
James Victor Gbeho (Ghana)
Even Fontaine–Ortiz (Cuba)
Laurel B. Francis (Jamaica)

Housekeeping Committees make recommendations on the adoption of the agenda, the allocation of items, and the organization of work.

Some Housekeeping Committees:
(1) General Committee
(2) Credentials Committee
(3) Committee on Relations with the Host Country
(4) Committee on Conferences
(5) Committee on Contributions
(6) Committee for Program and Coordination

Other Bodies Include:
(1) Board of Auditors
(2) International Civil Service Commission
(3) Joint Inspection Unit
(4) Panel of External Auditors of the United Nations, the Specialized Agencies, and the International Atomic Energy Agency
(5) Administrative Tribunal
(6) United Nations Joint Staff Pension Board
(7) United Nations Staff Pension Committee
(8) Investments Committee
(9) Advisory Committee on Administrative and Budgetary Questions

SPECIAL COMMITTEES THAT REPORT ON SPECIAL ISSUES:

There are some 75 such subsidiary organs. Some of these include:

(1) Special Committee on the Situation with regard to the Implementation of the Declaration on the Granting of Independence to Colonial Countries and Peoples
(2) Committee on the Exercise of the Inalienable Rights of the Palestinian People
(3) Special Committee against Apartheid
(4) Ad Hoc Committee on the Drafting of an International Convention against Apartheid in Sports
(5) United Nations Council for Namibia
(6) Committee on the Peaceful Uses of Outer Space
(7) Special Committee on Peacekeeping Operations
(8) United Nations Scientific Committee on the Effects of Atomic Radiation
(9) Ad Hoc Committee on International Terrorism

COMMISSIONS:

Three major Commissions report to the General Assembly:

(1) International Law Commission was established in 1947 to promote the development and codification of international law. It meets every year in Geneva and consists of 25 experts elected by the Assembly for 5-year terms. It prepares drafts on topics of its own choice and on topics referred to it by the Assembly and by the Economic and Social Council.

(2) United Nations Commission on International Trade Law, established in 1966, is a 36-country body that promotes the harmonization of international trade law and drafts international trade conventions. It also provides training and assistance in international trade law to developing countries.

(3) Disarmament Commission, established by the General Assembly in 1952, reports annually to the Assembly. This deliberative body makes recommendations on various problems in the field of disarmament and inter alia considers the elements of a comprehensive program for disarmament to be submitted as recommendations to the Assembly and, through it, to the negotiating body—the Conference of the Committee on Disarmament.

GENERAL ASSEMBLY (Continued)

OTHER ORGANIZATIONS CREATED BY AND REPORTING TO THE GENERAL ASSEMBLY:

Office of the United Nations Disaster Relief Coordinator (UNDRO) is a clearinghouse for information on relief needs and assistance, and mobilizes and coordinates emergency assistance.

Office of the United Nations High Commissioner for Refugees (UNHCR) extends international protection and material assistance to refugees, and negotiates with governments to resettle or repatriate refugees.

United Nations Center for Human Settlements (Habitat) deals with the housing problems of the urban and rural poor in developing countries. It provides technical assistance and training, organizes meetings, and disseminates information.

United Nations Children's Fund (UNICEF) provides technical and financial assistance to developing countries for programs benefiting children. It also provides emergency relief to mothers and children. It is financed by voluntary contributions.

United Nations Conference on Trade and Development (UNCTAD) works to establish agreements on commodity price stabilization and to codify principles of international trade that are conducive to development.

United Nations Development Program (UNDP) coordinates the development work of all UN and related agencies. It is the world's largest multilateral technical assistance program, currently supporting more than 6,500 projects around the world, and is financed by voluntary contributions.

United Nations Environment Program (UNEP) monitors environmental conditions, implements environmental projects, develops recommended standards, promotes technical assistance and training, and supports the development of alternative energy sources.

United Nations Fund for Population Activities (UNFPA) helps countries to gather demographic information and to plan population projects. Its governing body is the Governing Council of UNDP, and it is financed by voluntary governmental contributions.

United Nations Industrial Development Organization (UNIDO) is an autonomous organization within the UN that promotes the industrialization of developing countries. It is in the process of being converted into a specialized agency.

United Nations Institute for Training and Research (UNITAR) is an autonomous organization within the UN that provides training to government and UN officials and conducts research on a variety of international issues.

United Nations Relief and Works Agency for Palestine Refugees in the Near East (UNRWA) provides education, health, and relief services to Palestinian refugees.

United Nations University (UNU) is an autonomous academic institution chartered by the General Assembly. It has a worldwide network of associated institutions, research units, individual scholars, and UNU fellows, coordinated through the UNU center in Tokyo. It has no faculty or degree students.

World Food Council (WFC) is a 36-nation body that meets annually at the ministerial level to review major issues affecting the world food situation.

World Food Program (WFP) is jointly sponsored by the UN and FAO. It supplies emergency food relief and provides food aid to support development projects.

II. SECURITY COUNCIL

The Security Council has primary responsibility within the UN system for maintaining international peace and security. It may determine the existence of any threat to international peace, make recommendations or take enforcement measures to resolve the problem, and establish UN peacekeeping forces. Its resolutions are binding on all member states. It has 15 members: 5 permanent members designated by the UN Charter and 10 nonpermanent members. The latter are nominated by informal regional caucuses and elected for two-year terms; five are elected each year. Decisions on substantive matters require nine votes; a negative vote by any permanent member is sufficient to defeat the motion.

Permanent Membership	Term ending Dec. 31, 1987	Term ending Dec. 31, 1988
China	Bulgaria	Argentina
France	Congo	Germany, Federal Republic of
USSR	Ghana	Italy
United Kingdom	United Arab Emirates	Japan
United States	Venezuela	Zambia

III. ECONOMIC AND SOCIAL COUNCIL

Under the authority of the General Assembly, ECOSOC coordinates the economic and social work of the UN and its large family of specialized and affiliated institutions. ECOSOC usually meets in plenary session twice a year for a month at a time, once in New York and once in Geneva. The 54 members of ECOSOC are elected by the General Assembly for three-year terms; 18 are elected each year.

Term expires: Dec. 31, 1987		Dec. 31, 1988		Dec. 31, 1989	
Bangladesh	Morocco	Australia	Jamaica	Belize	Poland
Brazil	Nigeria	Belgium	Mozambique	Bolivia	Rwanda
Colombia	Romania	Byelorussia	Pakistan	Bulgaria	Somalia
France	Senegal	Djibouti	Panama	Canada	Sri Lanka
Guinea	Spain	Egypt	Peru	China	Sudan
Haiti	Turkey	Gabon	Philippines	Denmark	United Kingdom
Iceland	Venezuela	East Germany	Sierra Leone	Iran	Uruguay
India	West Germany	Iraq	Syria	Norway	USSR
Japan	Zimbabwe	Italy	United States	Oman	Zaire

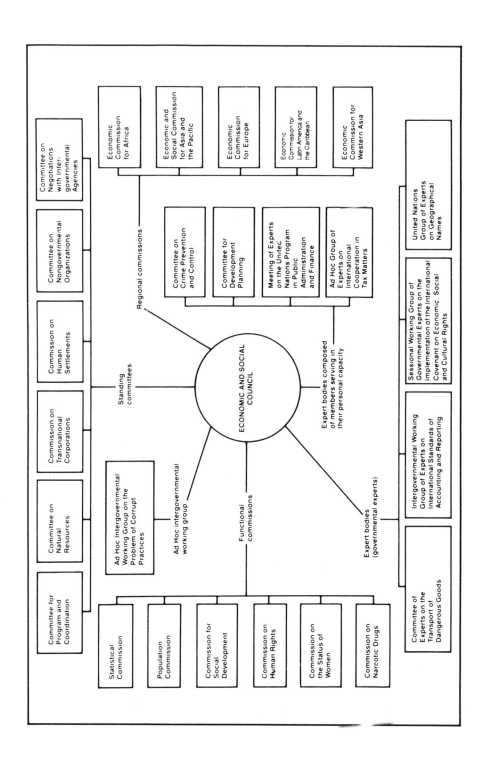

ECONOMIC AND SOCIAL COUNCIL

Standing committees

Committee on Negotiations with Inter-governmental Agencies

Committee on Nongovernmental Organizations

Commission on Human Settlements

Commission on Transnational Corporations

Committee on Natural Resources

Committee for Program and Coordination

Regional commissions

Economic Commission for Africa

Economic and Social Commission for Asia and the Pacific

Economic Commission for Europe

Economic Commission for Latin America and the Caribbean

Economic Commission for Western Asia

Functional commissions

Statistical Commission

Population Commission

Commission for Social Development

Commission on Human Rights

Commission on the Status of Women

Commission on Narcotic Drugs

Ad Hoc Intergovernmental Working Group on the Problem of Corrupt Practices

Ad Hoc intergovernmental working group

Expert bodies composed of members serving in their personal capacity

Committee on Crime Prevention and Control

Committee for Development Planning

Meeting of Experts on the United Nations Program in Public Administration and Finance

Ad Hoc Group of Experts on International Cooperation in Tax Matters

Expert bodies (governmental experts)

Committee of Experts on the Transport of Dangerous Goods

Intergovernmental Working Group of Experts on International Standards of Accounting and Reporting

Sessional Working Group of Governmental Experts on the Implementation of the International Covenant on Economic. Social and Cultural Rights

United Nations Group of Experts on Geographical Names

IV. TRUSTEESHIP COUNCIL

The five members of the Trusteeship Council—China, France, the USSR, the UK, and the US—are also the five permanent members of the Security Council. Only the US still administers a trust territory, the Trust Territory of the Pacific Islands. Originally, the Trusteeship Council had more members and administered 11 trust territories, but as the latter achieved independence or became parts of other states, the membership of the Council was reduced. China does not participate in the Council's work.

V. INTERNATIONAL COURT OF JUSTICE (WORLD COURT)

The International Court of Justice has 15 members, who are elected by an absolute majority of both the Security Council and the General Assembly for nine-year terms. The Court hears cases referred to it by the states involved, and provides advisory opinions to the General Assembly and the Security Council at their request. Five judges are elec'ed every three years.

Term Expires:
Feb. 5, 1988

Jose Sette Camara (Brazil)
Platon Dmitrievich Morozov (USSR)*
Roberto Ago (Italy)
Stephen Schwebel (USA)
Mohammed Bedjaoui (Algeria)

*Resigned, 1985

Feb. 5, 1991

Nagendra Singh (India)*
Jose Maria Ruda (Argentina)
Robert Jennings (U.K.)
Guy Ladreit de Lacharriere (France)**
Keba Mbaye (Senegal)

*President of the Court
**Vice President (deceased March 1987)

Feb. 5, 1994

Taslim Olawale Elias (Nigeria)
Manfred Lachs (Poland)
Shigeru Oda (Japan)
Jens Evensen (Norway)
Ni Zhrengya (PRC)

VI. SECRETARIAT

The Secretariat administers the programs and policies established by the other UN organs. It is headed by the Secretary-General (currently Javier Pérez de Cuéllar of Peru), who is elected by the General Assembly on the recommendation of the Security Council for a five-year term. The Secretary-General is authorized by the United Nations Charter to bring to the attention of the Security Council any matter that he believes may threaten international peace and security (Article 99), and may use his good offices to attempt to resolve international disputes. Under the Secretary-General are the Director-General for Development and International Economic Cooperation (currently Jean Louis Ripert of France). 26 Under-Secretaries-General, and 29 Assistant Secretaries-General. Further, the Secretariat contains a 16,000 international civil service staff (11,000 worldwide and 5,000 in New York), which carries out the day-to-day activities delegated to the Secretary-General. In the field, technical experts and economic advisers oversee economic and peacekeeping projects. Under Article 100 of the Charter, member states must recognize and respect the international character of the duties assigned to the Secretary-General and his staff.

SPECIALIZED AGENCIES

The specialized agencies are autonomous intergovernmental organizations related to the UN by special agreements. They report annually to the Economic and Social Council.

Food and Agriculture Organization of the United Nations (FAO) works to increase food production and to raise rural standards of living, and to help countries to cope with emergency food situations.

Edouard Saouma (Lebanon), Director-General
Via delle Terme di Caracalla
Rome 00100, Italy
Washington, DC Office:
1776 F Street, NW
Washington, DC 20437

International Civil Aviation Organization (ICAO) works to facilitate and to promote safe international air transportation by setting binding international standards and by recommending efficient practices. ICAO regulations are the rules that govern international flying.

Yves Maurice Lambert (France), Secretary-General
Place de L'Aviation Internationale
1000 Sherbrooke Street W.
Montreal, Quebec, Canada H3A 2R2

International Fund for Agricultural Development (IFAD) lends money on concessional terms for agricultural development proj-

ects, primarily to increase food production for the poorest rural populations.

Idriss Jazairy (Algeria), President
Via del Seratico 107, 00142
Rome, Italy

International Labor Organization (ILO) formulates international labor standards and provides technical assistance training to governments.

Francis Blanchard (France), Director-General
4 Route des Morillons, CH-1211
Geneva 22, Switzerland

International Maritime Organization (IMO) promotes international cooperation on technical matters related to shipping and provides a forum to discuss and to adopt conventions and recommendations on such matters as safety at sea and pollution control.

C.P. Srivastava (India), Secretary-General
4 Albert Embankment
London, SE1 7SR, England

SPECIALIZED AGENCIES (Continued)

International Monetary Fund (IMF) provides technical assistance and financing to countries that are experiencing balance-of-payments difficulties.

Jacques de Larosière (France), Managing Director
700 19th Street, NW
Washington, DC 20431

International Telecommunication Union (ITU) promotes international cooperation in telecommunications, allocates the radio-frequency spectrum, and collects and disseminates telecommunications information for its members.

Richard E. Butler (Australia), Secretary-General
Place des Nations
CH 1211 Geneva 10, Switzerland

United Nations Educational, Scientific and Cultural Organization (UNESCO) pursues international intellectual cooperation in education, science, culture, and communications, and also promotes development by means of social, cultural, and economic projects.

Amadou-Mahtar M'Bow (Senegal), Director-General
UNESCO House
7 Place de Fontenoy, 75700
Paris, France

Universal Postal Union (UPU) sets international postal standards and provides technical assistance to developing countries.

Mohamed I. Sobhi (Egypt), Director-General
Weltpoststrasse 4
Berne 1, Switzerland

The World Bank is actually three institutions: the International Bank for Reconstruction and Development **(IBRD)**; the Interna-tional Finance Corporation (IFC); and the International Develop-

usually for specific, productive projects. IFC lends to private corporations without government guarantees. IDA provides interest-free "credits" to the world's poorest countries for a period of 50 years, with a 10-year grace period.

Barber B. Conable (United States), President
1818 H Street, NW
Washington, DC 20433
New York office: 737 Third Avenue, 26th fl
New York, New York 10017

World Health Organization (WHO) conducts immunization campaigns, promotes and administers research, and provides technical assistance to countries that are improving their health systems.

Dr. Halfdan T. Mahler (Denmark), Director-General
20 Avenue Appia, 1211
Geneva 27, Switzerland

World Intellectual Property Organization (WIPO) promotes the protection of intellectual property (e.g., patents and copyrights). It encourages adherence to relevant treaties, provides legal and technical assistance to developing countries, encourages technology transfer, and administers the International Union for the Protection of Industrial Property and the International Union for the Protection of Literary and Artistic Works.

Dr. Arpad Bogsch (United States), Director-General
34 Chemin des Colombettes
CH-1211 Geneva 20, Switzerland

World Meteorological Organization (WMO) promotes the exchange and standardization of meteorological information through its World Weather Watch, and conducts research and training programs.

G.O.P. Obasi (Nigeria), Secretary-General

OTHER AUTONOMOUS AFFILIATED ORGANIZATIONS

General Agreement on Tariffs and Trade (GATT) is a multilateral treaty establishing rules for international trade. As the postwar plans for an International Trade Organization never materialized, the GATT evolved into a forum for negotiations on international trade.

Arthur Dunkel (Switzerland), Director-General
Centre William Rappard
154 Rue de Lausanne
1211 Geneva 21, Switzerland

International Atomic Energy Agency (IAEA) was established under UN auspices but is autonomous and is not formally a specialized agency. It promotes the use of peaceful nuclear energy and provides safeguards on most of the world's peaceful nuclear materials to ensure that it is not diverted to military use.

Dr. Hans Blix (Sweden), Director-General
Vienna International Center
PO Box 100
A-1400 Vienna, Austria

THE 159 UN MEMBER STATES

Since the United Nations was founded in 1945, membership in the organization has more than tripled. There were 51 original member states; today, the membership numbers 159 countries. In the past decade, most new members have been ministates, which have joined as they have become independent—the end of the wave of decolonization that began after World War II. The vast majority of the world's nations are UN members. During the 39th General Assembly, Brunei became the newest member.

Afghanistan, Democratic
　　Republic of
Albania, Socialist Republic of
Algeria, Democratic and Popular
　　Republic of
Angola, People's Republic of
Antigua and Barbuda
Argentina, Republic of
Australia, Commonwealth of
Austria, Republic of
Bahamas, Commonwealth of The
Bahrain, State of
Bangladesh, People's Republic
　　of
Barbados
Belgium, Kingdom of
Belize
Benin, The People's Republic of
Bhutan, Kingdom of
Bolivia, Republic of
Botswana, Republic of
Brazil, Federative Republic of
Brunei (Brunei Darussalam)
Bulgaria, People's Republic of
Burkina-Faso (formerly Upper Volta)
Burma, Socialist Republic of the
　　Union of

Grenada
Guatemala, Republic of
Guinea, People's Revolutionary
　　Republic of
Guinea-Bissau, Republic of
Guyana, Cooperative Republic of
Haiti, Republic of
Honduras, Republic of
Hungary (Hungarian People's
　　Republic)
Iceland, Republic of
India, Republic of
Indonesia, Republic of
Iran, Islamic Republic of
Iraq, Republic of
Ireland
Israel, State of
Italy (Italian Republic)
Ivory Coast, Republic of
Jamaica
Japan
Jordan, Hashemite Kingdom of
Kampuchea, Democratic
　　(formerly Cambodia)
Kenya, Republic of
Kuwait, State of
Laos (Lao People's Democratic
　　Republic)

Romania, Socialist Republic of
Rwanda, Republic of
St. Christopher-Nevis
St. Lucia
St. Vincent and the Grenadines
Samoa, Independent State of
　　Western
Sao Tome and Principe,
　　Democratic Republic of
Saudi Arabia, Kingdom of
Senegal, Republic of
Seychelles, Republic of
Sierra Leone, Republic of
Singapore, Republic of
Solomon Islands
Somalia (Somali Democratic
　　Republic)
South Africa, Republic of
Spain (Spanish State)
Sri Lanka, Democratic Socialist
　　Republic of
Sudan, Democratic Republic of
Suriname, Republic of
Swaziland, Kingdom of
Sweden, Kingdom of
Syria (Syrian Arab Republic)
Tanzania, United Republic of
Thailand, Kingdom of

Burundi, Republic of
Byelorussia (Byelorussian Soviet Socialist Republic)
Cameroon, United Republic of
Canada
Cape Verde, Republic of
Central African Republic
Chad, Republic of
Chile, Republic of
China, People's Republic of
Colombia, Republic of
Comoros, Federal Islamic Republic of the
Congo, People's Republic of the
Costa Rica, Republic of
Cuba, Republic of
Cyprus, Republic of
Czechoslovakia (Czechoslovak Socialist Republic)
Denmark, Kingdom of
Djibouti, Republic of
Dominica, Commonwealth of
Dominican Republic
Ecuador, Republic of
Egypt, Arab Republic of
El Salvador, Republic of
Equatorial Guinea, Republic of
Ethiopia, Socialist
Fiji
Finland, Republic of
France (French Republic)
Gabon (Gabonese Republic)
Gambia, Republic of The
German Democratic Republic (East Germany)
Germany, Federal Republic of (West Germany)
Ghana, Republic of
Greece (Hellenic Republic)

Lebanon, Republic of
Lesotho, Kingdom of
Liberia, Republic of
Libya (Socialist People's Libyan Arab Jamahiriya)
Luxembourg, Grand Duchy of
Madagascar, Democratic Republic of
Malawi
Malaysia
Maldives, Republic of
Mali, Republic of
Malta
Mauritania, Islamic Republic of
Mauritius
Mexico (The United Mexican States)
Mongolia (Mongolian People's Republic)
Morocco, Kingdom of
Mozambique, People's Republic of
Nepal, Kingdom of
Netherlands, Kingdom of the
New Zealand
Nicaragua, Republic of
Niger, Republic of
Nigeria, Federal Republic of
Norway, Kingdom of
Oman, Sultanate of
Pakistan, Islamic Republic of
Panama, Republic of
Papua New Guinea
Paraguay, Republic of
Peru, Republic of
Philippines, Republic of the
Poland (Polish People's Republic)
Portugal, Republic of
Qatar, State of

Togo, Republic of
Trinidad and Tobago, Republic of
Tunisia, Republic of
Turkey, Republic of
Uganda, Republic of
Ukraine (Ukrainian Soviet Socialist Republic)
Union of Soviet Socialist Republics
United Arab Emirates
United Kingdom of Great Britain and Northern Ireland
United States of America
Uruguay
Vanuatu, Republic of
Venezuela, Republic of
Vietnam, Socialist Republic of
Yemen Arab Republic (North Yemen)
Yemen, People's Democratic Republic of (South Yemen)
Yugoslavia, Socialist Federal Republic of
Zaire, Republic of
Zambia, Republic of
Zimbabwe

The following countries maintain offices of permanent observers at the UN:
Korea, Democratic People's Republic of (North Korea)
Korea, Republic of (South Korea)
Monaco, Principality of
Switzerland (Swiss Confederation)
Vatican City, State of the

Index

Let UNA-USA put you in the corridors of power.

If you are among the 85% of Americans who say they want a stronger United Nations so it can do a better job solving the world's problems, then UNA-USA is for you! The United Nations Association of the USA is dedicated to making the U.N. work. In an increasingly dangerous and chaotic world, peace and prosperity cannot be secured without better international institutions and stronger U.S. leadership. UNA-USA is helping to achieve both through a unique blend of policy research, international dialogue, and public outreach.

UNA-USA is a national, nonpartisan, nonprofit "citizens' think tank." Through it, thousands of Americans come together to weigh the choices facing U.S. foreign policy makers; and for more than twenty years, decision-makers at the highest levels of government have listened to them. Join us and you too can be heard.

UNA-USA has over 175 local chapters, each with a lively program of discussions, debates, speakers, and special events designed to inform and entertain you.

With your membership comes a subscription to *The Inter-Dependent*, UNA's acclaimed bimonthly publication. Its timely investigative reporting takes you behind the headlines of today's news, and offers a range of views seldom found in the domestic press.

Also available, on request, are Fact Sheets, Reports, and Alerts derived from UNA's ongoing coverage of the United Nations, from its close contacts with business, labor, and government leaders, and from its high-level bilateral programs with the Soviet Union, Japan, and the People's Republic of China.